Tending the Spark

Lighting the Future for Middle School Students

Betty Staley brings to light what is relevant about human development during the middle school years... She embraces the middle school years with flare, sharing wisdom, experience, intellect, humor, and personal stories to remind the reader that the struggles of adolescents ignite the flames of adulthood. Ever wonder, "What were they thinking?" in reference to an adolescent? Staley answers in *Tending the Spark*. Educational research, neuroscience, and child development intersect with current societal demands to illuminate the impact on today's youth.   *–Mechelle Horning, M.A. Principal*
                         Alice Birney Waldorf Public School K 8

...I find that the most meaningful influence anyone can have on a child is rooted in a relationship founded in deeper understanding of human development ... *Tending the Spark* offers critical perspective into an often misunderstood and sometimes underestimated period of intense social, emotional, physical, biological, and spiritual growth... As a practicing clinician, I find Betty's book, like many of her others, to be a source of ongoing reference. *Tending the Spark* gives practical educational and parenting advice rooted in the "why" of middle-childhood development.
                 –Jeff Lough, MS, Nationally Certified School Psychologist

Tending the Spark

Lighting the Future for Middle School Students

Betty Kletsky Staley

Waldorf
PUBLICATIONS
RESEARCH INSTITUTE FOR Waldorf EDUCATION

Printed with support from the Waldorf Curriculum Fund

Published by:
Waldorf Publications at the
Research Institute for Waldorf Education
351 Fairview Avenue, Suite 625
Hudson, NY 12534

Title: *Tending the Spark: Lighting the Future for Middle School Students*
Author: Betty Kletsky Staley
Editor: Patrice O'Neill Maynard
Proofreader: Ruth Riegel
Layout: Ann Erwin
Cover art: *Awaken* by Ursula Stone, oil on canvas, 80x80cm
Used with kind permission of the artist

Table of Contents

Dedication

This book is dedicated to my grandchildren:
Ben, Adam, Louisa, Katherine, Charlie, and Misha

Introduction

Since the 1990s, there have been excellent books calling attention to the loss of childhood in society, to the effects of children growing up too quickly, to the influences of technology, advertising, and materialism. Why another book? What has changed?

The age of middle-schoolers, eleven to fourteen years of age, is an in-between time. They are no longer children and not yet adolescents. Puberty is happening earlier than in the past, averaging at age twelve years, when girls begin menstruating and boys experience wet dreams.

At the same time, major neurological changes are happening. Research from neuroscience beginning in the 1990s has demonstrated how different parts of the brain are affected through growth spurts of neurons, myelination, and frontal lobe development in youngsters of middle school age. Starting around eleven in girls and twelve in boys, growth spurts and pruning in the brain and the physical body are affecting the way youngsters think and understand. The secondary growth spurt and frontal lobe development in mid-adolescence starts the youth on the path to executive function or maturity.

As Frances E. Jensen, an internationally respected neurologist, writes in *The Teenage Brain*:

> The frontal lobes are the seat of our ability to generate insights, judgment, abstraction, and planning. They are the source of self-awareness and our ability to assess dangers and risk so we use this area of the brain to choose a course of action wisely. ... [T]he connectivity to and from the frontal lobes is the most complex and is the last to fully mature. This "executive function" thus develops slowly: we certainly are not born with it.

In fact, the teen brain is only about 80 percent of the way to maturity. That 20 percent gap, where the wiring is thinnest, is crucial and goes a long way toward explaining why teenagers behave in such puzzling ways—their mood swings, irritability, impulsiveness, and explosiveness; their inability to focus, to follow through, and to connect with adults; and their temptations to use drugs and alcohol and to engage in other risky behavior. (Jensen, pp. 36–37)

Daniel Siegel in *Brainstorm* writes:

When our adolescence begins, even more dramatic changes in this frontal region occur.... In this way, the frontal area is involved in both the shaping of our own internal mental processes such as thinking and decision-making as well as the social processes such as empathy and moral behavior. So when we speak about changes in the adolescent brain, we'll see that many of these important changes involve increasing levels of integration, especially carried out in the cortex. This increased cortical integration enables such diverse abilities as cognitive control, emotional regulation, gist thinking, self-understanding, and social functions to change and emerge throughout adolescence. (p. 88)

Elkhonon Goldberg, clinical neuropsychologist and cognitive neuroscientist, described the mid-adolescent prefrontal growth spurt "that allow us to rise and go beyond the limitations, constraints, and shortcomings of the earlier neural system." (Pearce, *The Biology of Transcendence*, p. 47) Goldberg continued his exploration of the changes in the brain throughout life in *The Wisdom Paradox*, 2005.

After sixteen, adolescents begin the path to adulthood, learning by experience and role models how to manage these changes, how to take responsibility, and how to assume their role as members of the community.

Since middle-schoolers have only completed part of their emotional and neurological maturity, it is no wonder that they are erratic and confused. Everything seems new and exciting, but they lack discernment in how to identify priorities or gain control over newly experienced instinctual drives.

The 19th-century artist William Blake designed a lithograph titled "The Good and Bad Angels Fight for the Soul of the Child." Without becoming overly dramatic, it feels as if we are in the midst of such a battle with powerful negative forces specifically aimed at this age group—through sexualization and violence in movies, overload of internet information, video games, cell phones, and commercials, as well as the flooding of advertising and consumerism.

All these negative influences have a common aim—to reduce the human being's spiritual potential to an animal, a machine, an interaction of chemicals, or a computer. But that is not what a child is.

Throughout the book I refer to the phrase "tending the spark"—referring to highest human qualities that every child has in potential. Each child carries the spark of spirit, the promise of goodness, beauty, and truth—unfolding at each stage of childhood.

Protecting this spark is the serious task we take on as parents and teachers, and we must never forget this. The attack is on all ages of childhood, but the openness of middle school children makes them especially vulnerable to losing what is highest in human ideals—with the sense of self-worth that follows. Each middle school child carries the potential of being a healer, a shaper, a carrier of humanity. What happens in the middle school years will strongly influence the future.

Over the course of history, the strength of the community, the group, has shaped the individual. Wisdom was embodied in traditions that guided each stage of life. We trusted those traditions because we experienced the deeper wisdom within them. As centuries passed, when people no longer had access to higher knowledge, the traditions no longer had meaning, but were followed out of habit.

Since the 15th century, the dawn of the modern age, Western societies have put increasing emphasis on the individual with lessening emphasis on the group. The role of the individual has grown stronger and stronger until the 20th century, when the disconnect from the community became severely problematic. Historian Franklin Baumer called the 20th century "the Age of Anxiety, Absurdity, and Alienation." This has intensified as we have moved into the 21st century. Under the influence of western values, individualism is also becoming more common in eastern cultures, and some of these issues are now frequent there.

What has been an adult expression of individualism has spread to adolescents and middle-schoolers and has loosened their connection with the family. In addition, the pace of life has sped up as adults find themselves stressed and struggling to meet the needs of children. Individuals feel freer to decide their own beliefs and their own values. There is freedom to choose one's own community, one's own occupation, one's family situation, and even one's gender.

Researchers, teachers, sociologists, and psychologists have identified that within the last fifty years the increase of individualism among children has become common. Even young children are choosing what they want to do or eat, or when they want to go to sleep. This intensifies as children reach middle school age.

For adults, individualism is positive, allowing for creativity, new initiatives, and finding a path that works as long as they keep a connection with their community. The difficulty is that when children become too individualistic before they have established roots in their family and community, there is a tendency towards isolation, egotism, and lack of compassion. They only know what they want and what satisfies them without recognizing the needs of others. This may work for a while, but human warmth and connectivity are deep human needs for social health.

BIG CHANGES IN SOCIETY

Three big changes—technology, big business, and changing parental and teaching styles—have affected middle school children's development.

Inappropriate use of technology has robbed children of time needed for healthy play, experiences in nature, and time for reflection. Technology as a tool, which has so many positive aspects when used well, has brought children face-to-face with images and information beyond their capacity to understand. They are able to engage in activities such as internet bullying, smartphone photo sharing, texting, video games, and pornography. Busy parents have turned to technology as baby sitter and baby distracter for children, but also for middle-schoolers who have been seduced by the allure of the screen. The long-term effect of children being on screens is only beginning to be identified.

Big business is making big money from advertising to middle-schoolers who are eager to join the teenage world. Using sophisticated techniques, they secure brand loyalty from the "tween market," those youngsters between ten and thirteen who cannot differentiate fact from fiction. Big business, not interested in the laws of child and adolescent development, treats children as products from which to gain profit.

Parents and teachers have lost confidence in their authority to make decisions based on healthy child development. Because they fear their children will not succeed in the adult world, they choose approaches and methods that exert pressure earlier and earlier. Middle-schoolers are treated as young high school students although they lack the capacity to handle the responsibilities. The stress of families and teachers trying to slow life down for their children's benefit continues to be overwhelming.

There is a sharp increase in child illnesses, anxiety, and learning issues with large numbers of children on medication. Popular culture, billboards, television, movies, music, and video games are filled with sexualized imagery. There is an increase in aggression and violence surrounding children. However, despite all of the negative influences from technology, big business, and changing parenting styles, children are children with their delightful openness and excitement for life.

It is during this critical time of the middle school years that children are preparing the "civilizing mind"—a term neuroscientist

Elkhonon Goldberg named for the time when middle-schoolers are shaping whether they will be a victim of their biological instincts or whether they can master their instincts and develop compassion and empathy, the spark that will flame in their adult lives.

Middle-schoolers still have an innocence about life. They have ideals and want the world to be a peaceful place. They are open, enthusiastic, and creative. They have not yet limited themselves to what they can or cannot do. With teachers or parents who stimulate their interests and guide them, there are no limitations to what they will try. Everything is possible. Yet because of the stage of their brain development, they do things that often don't make sense.

In my travels, I experience the same question from parents: What can we do to fight the overwhelming influences from popular culture? It is as if an unwelcome stranger has entered our homes and we are no longer in control.

Let us meet some middle-schoolers as examples of the disconnect between their deeds and their capacity to understand the world.

Eric, an exemplary seventh-grader, was on a field trip. But, standing by the side of the road, he picked up a rock and threw it at a school bus. Luckily, he did not hit the bus, and the driver, oblivious, continued on. But Eric stood transfixed, staring at his hand, as if to ask, "Does this hand belong to me? Did I just do that?" He was stunned by this impulse that seemed to come out of nowhere.

Elizabeth was annoyed at Jocelyn for not inviting her to her party. To get even, she decided to send a picture of Jocelyn from a time when they had playfully taken seductive pictures of each other. When Elizabeth was caught and questioned, her response was, "Well, I didn't think it would be a big deal. Anyway, she should have invited me to her party."

Lenny was getting a ride to a baseball game with a classmate's mother. He was upset by the mother's body odor and proceeded to tell her that he could recommend a very good soap that she could use. When he noticed the mother in his schoolyard, he walked around holding his nose and getting other classmates to do the same. When questioned, he explained, "I was just trying to help her, but she hadn't listened."

Felipe asked one of the seventh-grade girls to send him pictures of her nude. He promised he would delete them. She had a crush on him and wanted him to like her, so she sent them. He then texted them to all of his friends. She said, "But he said he would delete them." She could not understand why he had betrayed her trust.

Because middle-schoolers have struggled with developmental issues historically, some things have not changed. However, we need to realize that because of the powerful influences affecting children, life has changed, causing middle-schoolers to be vulnerable and in need of our support.

This book is an attempt to examine what we know about child development through educational researchers, including what Rudolf Steiner brought from his insights into the development of Waldorf education; what we have learned from research in neuroscience; and how changes in society are affecting middle-schoolers—and then figure out what we can do about it.

I have always been interested in child development and have spent fifty years as an educator, mostly in middle and high schools. My classroom experience has been mainly in Waldorf schools (an international educational movement based on the insights given by Rudolf Steiner). I was involved in adapting Waldorf education to public schools, particularly in inner city situations. In addition, I have worked with teachers from public and other private schools for over twenty years and shared their concerns, struggles, and commitment. I have also worked with teachers in court and community schools adapting Waldorf educational methods for youngsters who have been in trouble with the law and ended up in special schools and juvenile halls.

There are aspects of child development that are universal, and there are aspects that are unique to particular populations. With the advent of the internet and globalization, issues that were particularly problematic in the West are now to be found all over the world. In this time of globalization, the concern for middle school children is shared worldwide. In this book, I will explore the Vulnerability Gap and bring the image of tending the spark to prepare for "the civilizing mind."

Note: The term "middle-schooler" is used throughout this book. It seems to be more inclusive than to write "boys and girls" or "11- to 14-year-olds" each time.

CHAPTER 1
When Did Middle School Arrive?

Middle school youngsters can generally be grouped between the ages of eleven and fourteen. No longer young children, they are not yet adolescents. This in-between time is challenging for them and for the adults responsible for them. Understanding how life around this age group has changed will help illuminate how we can spark in them higher human capacities.

In past centuries and even decades, this age group was not separated from the rest of their childhood years. Two influences have worked on them to create the situation we experience today: The first is *biological*; the second, *cultural*. Societal and cultural—particularly "pop" cultural—forces have become powerful shapers of our lives.

Looking at these periods of change in the life of a young person, it is worthwhile to remember our own teenage years and the cultural influences shaping our lives.

Focusing on changes from 1900 to the present, demonstrating more changes than in recent centuries, will offer insights into this question. In the early 1900s, puberty arrived at age sixteen or so; today, it arrives closer to age twelve. Until the Industrial Revolution, children worked on farms with their families. Once children began to work in factories, they were separated from their families, becoming part of the labor force.

By the 1920s, girls attained puberty closer to age fourteen. Gender roles were separated. The challenges for adolescents were to find a job, to marry young, and to start a family. Nothing more than basic education was needed to function in an industrial society—

a general understanding of arithmetic, reading, and writing was all that was necessary. Child labor was common, but after the age of fourteen.

Several important changes took place during the 1930s. The Great Depression pushed out the 14-year-olds working in factories, allowing the unemployed adults to have these jobs. The unemployed youth were then enrolled in high schools, which became common. By the end of the 1930s, and for the first time in the history of American education, most 14- to 17-year-olds were enrolled in high school. Out of this phenomenon, a separate group identity began to form.

World War II was the defining experience of the 1940s. During the war, children and young people contributed to the war effort. Young men were drafted. After the war was over, youths were seen as a valuable part of the community. The word "teenager" first appeared in print in a magazine article in April 1941. (Jensen, p. 16)

In the United States, the post-war years were optimistic, and society was stable and prosperous. Of course, minorities still struggled to gain economic stability and recognition. In the post-war years, an individual's experience was defined by the localized effects of the war. For example, were they and their country winners or losers? Were battles fought on their home ground? Were family members killed? Was their town or city devastated?

In the 1950s, a teen culture emerged. Teens became aware of themselves as a separate group through their music, image, and style. Typical music included songs that were sentimental, celebrating love and family, and these were enjoyed by both youth and adults. Television was becoming common in most homes with a few channels available. Children watched *Howdy Doody*, and teenagers watched and danced to *American Bandstand*. For the first time, youth were allowed to keep the money they earned and had purchasing power. It was just at this time that the world of advertising was developed and began targeting this group.

A big shift occurred in the musical scene. When Elvis Presley appeared on the Ed Sullivan Show on September 9, 1956, gyrating and singing "Hound Dog," it was as if a lightning bolt had struck. Teenagers took rock 'n' roll to be their music. They copied his hairstyle and fashions, creating a popular teen culture for the first time. Sexuality was now out in the open. Parents felt threatened by this unfamiliar and wild music, but teenagers embraced their separateness from the adult world. Over time, many parents came to enjoy Elvis's music and sang along. As John Lennon said, "…before Elvis, there was nothing."

The early and mid-fifties were my high school years. Even though we were a poor family, I could keep my babysitting money and use it to buy clothes. My friends and I carefully read *Seventeen* magazine that served as our guide to correct style. Examples? Don't mix plaids and stripes. Don't wear your shirt outside of your pants or skirts. Don't wear clunky shoes with skirts. Wear a starched crinoline under your skirt.

The parental response to the teen culture was to issue rules, rules, rules. The more adults disapproved, the more teens formed a subversive culture. Tension was building. Parents differentiated "good girls" from "bad girls," and we were warned not to get into the wrong group.

The 1960s was the era of teenagers. There was prosperity, money, and jobs. The Hippie Generation and the Drug Culture were in full throttle, and all societal rules and expectations were questioned. The rage was *Hair: The American Tribal Love-Rock* musical with nudity, sexuality, the use of illegal drugs, and irreverence toward the American flag. The audience was stunned by the nude scene and a racially integrated cast. The excitement was similar to that caused by the recent production of *Hamilton* on Broadway.

However, the optimism, wildness, and social commentary that had prevailed in the first part of the 1960s changed radically with the assassinations of President John F. Kennedy, Martin Luther King, Jr., and Robert Kennedy, as well as with the Vietnam War, which dragged on until it ended in 1975. Youth experienced these assassinations and the war played out on the televisions right in their own living rooms.

A gray cloud fell on the adolescent generation. They had been raised on the heroism of the "greatest generation," which had saved the world from Nazism. Teenagers protested the Vietnam War, but the ending of the war did not bring the feeling of triumph they expected. Was it a war or not a war? Who were the heroes? Who were the enemies? With this unclarity, they could no longer trust their elders. With the Watergate scandal and the resignation of President Richard Nixon in 1974, a feeling of distrust permeated the youth population.

When these youth became parents, they were confused. There had been a breakdown in rules and societal structure. How were they to raise their children now that traditional society was seen as passé? They were torn between setting limits for their children and giving them the freedom they themselves had fought for and won. Their children were even more confused. They wanted to be rebellious as their parents had been, but against what? Most of their parents let them do anything they wanted anyway. Their parents were caught up in the "me" generation and were busy searching for their own fulfillment, leaving their children on their own as "latchkey kids," expected to let themselves into their houses after school to fend for themselves until their parents came home from work. Family values changed to individual values. People could choose whatever they wanted—their own religion, sexual identity, food, entertainment, or living arrangements.

Television was available in most homes, and commercials were catchy and often remembered better than the programs themselves. With the advent of Public Broadcasting, *Sesame Street* was introduced in 1969, and children from then till today have grown up with its characters without being bombarded with commercials.

During the 1970s the definition of "teenager" began to shift to younger children, and the term "teenybopper" was coined. The freedom that had been given to adolescents was now given to ten-, eleven-, twelve- and thirteen-year-olds. Parents became more uncertain about their role as an authority in their children's lives.

With the rise of cable TV, families had choice of dozens of channels. I attended the International Design Conference in Aspen, in which one of the founders of *Nickelodeon* (a children's program that began in 1979) described how the program began with the intention to have healthy images for children without violence or sex. However, the youngsters of ten years of age and up wouldn't watch it. It was too babyish and too slow moving. As the producers worked with focus groups, they found they had to speed up the movements and add elements that would attract children who were also to be buyers of their sponsors' products.

Cable television also made it possible for sports events to be seen in the home, from which children and teenagers could emulate the physique, actions, and attitudes of sports figures.

As a teacher at that time, it was difficult for me to count on parents to support structure, discipline, or community values. Children and teens could wear what they wanted, although most of their dress styles were copied from young adults. This was a time of getting rid of bras, wearing grungy and ripped jeans, and feeling a general sense of undirected anger. Rules were considered vestiges of middle-class values, and disciplinary action was frowned upon.

In the 1980s, families were under stress with on-going battles between teens and parents. The world of the teenager was filled with sex, drugs, videos, and rock 'n' roll. If parents wanted to exert or regain control, they had a difficult time because teenagers now had a strong culture of their own, and parents felt helpless to give direction. Materialism and entertainment penetrated all areas of life, and having the right brand was more important than parental values.

In 1984, noted psychologist David Elkind lamented, "There is no place for teenagers in American society today—not in our homes, not in our schools, and not in society at large."

The recognition of the importance of time for teenagers to mature was no longer valued. Everything was moving very fast in the '80s, and teenagers had to be ready to deal with whatever came at them. Parents were busy with their own lives and had no time. Although media and merchandisers had stayed away from the preteen market, recognizing their need for protection, now they dove into the "tweens" and marketed to them directly, playing on their immaturity to discern what was attractive to them or not. The idea was that through advertising these preadolescents would be enticed to join the popular culture, to be trendy, and to dress with the latest clothing that was guaranteed to do this for them. The Frontline episode "Merchants of Cool" describes the clever ways in which advertising developed brand loyalty by touching in on the vulnerabilities of this age which, more than anything else, wants to be accepted and cool.

With the introduction of home video cassette recorders, youngsters could record and replay programs, rent and watch movies. Parents could not keep up with the content of all the videos available to be able to approve of what their children watched. Birthday parties often included movies that parents would not have approved taking their families to in the theater. Young teens could pass around sensational videos to watch on the sly.

The key here is that in the '80s, society no longer understood adolescence as a time of transition from childhood to adulthood, a fragile time in which teenagers' emotional maturity was not yet directing their actions. Instead, teenagers were treated as adults, with all of the responsibilities and freedom to find their way. Furthermore, society did not distinguish between early adolescence, middle adolescence, and late adolescence. When children turned thirteen, they were welcomed into the teenage/adolescent world.

However, it is only after age sixteen that teenagers have the mental abilities to integrate their roles, their abilities, their likes and dislikes, and their attitudes towards family, religion, society, and possible professions. The teen generation of the '80s was not given time to develop self-identity, and at the same time they were confronted with an unclear set of values from the adults. Individuals were left to determine their own values, and there were many options. Family structure was dissolving, divorce had become a common experience. Teenagers, often torn by difficult custody battles, had to carry adult responsibility. They were rushed through the time needed for healthy development.

The 1990s was the information decade. With the introduction of the internet, information about AIDS, cancer, racism, homosexuality, women's issues, and teen pregnancy, youngsters from eleven years old and up were overwhelmed and having troubling processing all of this.

Parental complaints about content of movies and videos led to ratings being displayed with TV-14 considered unsuitable for children under fourteen. As complaints continued, V for violence, S for sex, L for coarse language, and D for suggestive dialogue were added to the ratings. Fourteen was considered mature enough to handle sensationalism, violence, and sex. In 1996 parents were able to add the V-chip to automatically prevent their children from watching television programs with inappropriate ratings.

With the rise of the computer, youngsters could see many of the programs their parents had barred them from on television until chips became available to prevent access to certain material on computers as well.

As the century changed, in 2000, girls were attaining puberty at an average of twelve years of age. The events of 9/11 defined this generation, and social media including the internet, texting, and video games became their drug of choice. This opened them up to the world of pornography and violence.

Without the social and emotional skills to deal with this onslaught, preteens were vulnerable to messages on the internet from people they didn't even know to either perpetrate cyber-bullying or become the victim of it. They became addicted to their devices so that they struggled to pay attention in school, to respect adults, to use their time wisely, and to develop healthy social relationships. Advertising had a strong hand in shaping the culture in which being cool was the key intention of "tweens," the new name given to this age group.

Just as parents in the '60s felt threatened by rock 'n' roll as a subversive force in their children's lives, parents today feel threatened by internet sites that children access without supervision and by their children's neglect of family and school interaction.

In the course of a hundred years, children have gone from being embedded in the family to belonging to a separate and alien culture. This group of 11- to 14-year-olds has adopted adolescent behavior without the skills to manage it. At the same time parents have hovered over their children, wanting them to be safe and cared for. Parents themselves, however, have succumbed to the seduction of technology and have become slaves to their smartphones. Even though they may be present physically with their children, their minds are often somewhere else. They still carry the feeling of wanting to be liked by their children and have difficulty setting boundaries.

The influence of available money, the teen and preteen market, the separate teen movies, clothes, language, and technology have created a gulf between adults and preteens. Preteens feel that adults do not understand them or have no time for them, and so they rely on their peers. They are surrounded by forces from outside that they cannot understand or manage. They are not yet developmentally able to discern how to find their way. The early adolescents have paid the stiffest price for the changes that have occurred. And these are the children we refer to as "middle-schoolers."

However, the problem is bigger than technology, marketing, changes in music, or the sexual revolution. The historical shift in the lives of our young people has been accompanied by a shift in the lives of parents. According to German sociologist Norbert Elias, this shift in the second half of the 20th century resulted in an attitude in which Western Europeans and Americans "became less comfortable with any sort of power differential in social relations." (Katz, p. 24) As human rights were extended to previously disenfranchised groups in the community, the legitimacy of any kind of authority became suspect. Parents and teachers lost standing as youngsters turned away from them as models, and turned to their peers for the basic rules of behavior and cultural values. This has resulted in what Dr. Leonard Katz calls the "culture of disrespect."

Dr. Katz has practiced for over twenty-five years as a family physician and psychologist and has traveled the world to experience how children and parents are changing. What he has found is that over the past three decades, there has been a massive transfer of authority from parents to children. Although he sees some aspects of this problem in countries around the world, what he calls "the collapse of parenting" has been especially true in North America, and most strongly in the United States.

The situation is further described by Dr. Neufeld, a Canadian psychologist, who recently retired from active practice after forty years of working with children and adolescents. He has observed a fundamental change in the ways children prioritize attachment. Where the primary attachment had been to their parents,

> for the first time in history, young people are turning for instruction, modeling, and guidance, not to mother, fathers, teachers, and other responsible adults but to people whom nature had never intended to place in a parenting role—their peers. ...Children are being brought up by immature persons who cannot possibly guide them to maturity. They are being brought up by each other. (Katz, p. 29, quoting from Neufeld and Maté, *Hold on to Your Kids*, p. 7)

Thus there has been a shift in the basic nature of relationships.

This book is an attempt to explore the middle school years, how youngsters have changed, how society has changed, and what we can do to tend the spark of each child's higher soul capacities.

CHAPTER 2
The Vulnerability Gap

Twenty years ago I gave a keynote address in Dornach, Switzerland, about the changes in children, particularly in the West. Teachers from European and American schools described that their young students were tired and lethargic, had decreased attention span, were unwilling to try harder, lacked the will to follow through, felt a sense of entitlement, and were reliant on drugs to address ADD and ADHD. Teachers had to teach less material each year because children were not able to learn what the previous generation had. At that time, the concerns were focused on lack of rhythm at home, lack of boundaries and expectations, passivity due to television watching, and unrealistic academic expectations. Although the situation was worse in the U.S., the problem was more widespread. This situation was not a secret. Psychologists and researchers were writing books such as *The Disappearance of Childhood, All Grown up and No Place to Go* (Elkind), *Children without Childhood* (Winn), *Nature Deficit Disorder* (Louv), etc., speeches were given, workshops were held.

> Whereas once ADHD was considered a mostly American phenomenon, awareness, diagnosis, and treatment have been growing in other nations. Increasingly, children are being diagnosed in every nation with compulsory schooling, at rates that are surprisingly similar throughout the world. (Hinshaw *ADHD, What Everyone Needs to Know,* p. xviii)

Increases in mental health problems now occur across all populations of children with increased medication to treat educational issues. Not only are children changing, but many parents are also undergoing change, including being emotionally unavailable, digitally dependent, unable or unwilling to set clearly defined limits, lacking attention to nutrition and sleep, spending less time in nature, resisting allowing their children to be bored or to experience delayed gratification. This is not a matter of blaming parents, but of understanding what it means to be an adult during a time of cultural redefinition.

Children make decisions to eat whenever they want, decide what foods should be served, go to sleep when they want, and demand entertainment. They are indulged, distracted, and entitled. Educational pressure to achieve standards inappropriate to developmental stages demands speeding up what children are supposed to know and leaves many children lacking self-confidence and feeling negative toward school and toward learning.

Life is changing in many areas—physical maturation is speeding up, societal pressures force youngsters to grow up too soon. Changing parenting styles, as well as environmental issues such as chemicals, pollution, and hormones in meat—deprive children of healthy development. Some of the changes can be dealt with through changing our habits and parenting styles. Others are affected by technology, particularly video games and social media, and still others may be affected by substances less easily controlled such as environmental estrogens and other toxic substances.

Yet youngsters in middle school continue to be interesting, fun, and idealistic, as they explore the new world in their bodies, their emotions, and their minds. Despite negative aspects and the temptation to be melancholic about all that is going wrong, there is much to celebrate with young people today. The burden is on us as adults to be flexible, open, willing to hold boundaries, and most of all, to be able to give children time and love.

WHAT IS DIFFERENT TODAY?

Most research shows that the conclusion of puberty in girls has changed from the beginning of the 20th century. (See Greenspan and Deardorff, *The New Puberty*, p. xii; Leonard Sax, *Boys Adrift*; Sax, *Girls on the Edge*, pp. 99–100; and Siegel, *Brainstorm*, p. 25)

In 1900, when pubertal and neurological changes happened around age sixteen, adolescents began to experience executive function, using new emotional and intellectual capacities to manage hormonal changes. Around 1920, the average age of puberty was fourteen, leaving a two-year gap between puberty and executive function. However, since 2000, the average age of puberty is around twelve, leaving a four-year span between puberty and executive function. This is a new normal.

I call this four-year span the Vulnerability Gap, a fragile time when youngsters are at risk of being strongly affected by cultural, emotional, and biological influences without having the emotional and intellectual capacity to handle what is happening within them.

HOW ARE BOYS BEING AFFECTED?

A general attitude that gender differences were insignificant was challenged through brain research. Michael Gurian in *Boys and Girls Learn Differently* (2001) and Leonard Sax in *Why Gender Matters* (2005) made the case that sex differences do affect attitudes, learning styles, aggression, classroom behavior, and social interaction.

Boys, in different ways from girls, have been affected by changes in the family, in school, in social dynamics, and by environmental factors.

Family life has gone through significant change, particularly the absence of fathers. Gone is the most significant male in a boy's life. In some cases, the father may be technically present, but he is so busy traveling for work that he hardly has a relationship with his son(s). In other cases, the father is absent either through divorce, death, or because he has never really been part of the family.

When I worked with a court school for delinquent boys, we found that the boy whose father was in prison had a stronger sense of self-identity than the boy who never knew his father, or if his father had disappeared. We see in this that even though his father was a negative role model, the son could experience consequences of his father's decisions and had to confront such behavior in his own life.

The growing number of boys living with their mothers as single parents creates another challenge in society. Boys are often given adult responsibilities to make up for the absent parent, or they struggle to figure out what it is to be a man within a feminine household. Mothers often make extra efforts to connect their sons with male relatives or community members to model healthy male examples. As hard as single mothers try, gender styles are different, and boys need men, male role models, to guide them.

Boys have always struggled during the middle school years trying to figure out their place in the group order. Who is the leader? What does it take to be accepted? How can I feel strong enough to take risks? Will I be able to defend myself if I'm picked on?

Some have used power over others either through bullying or being outstanding in school or sports. Others have felt victimized or shut out, not sure what it takes to be accepted. Although they may give the impression of handling the situation, these middle school years are a torture for many boys. (Middle school might just be a torture on some levels for *all* middle-schoolers!) They lie awake worrying about what will happen the next day at school or in their neighborhood. They are confused about the changes in their bodies, not clear about what is normal, and wanting desperately to have a friend.

There is a difference in boys' motivation and interest in school. We can trace this back to their time in preschools and kindergarten. With the early acceleration of learning in kindergarten, boys are struggling. They need movement—to run around, climb trees, test themselves physically against each other, and explore with their senses, but with the emphasis on academics and classroom work, they have difficulty sitting still for long periods. Soon they are separated and labeled as problem children. In many cases, this leads to diagnosis of ADHD, oppositional defiance disorder, bipolar disorder, depression, and medication. Once boys feel singled out in school because it is not meeting their needs, they come to hate school and give up, or become active underminers of what they have come to hate.

Teachers of elementary grades experience boys lacking motivation to complete their work, to exert effort, to express interest in reading or to work quietly on arithmetic. They either become hostile or they want to disappear into video games. This continues in middle school where they don't want to compete with the girls and would rather give up and pretend that they choose to not make an effort, with an attitude that expresses that they could really do well if they wanted to exert themselves.

As they become teenagers, many boys lack motivation, don't want to work hard, have less interest in sports, and may convince their parents to let them be home-schooled.

If they have been turned off in school or do not have strong interests in another activity, such as hobbies, sports, outdoor activities, or theater, boys are particularly vulnerable to being addicted to violent video games. In these games, they can be heroes in a state of constant excitability, killing, zapping, and destroying. As Dr. Leonard Sax states, "The more time you spend playing video games, the more likely you are to develop difficulties maintaining sustained concentration on a single item." Boys can take risks in aggressive video games that they avoid doing in real life. Because they are killing virtual human beings as if they are objects, this dehumanizes their personalities resulting in less caring and being more hostile.

In *Wired Child*, Richard Freed, PhD, a child and adolescent psychologist and authority on raising children in the digital age, points out that brain imaging techniques such as fMRI and PET scans reveal that video gaming impacts the mind in a similar way to drugs and alcohol. "Video gaming triggers the release of dopamine at levels comparable to an intravenous injection of amphetamine, a powerful and addictive psychostimulant." (p. 77) This addiction stimulates the sense of pleasure in the brain and affects areas related to motivation, insight, self-control, and decision-making. Doctor Freed also reveals that the work of Dr. B.J. Fogg at Stanford University has influenced the entire social media and video gaming industries with programming called "Persuasive Design," invented to make video games and social media programs deliberately addictive. "Let's keep them gaming forever!" was a slogan on one of Dr. Fogg's 42 websites. This slogan was removed after the breaking news of the Cambridge Analytica scandal that proved extreme invasion of the privacy of Facebook users.

Some boys have a more complicated experience of delayed puberty and/or problems in their sexual development. Although girls begin puberty around 9, boys begin around 12, and sometimes not until 14 or 15. This leaves a situation where "…many girls now have completed the process of puberty by age 11 or 12—an age when most of the boys are just getting started." (Sax, *Boys Adrift*, p. 134)

According to Greenspan and Deardorff (*The New Puberty*, pp. 55–60) and Sax (*Boys Adrift*, pp. 138, 142–143), endocrine disrupters affect girls and boys differently. There is growing evidence that exposure to synthetic chemicals, especially environmental estrogen, may disrupt or slow puberty in boys. Hormones that are usually released when puberty begins are released much earlier, stimulated also by hormones in commercially processed meats. This influence includes the time in utero and in early infancy. These can affect the boys in "blunting" or eliminating sex differences in behaviors.

It's interesting to note that Dr. Rudolf Steiner (1861–1925), in his lectures now called *Waldorf Education for Adolescence* (p. 59) explained that—to the extent that we can generalize, as every child is different—girls achieve puberty with more highly differentiated astral quality in their new capacities of judgment, while boys attain puberty without this refinement. This can tend to make girls more verbal, more mature in affect, more impatient with "those hopelessly immature boys." Girls often pull boys up by the scruff of their necks to "get with it" for the first years of middle school; however, by the ages of 16, 17, and 18, this turns, and boys (free of addictive encumbrances as those just described) are helpful to girls in ways of intellectual capacities. By the age of 21, young men can often step into adulthood easily, while some young women struggle with identity and cannot separate feelings from thinking abilities

HOW ARE GIRLS BEING AFFECTED?

Louise Greenspan, MD, a clinical pediatric endocrinologist, and Julianna Deardorff, PhD, a clinical psychologist and researcher in pubertal development, writing in *The New Puberty*, point to hormone-mimicking chemicals and the effects of stress in early life affecting early puberty and obesity in girls.

Girls have always relied on relationships for their social life. This is true from the early years. They generally tend to value being liked more than being good at something. When they reach the middle school years, they are particularly vulnerable to the dynamics of judgment. They struggle with their self-image, are nervous about being accepted, and can be adept in reading subtle clues from others. Are they wearing the right clothes? Will they be made fun of? How do they avoid being gossiped about? Who is the leader who can turn a group against them with the roll of her eyes or the whisper of judgment? The hierarchy of power in a circle of girls is fluid, and young girls never quite know if they are in it or outside it.

With the influence of social media, girls are significantly affected. In the past, they may have picked up a note shaming them, but now it is put on social media so everyone can see it. They are never sure of their place in the social group so being constantly connected through texting becomes vital to their feeling of participation and acceptance. Taking pictures of themselves to establish their self-image is a dangerous game because if they don't get enough "likes" they can feel devastated. Which group of friends do they want to be in, which group accepts them, what do they have to do to be in it? Their sense of self-worth is fragile at this time of the Vulnerability Gap.

Girls tend to be happy in school if they feel they are liked by their teachers. They take comfort in doing their work regularly and being praised. Whereas boys have trouble sitting still in the early grades, girls are able to do so more easily. If girls feel appreciated, they will work hard for their teacher. However, in middle school the changes they are going through may interrupt their commitment to their school work. Being concerned about being humiliated, hyper-aware of hair and clothing styles, not sure of her status with friends, she can easily be distracted. She is trying to be as perfect as possible, copying the popular girls or watching a YouTube video on how to dress or put on make-up. Having a best friend, even though it may change, can feel like the difference between life and death to a middle school girl.

With the earlier hormonal changes in puberty, girls become aware of their bodies at a younger time. They feel these changes in unusual feelings, not sure how to handle having their breasts develop or beginning menses earlier than others. At a younger age they would have been oblivious to their bodies and would have enjoyed running, jumping rope, and other physical games, but now they are self-conscious in these activities.

In their 2010 study, Greenspan and Deardorff showed that the onset of breast buds was showing around 7 and 8, but that first menstruation was around 13. They conclude:

> These studies all agree on one thing. The discrepancies cannot
> be explained entirely by changes in nutrition, body weight,
> or body fat percentage. Rather they point to the powerful
> environmental effects of changes that have taken place in
> lifestyle factors, and perhaps psychological conditions. (p. 12)

They conclude that there are three issues that may affect early beginning of puberty: excess fat, being overweight or obese; exposure to chemicals that disrupt healthy human biology, especially the hormonal system; and social and psychological stressors such as early childhood trauma and poor familial relationships. (p. 13) It seems a combination of these factors, some environmental and some psychological, act as triggers to begin the process of sexual maturity in girls. The two big changes for the girls in middle school now are the effect of early puberty and social pressure intensified by the strong influence of social media.

PARENTAL LIFE STYLES ARE CHANGING

As described earlier, parents are stressed and having difficulty coping with challenges. They are often obsessively connected with technology, and they might pay less attention to their children. At the same time, they can be very concerned with wanting their children to be protected and safe, even going so far as to be termed "helicopter parents," hovering over every action in a child's life; or the newer term "bulldozer parents," plain old pushing to get the best for their child.

This seems contradictory, but this contradiction is the reality. Visit a park where young mothers have taken their children for fresh air. The mother may be nursing or holding the infant and at the same time speaking on her cell phone. Or she may be listening with earphones. How can she be connected with the child, listening, sensing the child's needs, speaking to the child in reassuring tones? Often, these same mothers (and fathers as well) love their children very much, but are not conscious of the results of their distracted actions. I have seen children of three or four tugging at their parents' arms, crying, "Look at me!" frustrated at their parents' attention focused elsewhere. A twelve-year-old wrote a skit which he acted out with his friends in which they call upon their parents to get off the cell phone and be connected with their children.

There is no question that life is stressful today as the pace quickens with so much sensory overload, commercial bombardment in every venue, financial stress, and feelings of isolation. Yet there have been other times in history when life has been stressful. What is different? There are many reasons, but one frequently met around the world in my travels is the loss of the sense of inner authority, the responsibility of what it means to be an adult in relation to children. This leads to the adult's sense of feeling inadequate, looking for guidance elsewhere, in books, podcasts, experts, and popular figures. The materialistic tone of our time encourages parents to give toys, books, and "things" instead of attention to their children. Children's needs are not a matter of how many toys or gadgets they have, how many extra activities they partake in after school, or how much money is available. The quality of relationships, deep and meaningful, is what makes a difference to a child. This will help parents ignite and tend the spark within each child.

Both boys and girls experience a lack of adult guidance as they find their way to adulthood. Never before have children been left to be guided by peers not yet at the stage of adulthood themselves. This shows in a coarsening of public life, in language, gestures, treatment of each other, and disregard of adults.

WHAT IS HAPPENING IN THE MINDS OF MIDDLE SCHOOL CHILDREN?

What's going on behind the scenes? Middle school is a time of great drama. We experience the middle-schoolers in their everyday enthusiasm, frustration, moodiness, and excitement. However, behind the scenes of this great drama is the unseen development in the brain. Understanding some of the subtleties guiding middle school behavior helps us as parents and teachers to have patience, warmth, and, yes, even delight.

Neuroscience has been a formal science for only about thirty years. Already very important discoveries have been made, but it is still only in its infancy. Studies beginning in 2002 (the CYGNET study) and continuing additional studies were brought together in an article in *Pediatrics*, 2012, and more studies are continuing.

Changes in the brain stimulate other parts of the brain to begin the process of puberty. In the boy, the presence of androgens (male hormones) triggers the growth of pubic hair. In the girl, estrogen is responsible for the beginning of puberty. In pubescent girls, the gonadotropin hormone (GnRH), which is released by the brain acts like a switch that turns on the pituitary gland, which then sends a message to the ovaries to produce estrogen, which causes breasts to grow. (Greenspan and Deardorff, *The New Puberty*, p. 50)

The stages of puberty, whenever they occur, are part of a normal process that takes place in all young people and marks a transition from childhood to adulthood in which their bodies, their emotions, their social relations, and their behavior will be completely different once they have come through the process.

In trying to understand the middle school child, we need to consider the complexity of child development. Each part of the brain has its own time of maturing, which makes it possible for new capacities to arise. Rushing the child through these phases takes away the potential of healthy growth. A great dance occurs between the different parts of the brain's functioning and the child's experiences. When the child is ready and has an appropriate experience, new capacities and skills arise. The experiences work back on the brain and affect the development of neurons. Certain experiences can stimulate the cells and neurons to awaken prematurely. For example, sexualization of modern society may affect the sexual precociousness children experience in their bodies.

Although neuroscience has given us a great deal of important and useful information, there is a tendency to see children simply as a collection of neurons. This materialistic view can blind us from considering the human being as spiritual with a unique destiny. The brain is a magnificent physical vehicle, establishing the possibility of thinking, feeling, and willing. It is the physical foundation that the human "I" uses to make its way in the world. Without a healthy brain, the human being struggles to develop capacities. Without a healthy soul and spirit, the human being can use capacities for immoral goals. Tending the spark is supporting healthy soul and spirit development, as well as healthy physical development at this critical time in a child's life.

DEVELOPMENTAL STAGES AND THE VULNERABILITY GAP

We are born with an abundance of neurons and gain more during the first neural growth spurt. Throughout childhood, the experiences we have affect the building of neurons in our brains. Every few years there are smaller neural growth spurts. At each stage new experiences engender new neurons that are then activated; new capacities awaken, and children use their experiences to develop capacities into different kinds of intelligences.

It is essential for children to have balanced human adults during childhood to guide them on their path of development. Children imitate everything around them with the greatest trust that "this is exactly the way it should be." For the first seven years, children imitate unconsciously, absorbing the gestures, the language, and the attitudes of parents, teachers, and caregivers. From around seven to ten, children love to be taught new things. They follow the teacher, their parents, or another adult in how to organize themselves, use their tools (pencil, brush, etc.) correctly. They are happy to learn to sing, to do handwork, to learn another language, to do arithmetic, to make maps. Most children respond easily to the teacher's instructions, and if the teaching is artistic and enthusiastic, they respond with eagerness and joy.

Around the age of nine (anywhere from 8.5 to 10 years of age), children go through a time of separation, of beginning to see themselves from the outside and realize they are different. The magic is gone from the world, their imagination dries up, and everything seems ordinary and dull. This "nine-year-change" is for the child a mood of the soul as it begins to find a way in the real world.

After the nine-year-change the different parts of the brain begin to stabilize. Children continue to gain knowledge, storing up treasures that they will later come to understand in greater depth. This time after the nine-year change and before the ages of eleven/twelve is often referred to as the heart of childhood. With support and understanding, children come through this time ready to engage again and find new connections and satisfaction.

The four-year gap in ages between 11/12 and 14/15, the Vulnerability Gap, is a time of danger and opportunity. Here is the biggest growth spurt since infancy. It is a time of integration of the brain itself in which all neural systems are synthesized. Different parts of the body grow at different rates, which often results in physical awkwardness. Those neural connections that are weaker will disappear in a pruning process. Those experiences that have been repeated during childhood will endure as they are myelinated. Myelin is a fatty white substance that surrounds and protects a nerve axon so that nerve impulses to muscles are speeded up and so that communication between neurons is facilitated. During this time, different parts of the brain are linked, and all previous neural systems are integrated. This takes time.

Gradually children begin to realize that adults are different from each other and to question these adults to measure the different answers they are likely to receive. This becomes particularly strong during the years 11 to 14, when children's capacity to think heightens and they begin to consciously decide whom to imitate. They pick their stars, influenced by the books they read, the movies they see, the music they listen to, the older teenagers around them, their parents, teachers, and coaches who see them daily, as well as other adults in their environment.

Because of all the changes going on in the brain, the middle school age of eleven to fourteen is an unstable time in which the soul forces of thinking, feeling, and willing separate in different directions and go their own ways. Middle-schoolers experience thinking as a new power, arguing, exploring causes, gathering facts, collecting, and challenging. They are very sensitive in their feeling life, easily hurt, quick to feel isolated and unstable. They are active in their will, pushing against others, using strength to defend their position, competing, and sensing strength in different parts of their body. However, these three forces do not connect with each other just yet as the body processes the brain matter and the new changes in the body. This is very confusing for the child who might be out of control and sometimes feeling at a loss.

Psychiatric disorders often have a first major onset during this time, and we need to be observant when we see signs of disturbance. The child is particularly susceptible to stress because stability is needed for this time of synthesizing all the systems of the brain, the integration of the three soul forces. Supportive relationships, adult role models, and security are needed to stimulate integration. We could say that this period is a stabilizing of the "old mind," of all that came before puberty.

If this is normal development, why do I speak of the Vulnerability Gap? Aren't the middle school years just another stage like all the others? Aside from the growth forces in infancy, this is the most significant time of enormous growth in human life, never to be repeated again in a lifetime. Everything feels new. Everything is changing outwardly, whether it is the change in shoe size, the sharpening features of the face, or the gradual strengthening of the muscles. Everything is changing inwardly in thinking—youngsters strive to figure out how to make their way through the drama of this age, reflecting on experiences, waking up to who they want to be, and figuring out their identity, separate from parents and teachers they may have followed willingly up to this point in their lives.

This period of change has always been present in historical periods of the past, but there is a difference. Then children were then protected by family structure and conventions of society. Preteens were still considered to be children in the past and did not have as much freedom to choose their food, their clothes, when they wanted to do something, or when they didn't want to fulfill the expectations of adults. They didn't have influence on the family life the way they do today. Adults were adults and children were children. Apprenticeships were common at the age of fourteen or so, when a young person learned a trade under the strict guidance of a journeyman or master. Choices for them could happen after they had gone through the rite of passage and become adolescents or young adults.

In our time when so much change is happening within the physical body and the soul of the child, when they are struggling to adjust to these changes, our cultural norms of family structure and society have weakened in their understanding of what is needed. Children are making choices from the time they are very little, and parents are often overcome by the power children exhibit in demanding "I want" and "I need." Society does not protect children from experiences they are not ready for, and parents can feel overwhelmed trying to hold boundaries, working to have children wait before they get to do what they want. An example is the rating of movies. One would expect that a movie for children would be appropriate and not introduce sexuality, violence, coarseness of language, or rudeness. Yet there is more and more un-clarity of what the rating means when a movie is considered appropriate for a certain age. Does the parent have to watch each movie first before allowing the child to attend? It would seem so, but it isn't realistic given the demands of time on most parents.

Indigenous cultures had their own rites of passage, after which the young person was recognized as a member of the community with adult responsibility. In families guided by a religious teaching, a rite of passage was organized so that this would happen. These experiences did not happen by themselves or under the care of others their own age. These rituals or rites of passage happened because adults were guiding the process in which the child had to learn particular skills and gain knowledge, had to show a hard-won new capacity in front of the community. This was then followed by recognition and a clear welcome from the witnessing community. It was a lengthy process, involving hard work, separation, fear, worry, and relief. These kinds of rituals still go on today with more or less success in bar and bat mitzvahs in Jewish traditions, confirmations in Christian faiths, Eagle Scout status in the Boy Scout structure, and so on.

With earlier physical puberty in girls, and both boys and girls being prematurely sexually aware, they are vulnerable. They are still children, but they are needing to take responsibility for their sexual behavior before full emotional and social maturity has occurred. They are at the mercy of older children, teenagers or adults who can easily manipulate them. In their desire to be accepted, they will do things that bring harm. They are at risk physically, emotionally, socially, and intellectually just at the time when their brains are going through dramatic restructuring.

These cultural influences are unwelcome strangers who have moved into our homes during the Vulnerability Gap through screen technology including smartphones, iPads, computers, and flat screen TVs. They are strong, they are disruptive, and they affect the child's ability to complete remodeling in an effective way. In the past fifty years, the television was the unwelcome stranger, moving in, taking up space and time, and introducing values from popular culture. Now there are more strangers, and they are insidious—technology, pornography, group pressure, older teens taking the place of adults, deceleration of academic expectations, and the power of the dollar in advertising and marketing. They are pushing their way in, uninvited, just at this time when youngsters are most impressionable and lack the capacity to differentiate or regulate their influence.

Let's be clear—all aspects of popular culture might not be harmful and vicious. However, we must become guardians of our children seeking what is healthy, and we must protect them from what is not. If we do not tend the spark of higher human capacities, who will? Children cannot be abandoned at this time in their lives.

We can use the metaphor of a tight rope over a marsh with sharks threatening from either side when we speak about middle-schoolers. There are physical health risks, especially due to environmental or chemical influences, premature sexual activity, harmful foods, and beauty products. There are behavioral health risks including body-image issues, eating disorders, substance abuse, poor academic performance, delinquency, addiction, and aggression. There are soul health risks which include isolation, the crushing of innate idealism, (yes, again) premature sexuality, cynicism, poor self-image, bullying, and feeling objectified.

As we contemplate these challenges, let's not be disheartened. Remember, there is a tightrope over this marsh. The child has to walk on this tightrope, looking straight ahead, balancing arms and legs, and keeping a rhythm. What they are bringing with them is their open-hearted interest in the world, their willingness to explore new things, try out new opportunities, aspire to high ideals, and share their thoughts. They may make some erratic movements, almost fall off, but we adults must be there to catch them, support them, and believe in them. They are moving through the Vulnerability Gap until the time comes when they can catch themselves, reflect on what they are doing, and make necessary changes to find their balance.

That will come with adolescence, with its growth spurt of new neural pathways and a new awareness of their greater Self. Adolescence is filled with risks as teenagers go through the process of transforming instincts to a higher level of behavior, thinking critically, assessing risks, becoming capable of considering the big picture. Anything is possible as the new mind is being developed. The combination of pruning, myelination, hormones, genetic influences, and experiences all shape neural activity and serves as psychological support for the deepening soul of the teenager and young adult. It is a time of awakening. But that is more the story of the high school years.

CHAPTER 3
Preparing for the Civilizing Mind

In the last chapter I described the Vulnerability Gap, from ages eleven to fourteen, as a time of new and important possibilities, as well as risks.

The young child comes "trailing clouds of glory," as William Wordsworth described in his poem "Intimations of Immortality." As the journey begins on earth, the infant is deeply influenced by heredity working from the past and from the family environment that will influence the future. Gradually the child explores the world through the senses and crawls, walks, and speaks through imitating those in the environment. Trusting in the goodness of those who care for them, children act out their environment through play and singing games and in becoming social with others.

Around the age of seven, the child awakens to the world of beauty, living in the rhythm of seasons through nature and community activities, following the authority of adults who guide them into the world of thinking, feeling, and doing. This is a time of developing healthy habits, setting the foundations of learning, and being a helpful member of the community.

Around nine the child draws in and begins to feel a separation between himself and others. From within, children meet the world through their temperament, and from without they begin to sense the effects of their environment, coming to realize that each person is different and each family is different. The nine-year-change is a shift in the child's perspective, having been cast out of the magical time of childhood onto the earth with the sense of the real world. As each child resolves this imbalance, there is new energy to meet the world.

The child from nine to eleven years of age is experiencing the heart of childhood—achieving a balance between physical grace in their bodies and excitement for learning about the world through their feelings. Forces work from two directions—from the earthly influences in the body and from cosmic influences working in the soul life. This is childhood at its most glorious, and every child deserves to experience the crowning of this stage of life. The cosmic influences work from within as the child awakens to morality and a sense of being connected with everything. This is the spark that needs to be tended before puberty brings weight and gravity.

Usually about age eleven in girls and twelve in boys, bodily influences exert pressure from another two directions—an explosion of brain cell growth and intense hormonal activity. A new blast of brain cells surges to think with and many new things arise to think about. There are also things to feel through the surging hormones. And the heart stands between these two new influences as the youngster tries to balance during this period of consolidation. This process takes time and is occurring behind the scenes, out of sight of the adults who care for the child.

The soul of the child connects with the physical body as signs of puberty are occurring. Children experience strange cravings, desires, and discomfort. They feel temptation as their instincts push them to satisfy these cravings. They begin to challenge rules, sneak, or lie. Although they may have acted like that during the nine-year change, now these attempts to test the rules and to test their world are more conscious. At one moment, they give in to the temptation, another moment they resist. They know what the rules are, but they struggle to figure out what to do. No longer is the child innocent; now there is consciousness that everything the youngster does will have an effect on others. We might say that the young person is now responsible for the karma he or she causes and is in the infancy of an adult biography.

Then around the age of fourteen, something new begins to awaken in the heart, something that hadn't been felt before and cannot be expressed concretely. We see echoes of this when we observe how children of this age want to help the world. They want to save the rain forests, to help the poor; they want the world to be a better, more loving place. The fact that they do not have the skills and expertise to do this does not take away from the deep longing of the heart. This longing to serve others is the spark we help to kindle.

CHALLENGING THE OLD MIND

By the time children reach middle school, they have unconscious attitudes, prejudices, and assumptions about themselves and others. They have developed these from their parents, their teachers, and the general culture because they always assumed that what was said to them was true. These come to form what I call the "old mind." From bigotry we can experience in contemporary life, we know that the old mind is present and powerful.

As students experience perspectives of different cultures or different viewpoints, they are challenged to think differently. "I never thought about it that way" is a comment that lets us know that something is changing in the youngster's mind. This is not comfortable at first, as it creates differences between an innocent middle-schooler and the adults or classmates who think in a prejudiced way. Statements such as "All people are..." are statements of narrow-mindedness and fixed thinking.

During middle school, experiences can expose these assumptions and stimulate new thinking, new possibilities, and new vistas of moving out into the world.

Middle-schoolers can also experience the old mind in the way they think about themselves: "I can't do that" or "I'm not good at that." However, if adults encourage them, they can begin to expand their sense of themselves and feel that something new is possible. The kind of attitudes middle school children have about others and themselves will help form the kind of a civilization that is developing for the future.

Neurophysiologist Elkhonon Goldberg refers to the prefrontal cortex as providing the physical foundation for the "civilizing mind." Through the development of the prefrontal cortex after 14, the child has the chance to develop civility. As quoted in Pearce's *Biology of Transcendence*, p. 48, Goldberg says, "It is this civility that is a prerequisite for the development of our capacity to transcend, to fill our role in evolution as well as curb our suicidal violence, and to survive."

What is needed for the civilizing mind to begin to awaken? There are two key elements. From the physical point of view, youngsters will experience physical change through the prefrontal cortex as the vehicle for soul and spiritual change. From the cultural life, they need adults who model idealism and true civility.

In many ways middle-schoolers are still children. As I mentioned earlier, this need was recognized by religious traditions as well as indigenous cultures, which held a ritual when a child became thirteen and took on new responsibility in the community. The experience of making this step marked a new beginning of what would gradually become an inner change.

Once puberty has occurred, and such rituals have been marked, adolescents' earlier relationship to life in the community changes, and they begin to take on responsibility. It is the beginning of a new stage that will grow more strongly during the next seven years.

Middle-schoolers stand as a bridge between past, present, and future. Everything that has happened before this time was done unconsciously. They were not really aware of what they were doing. Therefore, we speak of them as being innocent and not yet responsible for what they do. They acted out of the "old mind." But after adolescence is reached, the young person is embedded in a struggle between instinct and a higher self that is calling forth a new consciousness.

BUILDING THE CIVILIZING MIND

Because of earlier puberty, youngsters are at risk of being overwhelmed by outside forces before they become aware of their sense of responsibility and are mature enough to respond to situations that arise. Usually after sixteen, the adolescent develops executive function while asking the difficult questions of life such as Who am I? Where did I come from? What happens after death? What is good, what is evil, what is freedom? What are the repercussions of my actions? What is my responsibility? These are the questions that high school students struggle with, searching for answers that will guide them. This is the time when the Self, the "I am" or ego (not to be confused with Freud's use of the word), is beginning to awaken in the young person.

On one hand, it is why adolescents turn inward into the darkness of the soul, and give rise to the highest percentage of suicides in history, or feel intense isolation and possibly strike outward in criminal behavior. In some youth, we can trace their acts to mental illness. For others, something arises unprovoked, unexplained, to carry out such acts. Another way of looking at it is that the destabilizing experience of this new awareness is like mental illness. Teens search for anchors to help them stay grounded. Some deal with the inward confusion by covering it up with addictions to drugs, video games, alcohol or sex to keep from feeling pain. New questions arise as to sexuality, to friendship, to love.

The problem is that with earlier puberty occurring—again, currently around 12 years of age—there is an unprotected time until around 16 when they are adrift, needing to have the awareness and help of adults in their lives. They cannot cross the Vulnerability Gap alone; as though on a raft without paddles, they swim in the strong currents of our present culture that toss them to and fro.

How are their thinking life, their feeling life, and their will life changing? At this time when their emotions are supercharged, overwhelming their thoughts and their actions, they are at risk. They are vulnerable. Their behavior is often like a call in the wilderness for adults to wake up and listen to the pain that lives below the surface.

During the middle school years children respond to adults in a kind of imitation by looking up to those who express values they admire.

Youngsters of this age might act as if they are not paying attention, not admiring, but they watch and listen very carefully. They choose their own role models, people who "walk their talk." Gradually, as they begin to think for themselves, they will find their own way to manifest these values they have emulated when they are out in the world.

During the earlier years the child's morality is shaped from outside, from the rules and expectations of parents and society. Around eleven or twelve they begin to separate the rules of the adult world from their own ideas of what should happen. They question everything. The challenge is to help them understand the social situation, that rules are helpful for guiding people's behavior. Because their executive function is not guiding them yet, they need opportunities to discuss behavior to exercise this newly dawning capacity of executive function. To tell them that they must simply obey adults does not work at this middle school age. They need opportunities to consider what would happen if there were no rules, what rules might be helpful in a classroom or in a family, what happens when people disobey rules. Having class councils, voting on classroom expectations, holding family meetings, and asking for their opinions engages them in the process. Gradually they begin to become awake to the need for social agreements.

Of course, the adults have the final authority here, but the more this process can be worked out collaboratively, the more strongly the young person can feel involved, and the more he or she will feel included in the process. Their thinking becomes active in sorting out problems and solutions. They transform the old mind as the spark of concern and awareness for others is activated.

During the following chapters, we will consider ways in which we can help middle-schoolers begin the process of developing the new mind, the civilizing mind, in which values of morality, empathy, and compassion can guide thinking, feeling, and action.

CHAPTER 4

The Development of Character

TENDING THE SPARK

Rachael Kessler, in her beautiful book *The Soul of Education,* understands the need to prepare for the civilizing mind. She writes,

> Geometry and history, English and science—places and times for these subjects in the contemporary classroom are secure. But the *soul*? Doesn't that belong in church? Aren't questions of the soul private, spiritual matters that are best left at home?
>
> If so, someone had better tell the children. While we adults continue to debate these questions, most students continue to bring their souls to school. Except for the very few who are so deadened by drugs, abuse, or neglect that their inner lives are numb, students of all ages come to school with their souls alive and seeking connection. (p. ix)

It is during this time of vulnerability that we focus on character development to nourish the souls of middle-schoolers and prepare for the civilizing mind. During this time, middle-schoolers may become aware of something special that lives within: the spark of compassion, connectivity, and purpose. They go through phases in which they feel their individual needs and wants, and at the same time, they experience themselves as members of the community.

I observed examples of character development in the sixth grades in a number of Waldorf schools, as they might be present in any school. Because the sixth grade class is learning about chivalry as part

47

of medieval history, they focus on virtues they need to develop during the year. They focus on what they want to strive for at school and at home, and they include their parents and teachers in acknowledging their successes and struggles. One month the theme was perseverance. The children looked up the definition of the word, discussed it, and set themselves a task of how they would develop perseverance. Later in the year, they examined their behavior to see how they were able to succeed with this virtue.

I visited another sixth grade when the virtue of the month was reverence. That particular teacher invited a parent to visit the class and bring his or her own thoughts on the topic. This parent gave the sixth-graders a list and asked if they could have reverence for the following: lollipop, acorn, snake, air, kicking a tree, mosquito, superhero, earthworm, newborn baby, Voldemort, rosebud, standing up for a friend, their desk partner, and reverence itself. The children were to quickly write yes or no. Then they discussed their answers. As I listened, I could see how they were stretching their minds to see the thing in a larger context. For example, an acorn because it will grow to be a tree, air because we couldn't live without it. *Superhero* brought different kinds of answers. Some said "yes" because they save human beings. Others said "no" because they are mainly there for entertainment. And so it went. When they finished discussing each one, the parent asked the children to look at the list again and make any changes they wanted. A number of them did make changes. They reflected that, by listening to each other, they had new ideas.

What was impressive was the earnestness of the children in their discussion. An older group might have dismissed this as silly or been unwilling to discuss it publicly, but the sixth-graders were open to their own thoughts as well as to those of their classmates. In addition to earnestness, humor was present and served as a relief. Exercises like this help kindle the spark that lives within each child.

RECOGNIZING VIRTUES

Another sixth-grade experience occurred just before parent conferences. The children were to write a letter to their parents (which would be given to them at the conference). They were to tell their parents what they felt they were really good at and what they still needed to improve. One of the boys had a broken arm and wasn't writing. When I asked if he'd like to dictate his letter to me, and I would write it for him exactly as he said it, he agreed. His letter was as follows:

Dear Mom and Dad,
I'm pretty good at reading. It is easy. I don't like the book we are reading because it speaks of the present and then it goes back five years, consistently. That makes it boring. Both of you already know all of this. I am distracted because there are so many things in my head and I am stressed. You know that already. That's it for now, Your son —.

Other children were writing long letters with lists of what they were good at and what they were still working on. But this young man was a taciturn fellow. Although he didn't say much, I could see that his mind was full, and the distractions bothered him. It would have been so easy to see him as uninterested, but the clue to what was happening inwardly offered opportunities to support him more warmly.

Working on their virtues was the children's experience of individual awakening and development. At the same time, the teachers were working to build a strong sense of community to form a social foundation. I could already see the beginning of individual awakening of criticism as one of the boys corrected the teacher's statement in a rather rude way. One of the classmates responded to this rudeness by saying, "He's being a jerk." Tension between individual sharpness in the newly awakened thinking and a feeling of social cohesiveness continues throughout the middle school years and makes teaching these grades (and parenting this age) a challenge and exciting.

A KNIGHTING CEREMONY—
BEING PART OF A COMMUNITY

Some Waldorf schools have responded to the need for a rite of passage in awakening a sense of responsibility through a knighting ceremony. This developed gradually in one school and was adopted by different schools that then added their own aspects to the process. I have adapted elements from various schools for the following description.

At the beginning of sixth grade, students discuss chivalry and what it means. They hear stories of knighthood or examples of virtue by male or female characters. They decide what virtues they wish to develop at school, at home, and in the community. Examples could be helping out at home by doing their chores without complaining, collecting recycling in their neighborhood, being consequent in doing their homework, being kinder to their younger sibling. There are countless ways to work on developing better habits.

Each month they write an account of what they have accomplished, and their parent and/or teacher also makes comments about their improvement. During this time, they also design their own shield that carries a symbol that they decide represents their values. Toward the end of the year, after students have completed their reports and have been considered successful, there is a special evening in which the sixth-graders do activities by themselves that take courage. After they are knighted, they spend the night at school either with their class or on their own. In some schools, after the knighting ceremony, there is a grand feast of celebration with parents and teachers. With encouragement, most students complete the tasks and are recognized.

Developing the community life is critical during the middle school years. If it is missing, and the middle-schoolers become too individualistic, it is difficult to create a strong social fabric. The time to develop the community and prepare for the civilizing mind is a specific time, before the second growth spurt of neurons and executive function. This is the potential of the middle school years.

After years of teaching middle school and high school, my colleagues and I realized that the feeling of community had to be nurtured before individualism rose to the forefront. Individualism is ultimately an anti-social gesture, and if the community experience has not been rich and supportive, the youngsters can become self-serving, picking at the mistakes of teachers and classmates, and dismissive of others' needs. Of course, the process of building community must continue even when it has not been developed earlier, although it is more difficult. Skillful teachers and others can do this with sports teams, religious groups, service organizations, and classroom team-building. We should be grateful for their efforts.

When children are young, they have a deep sense of what is moral, which leads them to be fair, do the right thing, and differentiate between good and bad. After eleven or twelve years of following rules, they wake up to the fact that these rules were set by adults and seem somewhat arbitrary. They start to challenge the adults and discover that adults are not perfect and are, in fact, flawed. This is disheartening and can lead to hopelessness. The mood becomes, "What is the purpose of following their rules? They don't know anything."

The challenge for middle-schoolers is to understand the difference between what the community needs and what the individual needs. Here the teacher has the opportunity to work with the class in developing rules for classroom behavior, not rules that are imposed from without, but rules that have to do with the well-being of the class community. These discussions are priceless because youngsters gradually begin to see that rules are important for protecting the rights and needs of all.

These discussions create opportunities for the middle-schoolers to reflect on a particular behavior. What was the behavior? How did it affect the group? How does my behavior affect my classmates? Why? What can I do about it? Not every teacher has these skills, and it can be helpful to have another adult in the school who can work with a class in social and emotional development.

When the youngsters move into the next developmental phase, around age 15 or 16, they begin to understand the complexity of moral life, and they can approach rules in a different way, including dealing with the exceptions.

THINKING, FEELING, AND WILLING IN THE DEVELOPMENT OF CHARACTER

Living in Their Thinking

Middle school children's thinking is expanding and exploding with the bursts of brain cell production and the pruning of old ones. They can retreat into their thinking, aloof from others, living in their imagination, in their competitive dominance over others, and only be concerned with their own ideas. They can be one-sidedly living in their thinking.

"How do I differentiate my ideas from what other people think?" "How do I focus my thinking so I am not distracted by others?" Middle-schoolers and young teenagers have to manage the changes in their thinking and learn to use new capacities, yet their brains are only half-way developed. They have irrational misunderstandings that cause confusion and risk.

The challenge is for them to develop critical thinking, effective problem solving, and self-reliance. They have logic but no experience. They often come to a conclusion first and then try to fit in the evidence. Because they are emotionally immature, they hold tightly to their conclusion even though it is irrational. Try arguing with a thirteen-year-old. There is usually no conclusion except the age-old "Because I'm your mother" or "Because that's the way it is." They have trouble remembering things and often forget their homework, their shoes, or what you just told them. Be kind to them. They aren't doing this on purpose.

As they approach age fourteen years (often in eighth grade, but also in ninth grade), they seem more settled. Not only do they seem bigger but more solid and stable. They have more energy. Their language is more complex. As they have taken hold of their bodies and emotions, they enjoy their new thinking and are a lot of fun to be with. It is time to take a breath and feel a reprieve from the storm of the past two years. Yet, make no mistake, they are still mostly guided by their feelings while their thinking is awakening. We can be fooled by assuming they are adolescents, responsible for their actions. But that is not the case.

It is during this time that deceleration or *the downward extension of school* appears again as it did when first-grade expectations were put upon children in kindergarten. Although youngsters look like adolescents, they are still children and need time to consolidate the changes they are experiencing. Policymakers and educators, as well as commercial marketers, misunderstand this and take advantage of them, treating them as if they were older. In the rush to have them grow up quickly, they are often treated as high school students, expected to exert some degree of self-control and led into temptations that they are incapable of managing.

If middle-schoolers tend to live one-sidedly in the world of thinking, in ideas, they can become loners, cool and aloof. Some may be brilliant but unable to relate to their friends or classmates. Others may hatch wild plans to get even with opponents or live in illusions of grandiosity. They are open to virtual worlds of fantasy either through technology or in their own imagination.

It is difficult to reach such children, as their social skills are lacking. They may be on the autistic spectrum or they may simply be lost, waiting to be helped out of their own world into that of the community. They may feel safe taking refuge in their thinking, but become reclusive, lost in imagination, and unable to bring their thoughts down into real life, which will isolate them and create problems as they move into adolescence.

Adults need to help them experience safety, express their ideas, find connections with others, feel the warmth of companionship, and carry their ideas out through their will. They may invent new games, write articles for a magazine, play music together, experience the beauty of ideas when shared with others, and gradually find their way into a balanced life.

There are dangers to one-sidedness in thinking. Middle school students can take hold of this new brain thinking in a one-sided way and be smart, clever and aloof, or they can take hold of the will by giving in to unconscious instincts and impulses. The challenge is to create a bridge between the thinking and the will so that the heart realm mediates the two extremes, bringing balance and health. They cannot do this without adult guidance, guidance informed by idealism. They need adults who carry in their hearts seeds for the renewal of culture, who demonstrate deeds of love, of care for the other human being, of respect and reverence for others and for the earth itself. These are the gifts the adult world needs to give to middle school children in a way that tends the spark.

Living in Their Will

"How do I manage this body in which I dwell?" "What are the operating rules?" "Who is in charge?" "How does my body influence my feeling life?" "How is my behavior influenced by instinct and impulse?"

Instinctive urges stimulated by the newness of hormones are like fireworks sparking new feelings and desires. Middle-schoolers can live in a one-sided experience in their will in which they are tossed and turned by these new unfamiliar feelings, reacting quickly to what meets them, acting without thinking.

Often it is only after middle-schoolers make mistakes that they wake up to responsibility. As painful as it is to hold up a mirror so they will see themselves and recognize their misdeeds, these are opportunities for growth and maturity. They commit irrational acts even though they know better. Yet in the moment, they cannot predict the consequences. When an adult asks, "How could you do this? Didn't you think?" the youngster doesn't know what to say. Adults often don't realize how weak their children's or students' thinking skills are at this age. Regardless of how smart, thoughtful, and respectful they may be, they still act impulsively. We could easily fill a delightful and possibly embarrassing evening sharing the things we did in sixth or seventh grade! Now we look back at these events in our own preteen years, grateful we didn't cause permanent harm or complete chaos.

If middle-schoolers tend to live one-sidedly in the world of will, in action, they will react quickly to what comes to them rather than thinking first. They feel their sense of power, but it is usually power *over* others rather than power *with* others. Hot-tempered and aggressive, they get into trouble because they feel attacked, defensive, or self-righteous. Cool and calculating, these young people can get into trouble because they are isolated. They have wonderful energy, but it can be used in the wrong way. Left on their own, they either join with others who are similar and form gangs or act on their own using their energy to intimidate. They are the great challengers who confront their peers or the adults. They need help to calm down, think before acting, and most of all have channels for their energy.

By getting involved in athletics, outdoor challenges, or other physical activities, they have to learn to work as a team and enjoy the appropriate use of power. The adults guiding them need to sensitively work on team building and collaboration with the middle-schoolers so that they don't become stuck on being the first, best, and only. Learning to rely on others for the good of the group gradually helps them transform their will into service for others. Building a playhouse for younger children, transforming an empty lot into a garden, cleaning a trail are all examples of ways to harness the energy of the will. If not, as they move into adolescence, they are at risk of becoming brutes, and their hot-headedness will get them into big trouble. Or their cool, icy attitude can lead to disconnected harm to others.

Middle-schoolers don't recognize the difference between having an ideal and putting it into practice. Filled with hope and a sense of magical imagination, they want to eliminate pollution, stop global warming, save animals that are becoming extinct, and cure diseases. They benefit when their class has a practical project to improve part of the school campus, compost their food waste, pick up litter, or raise money for their favorite cause. They realize how much energy is involved, and how they have to keep at it day after day. Disciplining their will in this way keeps them from becoming disappointed when things don't change.

Living in Their Feelings

Between their thinking and will is the life of feeling, with new raw emotions, romantic notions, feelings of generosity, of jealousy, of compassion, of fantasy. This, too, can be an experience in one-sidedness. "How can I feel joy in life?" "How can I feel the beauty all around me?" "How do I take hold of my emotional life?"

The limbic system (the emotional part of the brain) dominates as youngsters experience new emotions and new feelings. They cry easily over small things, are overly sensitive, want close friendships, feel lonely, long for joy, feel as if nobody cares about them. They often care deeply about animals and want the world to be a happier place. But in the middle of it all, they are driven by unconscious feelings.

As Icard writes in *Middle-School Makeover*:

During the tween and teen years, other parts of the brain have to step up and take the lead role, while the prefrontal cortex is doing its job of getting stronger. Thus, the central part of the brain, the *amygdala*, takes the lead for our teens. It may come as no surprise that the *amygdala* is the emotional center of the brain. (p. 35)

Pressures at school and within peer groups can contribute to problems. Fighting for their own point of view, developing their sense of logic, and the need to shape their independent position often lead to angry and sassy interactions. "Talking back" is common, and to add to the problem, they are often sleep deprived.

All of these emotional changes are normal as they are still learning how to control and express emotions in a grown-up way, needing to have time to gain experience, to learn to read other people's emotions. What seems like insensitivity and rudeness is really awkwardness in trying out the new thinking that they are just getting used to. They don't yet have filters that sort out what is appropriate to say and what is not. Gradually, they become aware of their feelings that lead to unpleasant behavior. Then they may feel embarrassed and want to take responsibility to make things right again.

If they are one-sided in their feelings, they can become dreamers, overly sentimental or romantic. They may feel orphaned, victimized, hold illusions of carrying out a deed that cannot be accomplished, or made a fool. They may escape into their dreams and lose connection with their group. Their ideas are all over the place, and their will is weak.

Adults need to help them organize their thinking to carry out their dreams, make a plan, see what is possible, focus their will so that they can make a mark in the world. The ideals they long to follow may be worthy ones but, if unbalanced, may lead to nothing and cause a sense of frustration and hopelessness.

Feelings without clear thinking and purpose can toss the young person to and fro, with no place to land. Adults can help them recognize the importance of beauty in ideas, in feelings, and in actions that are realistic. They can bring to the youngster's attention the biographies of worthy human beings, helping them to enter the time of adolescence with grounding.

It is helpful for middle-schoolers to express feelings through talking or acting, developing a stronger sense of right and wrong, and more capacity for complex thought. Their task is to develop their heart-space through cultivating sympathy, compassion, and empathy—aspects of the spark that glows from within. This takes time and patience.

THE MIDDLE-SCHOOLERS WHO DO EVERYTHING RIGHT

Some middle-schoolers are more balanced in their thinking, feeling, and willing than others. They seemed easy to be around at the beginning of middle school. They are responsible and even-tempered in their responses. Adults may count on them to always do the right thing because they have been so steady. Teachers, parents, and other adults may expect them to be leaders, to offer new ideas, to set an example for their peers, and be counted on to get the job done.

But even these children will have times when their behavior makes no sense and they seem temporarily lost, erratic, frustrated, or unbalanced. Adults may feel disappointed when they don't come through, make mistakes, forget things, or act strangely. Remember that their brains too are changing, their hormones are firing, and they are at the mercy of powerful surges. It would be well to remember that within these children are young people full of promise. Do not hold on to the mistakes they make, the strange behavior at times, the poor decisions.

Believe in them. As they move into adolescence, they will regain that beautiful balance which adults had previously admired, but now it will develop out of their own inner intention.

THE NEED FOR BALANCE

Where would we be without thinkers, dreamers, or powerful doers? Society needs all of these capacities, but in balance. Because the youngsters themselves are going through a time of chaos, they can't find their way out of their one-sidedness without help. The integration of their thinking, feeling, and will is a challenging experience that takes time and support from the adult world. They will go through periods of loneliness, separation, and confusion. They will think without acting, act without thinking, and swim in their feelings.

We want to protect middle-schoolers from loneliness and sadness, but we can't. This experience is one of the most important to be worked through. To feel lonely means that you have come down to a sense of self. We have to help them along to self-regulate so they can begin to monitor themselves to know how much is too much.

What is the challenge? To integrate the three soul forces of thinking, feeling, and willing. Instead of being overly lost in one of the soul forces, youngsters need to build a healthy interrelationship of the three. How?

THE WIZARD OF OZ

One possible answer was given in Frank Baum's *The Wizard of Oz*. Baum described that the story came to him as a burst of inspiration out of nowhere. The story, first written as a book, has archetypal characters and has been interpreted politically, psychologically, and spiritually. Children loved the book and asked for more. Baum wrote many sequels to continue Dorothy's adventures. The production of the movie with Judy Garland helped make the story and its characters familiar in many homes. I find it a helpful imagination in understanding middle school children.

Dorothy lives with her aunt and uncle in Kansas. When she and her dog Toto are caught in a tornado, she is whisked away into "a land not like anything she has ever seen before." Unknown to her, her house has fallen on the evil witch and killed her. Filled with fear, Dorothy does not know where she is, she just wants to go home. The good witch instructs her to follow the yellow brick road to ask the Wizard of Oz the way back to her home. Along the way Dorothy meets the scarecrow who wants a brain, the tin man who has been rusted and wants a heart, and a cowardly lion who wants courage. Dorothy invites them to join her on the yellow brick road to ask the Wizard of Oz to give them what they long for.

Journeying through various lands that represent the temptations of the middle school child, Dorothy and her friends realize, as does the middle-schooler, that they already have what they were seeking. They just had to wake up to it.

Here we have three characters, each representing one of the three soul forces—thinking, feeling, and willing. Once Dorothy realizes she doesn't have to rely on a false authority like the wizard, she is whisked back to her home where she appreciates her aunt and uncle from a new perspective: "It's good to be home again."

I think the story has helpful images. The middle school child is going through many changes that destabilize their thinking, feeling, and willing. They are indeed in a land they have not visited before. Is it any wonder they are confused? They need to integrate their thinking, which is challenged by the millions of new neural connections; balance their feelings, which are overly stimulated by hormones; and direct their will, which is over-reacting to their unexplained experiences.

What is it that will guide them through this land where good and evil abide? The adults who love and care for this tender age will help them recognize that they have capacities that will help them find answers within themselves. However, they still need protection as they move into the next stage of the journey of adolescence, where they will awaken consciously to their Self, their "I." They will then take on the task of cultivating their spark by themselves that will illuminate their life journey.

CHAPTER 5

Preparing the Civilizing Mind:
The Four Essentials

There are four essential aspects that can help youngsters move through middle school, to bridge the innocent past and the responsible future, to balance between their thinking and their will through their feeling. These are the essentials that are important for character development that will help youngsters prepare their civilizing mind.

THE ROLE OF ADULTS

The first essential is healthy adult role models for young people to emulate. Repetition of this key point, noticeable in previous chapters, is intended to emphasize how necessary these role models are. The conventions of society used to hold children of this age until they came fully into adolescence. Already by thirteen or fourteen, children used to begin apprenticeships. A boy worked next to a man and learned a trade. A girl worked next to a woman and eased her way into adulthood. In our times, this stage of middle school is new. In the past, people were not free to choose their futures. One went from childhood to adult life without the transition adolescence now affords. Now, this preadolescent period of 11–14 and the adolescent period of 14–21 are two stages that form a new challenge. It is a great experiment. Can the youngster come to a sense of Self without support in society?

Who are the role models; who can the child look up to? As I describe elsewhere, adults are having their own problems, struggling to believe in themselves as authority figures, turning their children over to the guidance of older children, negating the wisdom and maturity they have gained through their own passage into adulthood.

Now that youngsters are in this stage, they are choosing their own role models, often beyond the close family members. They are looking outward to those they admire who will show them what it means to be a responsible, caring, altruistic 21st-century adult. Perhaps it is a teacher, a coach, a next-door neighbor, Uncle Joe, or someone they have heard about such as Martin Luther King, Jr., Mother Theresa, Nelson Mandela, Mahatma Gandhi or Jane Goodall. Eventually, they may also be looking up to a parent. But for now, they mostly need to separate from their parents to find a space for themselves.

In my own early adolescence, my role model was Jane Froman (1907–1980) with her song "I'll Walk Alone" from the film *With a Song in My Heart*. When World War II broke out, she was one of the first performers to volunteer to sing for the troops. In 1943 her plane crashed outside of Portugal, and she was one of the few passengers to survive, although she was badly injured. She went through years of suffering with one infection after another. She faced a possible leg amputation, but she could still rely on her beautiful voice. Her scars, the use of crutches, and repeated operations did not stop her. To add to the romance, years later she married the pilot who had rescued her in the plane crash. My girlfriend and I formed our own fan club, and we would listen to her music and feel filled with hope and joy.

I loved baseball, and Jackie Robinson was another idol of mine. He had the courage to be the first African-American to desegregate a baseball team. Inspired by his courage, I looked forward to the games, followed number 42, and wrote down every hit and every catch. It was helpful to have people such as these to admire and to wish for some of their qualities as my own.

Not only do we find our heroes in the popular culture, but we also find them in literature and music. Bringing biographies of heroes to youngsters in sixth through eighth grades is an important way of expanding the field from which they can find someone to admire.

In his recent book, *The Road to Character,* David Brooks speaks of the role biographies played in the life of General George Marshall.

> By cultivating the habit of reverence—for ancient heroes, for the elderly, for leaders in one's own life—teachers were not only offering knowledge of what greatness looks like, they were trying to nurture a talent for admiration. Proper behavior is not just knowing what is right; it is having the motivation to do what is right, an emotion that propels you to do good things. (p. 108)

In addition to real-life heroes described in books, there are also fictional heroes. Girls of my generation admired Nancy Drew for her courage and adventure. Boys read *The Hardy Boys.* Today, Harry Potter has inspired a whole generation to love reading and to feel excited about heroes who are teenagers confronting evil and doing the good.

Because popular culture surrounds middle-schoolers, they are flooded with images and examples of adults, good and bad. There are adventurers, inventors, fighters for justice, and sports heroes, but there are also adults they look up to, such as Kim Kardashian, who lead them into superficial worlds of appearance, or sports figures who become involved in domestic violence or drugs. Because information is so readily available, even heroes who work for the good are often exposed to be imperfect. We see media heroes, sports heroes, musicians, teen idols, and political figures crashing down from high public esteem through their connection with drugs, sexual misbehavior, or violence. But if middle-schoolers are lucky enough to find someone positive to emulate, this is worth gold.

THE ROLE OF STORY

The second essential is the role of story. Story has been important throughout history and especially for children. Stories fill the soul need to have heroes with humane intentions. Before middle school the Waldorf language arts curriculum is rich with mighty acts in myths, but once into the sixth, seventh, and eighth grades, biographies become an important means of education. In these life stories, human beings engaged in their striving have to overcome obstacles, develop self-discipline, and do something meaningful with their lives. These heroic stories show the middle-schooler that it is valuable to struggle against obstacles for the greater good.

Stories are important because they provide the ethical foundation of the culture. Through story, one learns about generosity, sharing, sacrifice, nobility, etc. Stories feed the soul; they tend the spark. I can sense in these stories that when good overcomes evil, the child inwardly says, "Yes!" The biographies of people facing moral challenges and rising to the highest are especially important now. Especially interesting are stories with siblings who were raised in the same family—one becomes a criminal, the other a police officer or a jail warden. What was the difference? Where did the inspiration come from that led one on a path of service and the other on a path of aggression and anger?

Unfortunately, much of the popular media portrays stories in which the "bad guy" wins, the good hero looks silly, and cynicism colors the quest. In reading some of the chapter books that are popular with middle-schoolers, I am struck by the level of sarcasm. This sophistication excites youngsters and keeps them constantly entertained. The sarcasm, as cynical judgment, leaves little space for reflection. Yet the hunger for heroes is still present and does help them look up to these figures with admiration.

Movies have become a strong contributor to the world of story. I was told that those who created *Star Wars* got together to create a modern fairy tale with archetypal characters. What about Superman and Spider Man? Now there is Wonder Woman. Why do they continually fascinate? There is something that touches young people in a visceral way. They might ask themselves, "Would I be a hero?" "Would I save someone?" "Would I serve the good?" "What would my super power be?"

Story is active in Waldorf education in the way we introduce geography and the cultures of other lands. Often unconscious judgments and biases are there, whether we realize them or not. I remember being told that there was nothing much happening down in Africa that was of much value. In fact, the introduction in a book from a well-known publisher stated that nothing of importance happened there until the European explorers landed on the shores. That set me on twelve years of research that resulted in my 400-plus-page book *Africa, a Teacher's Guide*. It also made me realize that the timing of subjects we teach can create a story filled with unconscious bias. For example, if we teach the Renaissance explorers and then teach African history and geography, that places African history in the context of European history. However, Africa has its own rich history, with tribal wisdom and medieval universities. If we teach that before the European explorers, we convey a completely different picture in which children can appreciate what had been in Africa before the European explorers came. With a more mindful approach, there is less opportunity for colonial arrogance.

It is during the middle school years that children become aware of their own story, of their individual journey. Having them interview family members can help them experience the complexity of their own story.

THE ROLE OF SERVICE

The third essential is the area of service—what children do with their hands so that they express concern for another. During the middle school age, it is easy to be concerned primarily with oneself. But to give service to others helps shift this focus. The fact that I can do something to make a difference for others brings purpose into my life.

Middle-schoolers need to begin to engage the world, be active in projects, and work together to accomplish meaningful deeds, but unfortunately, they are often brought into making judgments too early. Abstract education and an emphasis on asking youngsters their opinion about everything gives them a false sense of importance while leaving their souls empty.

Organizations such as Scouts and 4-H recognize the need at this age for guidance and structure. For example, the Boy Scout oath and law are:

On my honor, I will do my best to do my duty to God and my country and to obey the Scout Law; to help other people at all times; to keep myself physically strong, mentally awake, and morally straight.

A Scout is trustworthy, loyal, friendly, courteous, kind, obedient, cheerful, thrifty, brave, clean, and reverent.

The Girl Scout promise and laws are similar.

Adults can sometimes become sarcastic about these intentions because these words are so lofty and difficult to carry out, but they are more than words. They offer a path for middle-schoolers to find their way to becoming useful citizens of our world.

The path of Scouting is to achieve badges representing different skills and interests. The goal of each badge is clear and well structured. The leaders are there for help, but the boy or girl sets the goal and works to achieve it. I was a Girl Scout for only one year in seventh grade, and because it wasn't a natural next step in my high school, I didn't continue. Yet even this one year provided me with a structure and goal for that time of insecurity. I can still remember the badges I worked for and how meaningful each was.

Other young people, especially in rural areas, may join 4-H, an organization based on Head, Heart, Hands, and Health. Their oath is, "I pledge my head to clearer thinking, my heart to greater loyalty, my hands to larger service, and my health to better living, for my club, my community, my country, and my world." The 4-H motto is: "To make the best better." Their projects are usually related to farming, raising sheep or rabbits, training a horse, preserving food, sewing or quilting, etc.

As a teacher of middle-schoolers, it was obvious that self-discipline and clear goals lived in my students who were Scouts. They could be relied on to make a successful campfire, to know how to care for tools, or to be ready to participate in service projects. My students who were in 4-H had self-discipline, compassion, and persistence in serving others, most often because it had been developed through careful attention to the raising of animals.

Dave Kovar, a former high school student of mine, developed Kovar's Satori Academy of Martial Arts where he combined self-defense and life skills. His creed is, "I intend to develop myself in a positive manner and avoid anything that would reduce my mental growth or my physical health. I intend to develop self-discipline in order to bring out the best in myself and others." His students pledge themselves to humility, modesty, courtesy, integrity, perseverance, courage, and indomitable spirit. Dave has been a role model for thousands of young people. The Academy has opened many new locations, received prestigious awards, and gained national recognition for the example it has set for students as they combine street safety, confidence, and effective self-defense skills along with character development.

What is common to these groups is that the young people are focused on developing themselves, setting priorities, and living values which better the community. These organizations offer different levels of service: class projects, individual projects, and those that include the greater community. These types of experiences during middle school offer guidance and intentions with which to meet life's challenges at this time or in the future.

Volunteering fosters a sense of purpose and meaning. Gathering food for families in need, helping out in the community garden, identifying a neighbor who could use support are all ways middle-schoolers can do service. It helps if the project is more than collecting money, although that is also a good thing to do. Service is most effective when there is face-to-face involvement.

In my own eighth grade, my friends and I did a project for the American Red Cross. We were too young to give blood. Instead, we washed car windows in a parking lot and put notes on the windshields that read, "We hope you can see your way clear to donate blood." When we finished doing this, we reported back to the blood-donor center and happily received donuts and orange juice. We felt we had grown two feet higher.

In his book, *Amusing Ourselves to Death*, Neil Postman describes how each time a new form of communication is developed, our relationship to the world is affected. Whether by the newspaper, the telegraph wire, the telephone, the television, and now the computer, we have access to more information beyond our immediate surroundings. When we learn about a disaster or suffering in another part of the world, we want to do something to help. If we can do something, no matter how small, our will is connected with our feelings and thoughts. We feel that connection to others in our sense of well-being. However, if we only hear about something happening and we can't do anything about it, we are lamed in our will. The result is that we can be overwhelmed by all the problems and give up or only be concerned about ourselves. Volunteering helps us feel connected with our community and world by helping.

Participating in projects that are appropriate for each stage of childhood develops good will and leads to empathy. Service is a way of connecting to the world, staying engaged, learning about the needs of others, and understanding how we can help.

In one school seventh-graders go to a retirement home every week and interview their "buddy." Before leaving the school, the students often complained they really didn't want to go, and the elderly in the retirement home also felt lethargic about the visit. But after the visit, both groups were full of life, felt they had had a wonderful day, and excitedly shared stories of their experience.

THE ROLE OF ARTS AND CRAFTS

In addition to service projects, another aspect that affects the will, as well as thinking and feeling, is the whole realm of arts and crafts. Music, sculpture, drawing, painting, woodworking, handwork, and metal work offer the youngsters skills. With these skills come ideas, the expression of feelings with color and tone, and a beautiful gift for others in the result.

Art projects usually require an element of risk with a step into the unknown. How will this painting end? How can I chisel the wood so I don't split the grain? How do I bring care to my work with the hot fire of the forge when I am blacksmithing? Once children have learned to make things, they have gifts for their lives which they can share with others, and they can experience beauty and transformation.

In his book, *A Hawaiian Life*, George Kahumoku, Jr., a Grammy award-winning musician, describes the impact of his art teacher in grades six, seven, and eight.

He thought I had talent, but I also think he saw in me a kind of wild streak that we had in common. He let me do stuff no one else in the class was doing. He introduced me to batik. He had me doing ceramics. He put me on the potting wheel one time, and from that experience I knew I wanted to do this for the rest of my life. He showed me books by sculptor Henry Moore and all these other guys, Matisse, Cezanne, Dali, Picasso, whatever. I had no idea what I was doing. I made blocks of clay. I'd just stack them together and he let me go crazy. He even lent me oil paint and taught me how to stretch canvasses that I took home....

At a young age, I watched my grandfather Willy Kahumoku carve canoes out of koa logs he cut down himself. Grampa Willy would make poi boards out of felled ulu (breadfruit) trees and carve poi pounders out of stone that had reached the sea.

Finally, I could see the connection between what I learned at home and what I was being taught at Kamehameha Schools. I discovered this connection through the arts. I learned how making something out of nothing using only your own imagination, raw materials, and subject matter you found in nature. Using your own two hands and hard work you could create something out of nothing. I was on my journey towards becoming an independent thinker, a hard worker, and an artist. (p. 36)

Kahumoku reflected on his friend Kanialu who did not have this experience. "With the right kind of teacher, he might have been able to take advantage of the opportunities that were just around the corner. I came close to missing them myself."

George Kahumoku has gone on to be a well-known musician sharing Hawaiian culture. He is also a farmer, a teacher of students with special needs, a foster parent, and a mentor. Just as his art teacher had tended the spark in George, he has gone on to do that for many others.

These four essentials—adult role models, story, service, and the arts—integrate the thinking, feeling, and will. They are based in connectedness, in community, in belonging and caring.

The next big shift in adolescent development comes around sixteen. This is the time of the further development of the frontal lobes, heralding a new sense of responsibility, the ability to see the consequences of one's deeds. Through executive function the soul begins to direct and integrate the other parts of the brain.

It is with this new development around sixteen that Rudolf Steiner refers to the birth of the "second man" or "higher self," the chalice that is being formed for the incoming "I." It is at this time that the development of will forces more consciously stream into the head region and the teenager begins the process of maturing by consciously bringing together thinking, feeling, and will. This sets in motion the stage that will be completed in the twenties. With this comes the celebration of what it is to become a full human being, striving to act out of the civilizing mind.

CHAPTER 6
The World of Middle School Boys

Boys and girls from ages eleven to fourteen experience conflicting emotions, awkward body growth, and incomplete thinking patterns; yet they respond to these differently. There is no one way that is right. However, there are differences in the brain that point to certain behaviors as well as the effects of cultural and social influences.

DIFFERENCES BETWEEN PUBERTY AND ADOLESCENCE

Puberty refers to physiological changes involved in the sexual maturation of a child, as well as other bodily changes that may occur during this time. Puberty is completed when the girl begins menstruation (11–12/13/14), the boy when his sexual organs are complete (11–15/16). Puberty is the end of something, a completion of biological processes that have been going on since birth. These youngsters may be ready to conceive, but they do not yet have an identity.

Adolescence refers to the stage from puberty to adulthood and includes the key psychological experiences of the young person starting from the time of the secondary growth of the prefrontal cortex (15/16–21). Adolescence is a new beginning, a time to explore, the beginning of an individual spiritual development, to find the "true me."

In many cultures, particularly indigenous ones, once puberty is complete, it is time to leave home and find an individual way in the community. Adolescence is a state in which the person moves beyond the physical maturity to psychological maturity and developing an identity.

During childhood boys and girls go through many similar changes, but once past eleven years of age, the differences become more separate. In speaking about gender differences, we need to remember that there is a whole spectrum of development of maleness and femaleness. "We all know that there is an immense overlap between the genders, and that each child is an inherently sacrosanct individual not to be limited by a gender stereotype, but we also know that boys and girls learn differently." (Gurian, p. 9)

The challenge of including separate chapters on boys and girls always runs the danger of stereotyping. Although we've learned how much the brain influences gender, there are many other factors such as culture, family life, economic class, and generational differences influencing attitudes, preferences, and social dynamics.

THE WORLD OF BOYS

Walking into a sixth grade classroom is like taking a seat at a variety show titled "Stages of Puberty." It features all sizes of boys—tall, medium-sized, short, chubby, lean. The show goes on. Boys open their mouths. A deep booming sound from some fills the room. A high shrill emanates from others. Everyone is on a continuum of normal.

PHYSICAL DEVELOPMENT

Signs that puberty is approaching in middle school boys is often seen in facial hair that usually appears in the form of a dark shadow above the lip. The face changes. Gone is the baby face in boys. The chin lengthens and the nose grows, becoming wider and longer. The development of muscles and bones in the face is clearly seen, giving boys a lean look.

Between the ages of eleven and thirteen, boys become muscular and develop their gross motor skills which they exercise in testing their limbs, running, jumping, wrestling, and climbing. With their fine motor skills, they can control their handwriting, draw, use a compass and ruler, play an instrument, carve wood, sew, or put together model airplanes. After twelve, boys' hands and feet grow faster than their arms and legs—as if they have a life of their own, racing ahead of their torso and creating awkwardness in their walking and running.

The heart participates in the growth spurt like the other muscles of the body, and its weight nearly doubles. This happens more significantly in boys. The size of lungs and respiratory capacity increase. The amount of air that can be taken in at a single breath or in a given time increases markedly in adolescent boys. Because the heart and lungs have become larger and more efficient, boys especially can handle the demand placed on them by exercise. They also make a quick recovery from its effects. They need to constantly use these limbs, to test them in every way possible.

The remarkable deepening of a boy's voice is one of the most noticeable changes he must manage, with many months of cracking and squeaking in the process, much to the young man's embarrassment. A boy's "voice box" will grow up to seven times its original size in an 18-month time period, causing the major change in his voice.

At the same time as the growth spurt around eleven/twelve/thirteen begins, boys experience their first emission of semen (wet dreams), from masturbation or sexual dreams at night. The sexual organs begin to increase in size. It is only later, usually between 16 and 21, when the growth spurt is completed, along with the development of both primary and sexual characteristics, that fertility is possible.

Boys' skin becomes coarser with the sebaceous glands becoming more active, producing oily secretions usually resulting in acne or blackheads. Those frustrating zits announce to the world that the boy is undergoing pubescent change.

Because boys develop their muscular bodies during this time, most sports in middle school and high school work to the advantage of boys' physical bodies. During the years of 11–14 many boys are choosing a sport. Parents and youngsters should be aware of the dangers of particular sports before signing up. Not surprisingly, football and soccer account for the most injuries. As it has taken so long to learn about the effect of concussions on football players, we do not want to risk another generation of children's well-being.

The pituitary gland increases the amount of sex hormones in a teenage boy's body. The hormone testosterone causes most of the changes that occur in a boy's body including sperm production, increased lean body mass and muscle tissues, and rapid body growth.

The boy is struggling to find a right relationship with his physical body. He begins puberty with high doses of testosterone. Over just a few years he needs to learn to manage up to 20 times as much of the sex and aggression hormones as females do. The hormonal systems are flooding the body. He is dependent on others to help him manage the powerful surges coming from instinctual force. He experiences strange moods, anger, aggression, clumsiness, and awkwardness. He responds with extreme reactions—immediate and explosive, without thinking first. Three areas where he needs to take hold are a tendency toward aggression and dominance, a strong urge toward impulsive risks, and a short-term cycle of tension and release.

Boys worry about their physical development. Will they be strong enough to defend themselves if they are bullied? When will their muscles grow? They may look at advertisements of men with bulging muscles and ask to go to the gym to begin training. Rudolf Steiner urges, in his discussions in *Waldorf Education for Adolescence*, that teachers help boys avoid devolving into an egotistical sense of power and bullying with their new muscle strength by inspiring them to feel the higher possibilities in using their muscle power to serve others, instead helping them to understand the divine within themselves by telling inspiring biographies, instilling in them an appreciation for what is beautiful and good in the world and in themselves. (p. 62)

Some boys are more vulnerable than others. A short boy in middle school could take on several roles. He may become a mascot of the taller boys who carry him around, or he may resort to being the clown of the class. It is not easy to be a short boy. Even though he may gain his growth in tenth–twelfth grades, he still carries the feeling of being short and not up to par. One of the short sixth-grade boys mentioned to his classmates in the play yard, "I spoke to the doctor, and he said I will grow taller." His friend responded, "You shouldn't always believe doctors." So much for that advice.

Tall and big boys have a different vulnerability. They really don't know what to do with the mass they are carrying. While they may be well-behaved among adults, the moment they are with their peers or in the yard, the action begins. They throw their bodies around, testing themselves against each other, jumping, spinning, bumping up against each other.

Because a boy's identity is often based on what he can do, the sense of self is dependent on the skills he has and the things he masters. Boys test themselves through hiking, climbing, building, lugging, pushing, and all other challenges to their coordination. They can also discipline their bodies by developing skills working with wood, clay, stone or metal; fixing bikes, skateboarding, rock climbing, surfing or skiing. They make things; they take things apart and repair them. If they are on an athletic team, they discipline their bodies as they learn ways to use their strength and power. Gaining control over a changing body is a task during the middle school years.

COGNITIVE DEVELOPMENT

Critical thinking begins to appear during the 11–14 years when children see the world in terms of cause-and-effect. Boys are trying to understand concrete experiences and then apply logic to these situations and problems, often by confrontation. If parents set a curfew of 10 pm on the weekend, they will argue to push it to 10:30 pm. If they can't go out with friends until the chores are done, they'll negotiate strongly so that some chores can be left for later.

Their new kind of thinking focuses on the objective world. For example, how things work and what is real. They are not as interested in how people feel, but what they do. Their competitive attitude causes them to constantly assess each other to see who is "on top." They want to know who the winners are and how they gained that status.

They want to know what is important, why it is important, and what they have to do to learn it. When emotions are brought into the information, the boys may turn off, saying it is dumb. They separate information and compartmentalize it separately from their emotions.

The boy is more vulnerable to being manipulated by older boys who tell him he can be a hero if he takes on challenging tasks. For example, he will jump across buildings from one roof to another because Uncle Joe once did. He takes that as fact without asking further questions: If he can do it, he will be a hero. That is a big incentive for him. He compartmentalizes the excitement of competitiveness separate from any feeling of fear.

A seventh-grade class was discussing a list of words including consistent, misleading, stealing, cheating, defrauding, deceiving, honoring commitments, sincere praise, distortion, exaggeration, and admitting mistakes. They shared how each word related to honesty. It was impressive to hear how open the boys and girls were, as they distinguished subtle differences between the words and shared experiences. While they are in middle school, in a trusting environment, it is possible to speak about things or do things they wouldn't do later when they become more self-conscious. In a mixed-gender high school class, boys are usually sarcastic and cynical, protective of their personal experience.

As part of cause-and-effect thinking, boys tend to prefer non-fiction, facts, action-oriented plots, and how things work. They want hard evidence to back up what they hear. One of their pet phrases is "Prove it." They like to fix things: a problem or a physical puzzle. It is easier to get their attention if they can move around to look at the problem from different sides. Their sense of satisfaction when they solve a problem is often quietly expressed.

Their cause-and-effect thinking often leads to an interest in science, in understanding how things develop and how all this can be practically used. Although there are exceptions, it is noticeable how much satisfaction boys gain from working with physics, doing hands-on exploration, and gaining control of the objective world. However, when it comes to social situations, they may have difficulty understanding subtle interactions that go on within their group.

EMOTIONAL DEVELOPMENT

Boys hold their emotions inside their shell, not wanting to be exposed. They would rather do something physical than share their feelings. Often by the end of eighth or ninth grade, they enter the "grunt period" where they seem to have withdrawn inside a shell and become monosyllabic. It is as if they have lost the skill of expressing themselves through language. One of the joys of being a high school teacher was when I experienced those moments when boys regained their sense of spoken language. It wasn't that it had been gone, but something was holding them back from putting it out in front of others. When they ventured to describe their feelings or something sensitive in writing, the teacher had to be very careful not to share it with the class without their permission. Parents also have to be careful not to share their sons' feelings with others, unless permission has been granted. Otherwise, it is trespassing on the boy's privacy, and he will not risk sharing his feelings again.

Boys are influenced by society, by images on television and in movies, but also by older boys and men. They have to be superheroes, powerful, aggressive, not showing any tenderness. There are few examples of sensitive boys shown as heroes. This can sometimes lead to dangerous and even deadly "proving" ceremonies, in which older boys egg younger ones on to try risky stunts. In Los Angeles, for example, 14-year-old boys were prompted by older boys to lie down on the dividing lines on a busy highway to prove their courage. Some of those boys did not pass this test alive. When boys experience emotions, they move them down to "fight or flight" responses. Then they are more likely to respond to hurts by becoming aggressive or pushing themselves past rational limits.

When boys suffer abuse, ridicule, or hurt, they usually hold it silently within themselves and don't share it. That makes it difficult to prove something terrible really happened. Men have shared how they carried abuse silently for decades, afraid of being considered weak. A middle school boy was sexually abused on a middle school wrestling team. He mentioned it to his father but refused to give details and refused to speak with anyone in authority. Years later, he held it against his father for not protecting him.

Boys are more emotional than they let on. Often it is with one good friend that middle school boys show affection. If they are on a team and thus more secure in their masculinity, they will show affection with each other by putting their arms around their friend. Copying older boys, they may chest bump or slap each other's back. They are watching older boys to see how to express feelings of happiness or sadness. They struggle with any kind of shaming or being made the butt of jokes.

After speaking to hundreds of boys, William Pollack, in his book, *Boys' Voices*, gives us an insight into boys' emotions.

> I have discovered a glaring truth: America's boys are absolutely desperate to talk about their lives. They long to talk about the things that are hurting them—their harassment from other boys, their troubled relationships with their fathers, their embarrassment around girls, and confusion about sex, their disconnection from parents, the violence that haunts them at school and on the street, their constant fear that they might not be as masculine as other boys. (p. xix)

Why do they not speak about these things? The Boy Code that they have absorbed unconsciously or consciously tells them that boys should be stoic, not share feelings, not express weakness, nor do anything to call attention to vulnerability. They feel alone. Although their fathers may pay attention to them, wrestle or play catch, they are less likely to welcome sensitive conversations with their sons, or they themselves may not know how to deal with them and hold their own emotions inside. There is also an innate shyness that comes with the changes of puberty. This shyness underscores the reluctance to speak.

Where can boys turn for information and support? Although there are magazines for girls that deal with private issues, there are no magazines specifically for teenage boys except for *Boys' Life*, which is put out by Boy Scouts of America through subscription. Articles include: "Your Future, Astronaut? Artist? Firefighter? Chef? Here's How to Be What You Want to Be." But there are no articles about nervousness, about relating to girls, about worries about their bodies, etc. Publishers have made a decision that those magazines won't sell because boys only want to read about video games, snow-boarding, or skate-boarding. Instead, boys are reading men's magazines and some people think that's enough. If the boy is involved in Boy Scouts or another outdoor organization, he has many opportunities to take appropriate risks and show strength and persistence. He can feel affirmed and recognized by others by his achievements. If he does not have such opportunities, he has fewer outlets to gain confidence in his masculinity.

Ellis Rubenstein, editor-in-chief of *Seventeen* magazine, said, "I think of boys as the lost generation. Boys intuitively, and because of cultural norms, tend to go inside themselves. But they have those same struggles (as teenage girls), they're just a little harder to pin down."

The insights of Rudolf Steiner about the verbal ability of girls because of this ego quality that comes with the onset of puberty indicate this is not the case for boys and so the tools to articulate much of anything are missing for boys. One European high school literature teacher had the students in ninth grade (ages 14 and 15) read *The Sorrows of Young Werther* by Goethe. After discussing it in class, the teacher asked the students to write a summary of the story. One girl wrote 32 pages, while a boy wrote one sentence. When the teacher asked the girl to shorten the summary as it was too long, she carefully examined her own essay and responded, "Everything I have written is essential. What can I possibly take out?" The boy, on the other hand, was asked to expand on his one sentence, which read, "A man loved a woman and because she was already married, he committed suicide." He re-read his sentence and asked his teacher, "What else is there to say about the story?"

"No one's protecting teenage boys the way we do teen girls," said Jeff Csatari, current executive editor of *Best Life*, "The teen years are very scary times. You don't go to your mom and dad to answer these questions.... With a magazine it's just you one on one with the editors. You get real information that you can apply to your life." (www. huffingtonpost.com/eat-the-press/2006/06/27/teenage-wasteland-where-_e_23883.html)

The richness of emotional experience is present in boys, although it often doesn't seem so. Although both girls and boys are vulnerable to being hurt by other people's judgments, girls speak more often to other girls, which gives them more opportunities to discover that they are not alone. But boys also have much to say. They need to feel safe, be given enough time to speak about what bothers them or what is important to them, to talk in an unthreatening situation, shoulder to shoulder so they don't feel the eyes of the adult peering in on them, but instead feel love and admiration.

BEHAVIOR

From the time boys are young, they are focused on what they do physically. They are concerned about their physical strength, competition with their peer group, and feeling comfortable. As mentioned earlier, the academic expectations in the early grades leave many boys feeling rejected and uninterested in school. They opt out of the competition with girls and do things with boys that make them feel powerful. This sometimes leads to an obsession with video games where they can intensify the excitement by capturing, trapping, and killing the enemy. Overly stimulating, these urges keep them in a cyber-bubble that everyday school cannot compete with. They don't want to set high goals that they may not be able to achieve.

Boys whose family life offers other ways of their feeling powerful helps them as they move through these vulnerable years. As one twelve-year-old boy told me, "I think reading is cool. Some of my friends don't like reading, but they spend a lot of time on video games. I think that's stupid." His family leads a very active outdoor life—camping, skiing, swimming, and boating.

The lack of academic motivation in boys has become noticeable on many levels. Rather than sitting at a desk for hours, they want to use their large muscles, to run, jump, skip, push, pull, and hit. When the emphasis is on skill building, they are successful only if they are at the top. Group leaders who support team building and collaborative learning help boys monitor their need to be first and best. They learn to value being a member of the group, appreciating each other.

ADD and ADHD have become significant concerns with middle-school boys. Different countries have different levels of diagnosis and use of medication. Stephen Hinshaw, in his book, *ADHD: What Everyone Needs to Know*, says:

> The National Survey of Children's Health, a major US survey in 2011–2012—showed that roughly 15 percent of boys have been diagnosed, compared with 6.7 percent of girls, suggesting a ratio of between two and two-and-a-half to one.... It's a fact that boys are more at risk during grade school for behavioral problems, particularly of the *externalizing* kind (e.g., noncompliance, aggression, and impulsivity). (p. 80)

In looking at the prevalence of ADHD among different nations, Hinshaw writes:

> What's striking is that, outside of subsistence nations (for which ADHD has not yet registered as a concern) and outside of the United States, with its perhaps artificially boosted rates of diagnosis, a remarkably similar proportion of children around the world has clear trouble in handling the demands of classrooms. This fact lends credence to the notion that ADHD is a product of both biological vulnerability and increasing demands for attention and academic performance. When education becomes mandatory, underlying differences in self-

regulation and impulse control come to the fore at highly similar levels. ADHD is increasingly a global phenomenon—and one that we predict will remain in ascendancy as international pressures for academic achievement and job performance continue to rise. (p. 89)

As boys move through the middle school years, testosterone contributes to behavioral changes. Testosterone contributes to a boy's sex drive by enhancing arousal and sexual response mechanisms. Teenage testosterone may reduce a boy's communication and interest in socializing. His thoughts tend to be more focused on his body, athletic activities, and sexual attraction.

Boys have a lot of energy, but they often don't know what to do with it. This leads to risky behavior as they have too much bravado and little information or judgment to guide them. Their impulsive behavior, hormonal surges, restlessness, and aggression stimulate a willingness to try anything.

Eighth-grader Michael was climbing up sides of buildings, testing himself by balancing on tottering bridges of planks, throwing balls at the side of the house, breaking one window after another. He wasn't a violent boy, but he was always testing his capacities. At one point his mother said, "Michael, what is it with you?" Michael gave her a smile and said, "Oh, but I will have great stories to tell." I smiled as I looked at photographs of him, now age 20, on a family trip to the Middle East. He is climbing up the rocky side of mountains in the desert, jumping across chasms, and posing on a narrow strip of stone above a deep inlet. He is still gathering stories (if he survives).

Patrick had been a very open child, quick to share his thoughts and engage with the family. The summer he was 12 and getting ready to begin seventh grade, he continued being pleasant, but his responses were limited to one word. "Where are you going?" "Out." And so it went until after college, when he called his mother and said, "Oh, I've been wanting to tell you …," and on it went with much detail and engagement.

In a seventh-grade school dance class, the instructor who had earlier taught Swing was now introducing Renaissance dances. It was obvious that the girls who had matured earlier were in command of their bodies and could keep the rhythm. The boys had no control over their arms and legs. They twisted, turned, and slipped, with no connection with the steps required. Not able to do the simple steps, they became clowns and made fun of what they were supposed to be doing. The energy pulsed through their bodies, a smirk on their faces. It wasn't that they weren't trying, but they didn't know what to do to make their legs do what was needed. When the teacher asked them whether Swing made them more tired than the Renaissance dance, several of the girls responded, "What made me tired was trying to make my partner cooperate."

During the middle school years, boys especially need healthy male role models to guide them in developing skills. Through their actions they develop self-esteem. They need to know what the challenge is and how to meet it. When a boy meets it well, he feels much better. If he doesn't meet it well, he is devastated and feels worthless. His main model is his father, and he will go to great lengths to please him. The presence of his father is the most important influence during this time. Through his father he gets to know what it is to become a man and how to relate socially.

With the change in society from being more focused on agriculture to the industrial revolution and to the technological revolution, boys and fathers do less and less together in a natural way. It is an effort for the contemporary father to carve out the space to do things together, whether in nature through hiking, skiing, or fishing, through building and making things together, remodeling a car, building a skate board ramp, figuring out how to fix the lawn mower, or upgrading the computer. The key aspect is doing it together, with the father guiding the learning of skills. Recognizing the effort of his son is important before giving any kind of criticism.

If a father is not present, it is essential that the boy have a similar connection with another adult male who can serve as a mentor.

Organizations such as Big Brother often pair a male in the community with an adolescent boy. The earlier this happens, the more stabilizing it is for the boy.

The boy lives in the world of concrete polarities—one minute he is sweating from exertion, the next minute he is lolling around and will not lift a finger. Everything is experienced in black and white. It's all good or all bad. He just wants to be clear. Subtlety does not rule. Tell me what the rules are. If I break the rules, who is in charge? and What are the consequences? He is less inclined to see nuance so he needs to have a logical explanation. He will negotiate on and on, building one logical thought after another, and even bully until he gets his way. It is about dominance.

Boys respond to challenges or expectation by controlling physical reaction as a way to master their emotions—stomping away, hitting a wall. They explode or withdraw into themselves or into the tribe for safety.

Sixth-grader Alan played a video game based on horses. A classmate, Sarah, was part of his internet team. This game was played in the privacy of their homes. Yet, one day Alan walked over to Sarah's lunch table, expecting her to be friendly to him since they were on the same team. Instead, she looked at him and said, "What are you doing here?" He was crushed and couldn't figure out what happened. He had the school secretary call his mother because he said he was so sick he had to go home. Only with gentle questioning did the situation come out. He just could not figure out what had happened.

In a seventh-grade physics class the teacher was demonstrating the use of simple machines, in this case, how they could lift a car by the use of a screw (the car jack). He set up the jack under the frame of his 4000-pound car and called the students one by one to turn the crank. The boys made lots of jokes about it, turned the crank, laughingly asked for the keys so they could drive, and so on. They were engaged. This was REAL.

During another activity, the students were in groups of four and were to read instructions as to how to use different kinds of pulleys. In general, the girls on the teams read the instructions and tried to figure out what to do. Most of the boys didn't take it seriously until the end. They climbed on chairs, lifted themselves up over railings, whipped each other with ropes, jumped to touch the ceiling, tested their capacity to balance, and finally got to the assignment.

More intellectual boys use their strength to argue or make a point. For example, a math problem used the image of an astronaut landing on Jupiter. Eric who prided himself on his advanced knowledge of astronomy kept shouting, "Not Jupiter. It's a giant gas." Any time a student read the question and didn't substitute *Mars* or *Moon*, he shouted, "No, not Jupiter. It is giant gas." Using the power of his voice, he gained authority. Boys compete with each other with their bodies and with their verbal authority. Seldom does one have a glimpse of what is happening inside their inner sanctum.

The world of boys in middle school is exciting, stimulating, challenging, funny, intimidating, competitive, and poignant. Recognizing the tenderness underneath the bravado helps us support them at this critical time.

CHAPTER 7
The World of Middle School Girls

Middle school girls experience changes in their bodies, their feelings, and their thinking. Because they tend to have these experiences earlier than the boys, the gap between genders widens through middle school, and then narrows as boys and girls reach the end of high school.

DIFFERENCES BETWEEN PUBERTY AND ADOLESCENCE

Puberty refers to physiological changes involved in the sexual maturation of a child, as well as other bodily changes that occur during this time. Puberty is completed when the girl begins menstruation. Puberty is the end of something, a completion of biological processes that have been going on since birth.

Adolescence refers to the stage from puberty to adulthood and includes the key psychological experiences of the young person starting from the time of the secondary growth of the frontal lobes from ages fifteen to twenty-one. Adolescence is a new beginning, a time to explore, the beginning of an individual spiritual development to find the "true me."

Adolescence is a state in which girls move beyond physical maturity to psychological maturity, developing a role in the community. In many cultures, particularly indigenous ones, once puberty is complete, girls marry and begin bearing children, often embedded in the culture of the women who support them through the process.

During childhood boys and girls go through many similar changes, but once past eleven years of age, the differences become more separate. In speaking about gender differences, we need to remember that there is a whole spectrum of development of maleness and femaleness. We all know that there is an immense overlap between the genders, and that each child is an inherently sacrosanct individual not to be limited by a gender stereotype, but we also know that boys and girls learn differently. (Gurian, p. 9)

The challenge of drawing up separate chapters on boys and girls always runs the danger of stereotyping. Although we've learned how much the brain influences gender, there are many other factors such as culture, family life, economic class, and generational differences that influence attitudes, preferences, and social dynamics. In *Why Gender Matters* Sax states:

Every child is unique. I'm not saying that all boys are the same or all girls are the same. But the fact that each child is unique and complex should not blind us to the fact that gender is one of the two great organizing principles in child development—the other principle being age. (p. 35)

In *The Teenage Brain* Jensen says:

While hormones can explain some of what is going on, there is much more at play in the teenage brain, where new connections between brain areas are being built and many chemicals, especially neurotransmitters, the brain's "messengers," are in flux. (pp. 22–23)

PHYSICAL CHANGES

A parent takes her daughter to the pediatrician for her physical exam. An overly-protective parent is nervous that her daughter is showing signs of puberty. She wants to slow it down and keep her young, but biology has its own timetable. The pediatrician helps the parent understand that these changes are completely normal and assures the girl of ten, eleven, or twelve that there is nothing to worry about.

The pituitary gland increases the amount of sex hormones in a girl's body. As girls begin the path toward puberty, they develop breast buds and hair in the pubic area and in the arm pits. Hormone changes shape the puberty experience with a high dose of progesterone, estrogen, and prolactin. Progesterone is a growth hormone, contributing to musculoskeletal growth, sexual arousal, and sex organs. The early signs can begin as early as age eight or nine, although she may not menstruate until twelve or thirteen. With so much energy going into their growth, girls tend to get tired more quickly. They feel a kind of heaviness and find it hard to stand upright. Every organ in the body is growing, expanding, and maturing. There is a rounding and softening of contours of the girl's face and body. Her skin becomes coarser with the sebaceous glands more active, producing oily secretion that can result in acne or blackheads. It requires years to learn how to manage a new body and a new mind.

The slimmer or more athletic girls have energy to run, but the heavier girls or more physically developed ones tend to sit or lean against walls. Girls are often taller than boys during middle school. By age 15 or 16 they have reached adult height. They gradually put on weight as their hips fill out. This often leads to an obsession with dieting, food issues, and/or anorexia.

While a boy's vocal apparatus grows seven times its original size, a girl's larynx on average grows three times its original size, causing less obvious change, but still a deepening of the voice.

According to Rudolf Steiner, the whole of the female organism is organized toward the cosmos through the lunar cycle of menstruation. Her emotional life is more differentiated and she is more influenced by what goes on in her emotions. She is more subjective, swinging back and forth in moods, worried about how she fits in, concerned more with the quality of relationships, struggling to find herself in the midst of emotions swirling around her. It will continue to be this way until she experiences menopause as a grown woman. Of course, we can work with these issues along the way to develop objectivity and serenity long before menopause occurs!

Girls worry about whether they will get their period when all their friends have and how large their breasts will be. They have to figure out how to handle their bodies as they feel unfamiliar sensations during hormonal cycles. Their awkwardness is a soul state as well as a physical one. Some girls feel the weight of the changes, go inward and isolate themselves. Some girls put on height and bulk, and whereas they may be great soccer players, they struggle when they try to fit into the fashions of the day meant for slim girls. Girls who develop earlier than others are more sensitive to body image since American popular culture puts so much emphasis on being thin. On the other hand, girls who develop later have other pressures because they look like children and wonder when they will get their breasts and their period.

A girl makes most of her bone between 6 and 17 years of age. By 17, a girl has most of the bone mineral of her adult years. Jumping exercises rather than stretching are particularly helpful in building her bones.

When girls compete under the same rules and the same sports as boys, they experience more injuries. This is true even with the differences in the heads of boys and girls. Until 2006 most of the studies about concussions were based on boys. However, girls are at a higher risk of concussions in soccer, basketball, ice hockey, figure skating, cheerleading, and gymnastics.

Why are women more prone to these injuries than men? In summary, for example, the typical female athlete, as compared with her male counterpart, has:

- higher estrogen levels, along with less muscle mass and more body fat
- greater flexibility (due to looser ligaments) and less powerful muscles

- a wider pelvis, which alters the alignment of the knee and ankles
- a narrower space within the knees for the ACL to travel through
- a greater likelihood of inadequate calcium and vitamin D intake.

Women also tend to move differently than men. For example, when landing from a jump, women tend to land more upright and with the knees closer together. And when female athletes suddenly change direction, they tend to do so on one foot (perhaps due to their wider pelvis), while men tend to "cut" from both feet. (Robert H. Shmerling, MD, *The Gender Gap in Sports Injuries*, Dec. 3, 2015)

Dr. Leonard Sax points out that already as babies, girls hear better than baby boys. This difference increases as boys and girls age. Girls experience a parent's or teacher's speech as loud when boys don't hear it that way.

> That boy who's tap-tap-tapping his fingers on the desk might not be bothering other boys, but he is bothering the girls—as well as the (female) teacher. One reason for that difference, of course, is that eleven-year-old girls hear better. If you're teaching girls, don't raise your voice—and try to keep the classroom free of extraneous noise. Girls won't learn as well in a loud, noisy classroom. (Sax, *Why Genders Matter*, p. 18)

COGNITIVE DEVELOPMENT

With the recent use of PET scans and fMRIs, neuroscientists are exploring differences in brain structures of males and females. Although we don't really know why these differences exist, something did happen affecting the brains in different ways. They continue to change based on different influences. What is important to us as parents and teachers is to pay attention to the individuals and assess how they demonstrate a particular style of learning and respond to it.

Critical thinking begins to appear during the ages 11–14 so that girls see the world in cause-and-effect. As cause-and-effect thinking becomes less concrete, a new capacity develops: Girls tend to process information more completely because they connect it with their emotions.

Because girls are more focused on relationships, girls favor books and movies that involve people's feelings and motivation. They also focus on relationships in their groups: who likes whom, who is angry at whom, and why someone is moody. At the same time, they still have concrete thinking and believe what they hear. Because of this, they are particularly vulnerable to being manipulated by older boys. A girl will explain that "He told me I should send a nude picture of me to his phone, and he wouldn't show it to anyone." Of course, he does send it out, and the girl is in a pickle.

Girls tend to be able to sit longer and pay attention in school. With their stronger verbal abilities, cited earlier in Rudolf Steiner's indications that there is refinement involved in girls' arrival of puberty that is not present for boys, they work things out in everyday language, while boys tend to rely on nonverbal communication or use coded language. Boys prefer to have things they can touch and manipulate, which helps them understand the main principle. Girls can put up with long explanations.

Just because girls tend to be stronger in their feelings, this does not mean their thinking is less important. Girls need to think strategically, make good decisions, and be able to negotiate logically. Although they often rely on their intuition, they need to be able to hold their own with their intellectual skills. This is clearly happening more because girls are now the majority in law school and medical school. Situations that rely on problem solving enhance their thinking skills. Often it is their homework strategies that help them do better in school. They want to please and feel good about doing well, and they are willing to put in the extra time. However, they are sensitive to their relationships and other people's perceptions of them.

EMOTIONAL DEVELOPMENT

Girls have a rich emotional life, which they share with others. Or if a girl feels hurt or misunderstood, she will often speak about it with others to get their perspective. Because their feeling and thinking are connected, when girls experience emotions, they tend to move them upward to more complex thoughts. They want to understand why something is happening.

In the case of sexual abuse, girls are more likely to tell a trusted friend or write about it in their diary. Girls are more likely to use words to fight with others rather than throw their weight around, although this differs in different communities. Girls use emotional reasoning. If you believe or feel it is true, then it is true. It must be true. They can't sort facts from feelings. Thinking is still magical.

Parents and teachers should watch how middle-schoolers deal with emotions—do they react aggressively or shut down, refusing to discuss the problem, or do they try to figure out what caused the hurt and discuss how to react to it? That will offer a clue as to how to respond to them.

In general, both boys and girls experience huge swings in their emotional behavior as they are learning to control these new experiences caused by hormonal influences and by society. Over time they will take hold and bring their emotions into balance.

Even as recently as twenty years ago, we used to be very concerned about girls not having the same academic opportunities as boys. But that has changed, and girls are doing better in school. However, boys are showing less interest in school and in setting personal goals. As parents and teachers, we are trying to support both boys and girls in their educational and social development. But there are emergency signs that our sons and daughters are in trouble due to cultural influences.

Self-confidence, accepting oneself as is, and feeling connected drive girls. Although girls have more freedom of choice than their grandparents had, those who are highly motivated and success-driven cannot rest. They are more worried about being good enough, about whether they will achieve their goals and succeed. They obey an inner drive that keeps them up late at night studying or keeps them practicing gymnastics despite the pain in their body.

Often, they fall prey to superficial markers such as wearing the right makeup, having the right clothes, being perfectionists who obsess over their achievements. These are signs of seeking approval from the outside that cause inner problems such as anxiety and depression.

Because girls are surrounded by media images stressing how they should look, they try very hard to live up to these artificial and shifting standards. Girls have been defined sexually and accept this definition even before they understand it. Attention is on their bodies, how much skin they show, how they walk, how thin they are, how attractive they are to boys. It is not just being pretty, but pleasing boys to be accepted. The obsession with superficiality is seen in their constant connection with social media where they concentrate on how they are seen by their peers. They construct a persona that may have little relationship to how they feel on the inside. With all this anxiety, they don't seem to relax and have fun.

This is particularly problematic for girls from eleven to fourteen because in the Vulnerability Gap they look to peer acceptance to get them through, and so they lose the years when they need to be developing their authentic selves. By the time they reach maturity of executive function after sixteen, they may have developed habits of addiction, of sexual intimacy without relationship, or self-destructive acts such as cutting or taking pills. Parents need to be watchful and intervene before the situation becomes dire. Many girls end up in therapy or even hospitalization because their inner needs aren't being addressed.

It is important to keep in mind the attitude used in the Waldorf curriculum, which lies in developing sensibilities in girls for genuine beauty. This can be through classic paintings and sculpture of the human form and through music as well as artistic work accomplished by the girls themselves. This takes time and keeps girls engaged for long, concentrated periods of time—time not spent obsessing about and on social media!

One example of how social media socializes boys and girls is to look at images on magazine covers. For example, the cover of *Girls' Life* had titles such as "Fall Fashion You'll Love—100+ Ways to SLAY on the First Day," "Your Dream Hair," "Best.Year.Ever," "How to have fun, make friends, and get all A's," "Confessions! My First Kiss," "Real girls smooch and spill."

When graphic designer Katherine Young saw these, she created her own version of what the *Girls' Life* cover should look like. Her cover had titles of articles such as "Girls Doing Good, 100+ ways to help others in your community," "Wake up hungry? Healthy foods to power you through rough days," "Best.You.Ever," "Be yourself, work hard, and get better grades," "Confidence: My First Kiss," "Miss the big shot and still win." And "Your Dream Career, Next level planning and goals." (www.snopes.com?girls-life-vs-boys-life-magazine-covers)

That said, however, there were issues of *Girls' Life* that included stories about body acceptance, getting jobs, and dealing with bullies (and how not to be one).

The richness of emotional experience is present in both boys and girls, although it often doesn't seem so. Both are vulnerable to being hurt by other people's judgments. Both are afraid of not being accepted. Because girls speak more often to other girls, they have more opportunities to discover that they are not alone. They also enjoy curling up with a magazine as if with a close friend.

BEHAVIOR

Girls take in more sensory data than boys do: They hear better, smell better (pardon the pun), and are more sensitive to touch. They are better at controlling impulse behavior through self-regulation. Girls begin to assert themselves. Yet everything the girl does is affected by the emotional environment and relationships.

Stephen Hinshaw describes the impossible expectations that girls face in his book *The Triple Bind*. Although in many ways this is a good time in history to be a girl, from another angle it is a cruel hoax, "as though we'd invited our daughters to the world's most sumptuous banquet and then kept them from enjoying their meal." (p. 15)

What is the triple bind, and why is it putting girls at risk of self-mutilation, eating disorders, violence, depression, and suicide? "One-fourth or more of all U.S. girls between the ages of ten and nineteen face one or more of these threats..." (p. x)

The three aspects of the triple bind are:

1. Be good at all the traditional "girl" stuff such as empathy and bonding. Be nice, obedient, helpful, and nurturing.

2. Be good at the traditional "guy" stuff: Be aggressive, fight for top spots, prepare for a job, be athletic, competitive, assertive, and ambitious.

3. Conform to a narrow, unrealistic set of standards that allows for no alternative. The images are of ultra-feminine and overly-sexualized females.

The messages she encounters tell her that money, power, and status are what drive society, and she must strive to earn those goals. This gives her very few alternative identities she can embody in order to be successful. Starting already around age ten, the middle school girl feels trapped in the triple bind.

Social interaction rates very high on a girl's sense of security. She takes betrayal, being excluded, whining, talking back, and stubbornness personally. She needs more time to process her experiences, and she needs to talk about her feelings. She looks outward to see how people around her (especially her parents) are behaving, looks for limits, and begins to assume responsibility. She has a tendency to form small groups who listen to one another's feelings.

Girls want to have sensitive conversations, to discuss what makes them comfortable or uncomfortable. They respond to intimacy and can handle eye contact with adults. The girl has to cultivate relationships that allow her to connect meaningfully with others. She is dependent on being with other girls—something I call the "glue-girl" syndrome—so they can trade secrets and figure out the status of everyone around them. When girls are together, they get a huge rush of pleasure from the dopamine and oxytocin. This also why they get so much pleasure from connecting and bonding, playing with each other's hair, gossiping and shopping together, talking on the telephone, seeking connection with other girls and with boys. Girls are open about their ideals, and they search for meaning and order in the universe. They may discuss deeper questions such as: Is there is life after death? Girls often become annoyed that boys don't talk about intimate things.

Dr. Lou Ann Brizendine, in her book *The Female Brain*, says, "Connecting through talking activates the pleasure centers in a girl's brain. Sharing secrets that have romantic and sexual implications activates these centers even more."

The challenge for middle school girls is to express emotions that are appropriate responses to the demands of life. Without their executive function to direct them, they are at the mercy of uncontrolled feelings, verging at times on hysteria. They exaggerate situations, raising them to life-and-death proportions.

A seventh-grade girl was complaining that her older brother got a new cell phone after his was broken. Her temper tantrum went something like this. "My cell phone is not the newest model. How come he always gets the best and the newest? This isn't fair. I just want to die." At this point she was flailing around, knocking over a chair, working herself into a hysterical fit. The best thing was to let her play out her reaction because she wasn't responding to reason. The next day it was possible to have a reasonable conversation because her feelings had calmed down. Girls tend to take this extreme into language where boys more often clam up and then punch a wall.

The sexualization of our society pushes girls in elementary school to dress alluringly, justifying it as a means of self-expression. If girls have to do this to feel powerful, what else will they do as they shape their self-identity? Because of earlier onset of puberty, middle school girls have to take responsibility for their sexual behavior before full emotional and social maturity has occurred. They are at risk physically, emotionally, socially, and intellectually with issues of body image, eating disorders, substance abuse, poor academic performance, delinquency, and aggression.

Dr. Leonard Sax points to four factors that are driving the new crisis for girls—sexual identity, the cyber-bubble, obsessions especially with social media, and environmental toxins. When girls feel anxious and lost, they turn inward on themselves and create harm. "There has never before been any culture in which girls have had so many opportunities and yet receive so little structured guidance." (*Girls on the Edge*, p. 8)

Girls need supportive parents, useful information, close friends, physical safety, freedom to move about independently, and encouragement and respect for their unique qualities. This is all within the primary need to be embedded in relationships. Nothing else takes the place of a close friend, either a peer or a mentor.

The need to belong to a group drives the girl's behavior. This was brought home to me by Paula's behavior in my sixth-grade class. The group of girls had been together since first grade. Paula was very close to another girl in a pack of three. When Paula's family went on a trip for a few weeks, the other two girls bonded, and upon Paula's return, she felt shut out. I was a new teacher and tried to smooth things over. I took the girls bowling, had them over to my house, and found ways to bring them together.

Yet Paula was suffering. She was the youngest of a large family. Her mother was a very warm, creative person, and quite elderly by this time, and she couldn't bear the see Paula unhappy. In the mornings, Paula said she didn't feel well and couldn't go to school. At first her mother believed there was something physically wrong and let her stay home where she was cherished and the center of attention while her siblings were away at school.

As days went on, Paula still wasn't coming to school. I visited her at home and tried to convince her to return. It became clear there was no physical problem. As long as her mother felt so sorry for her and allowed her to stay home, Paula continued to stay home. The next year she went to another school to see if it would be easier with new classmates. She had many good school experiences, but a bad habit had already begun. When social issues arose, Paula escaped. This pattern continued into her adult life and she had difficulty settling into any career. When I spoke with her in her forties, she said to me, "I wish Mom would have just told me I had to go to school. I feel I would have worked out the problem even though it would have been hard. She protected me too much and I ended up just repeating the pattern."

In eighth grade Jamie started staying home from school. She was an excellent student, but she hadn't found a best friend. Although she had close relationships with her teachers and many friends in her class, she yearned for intimacy and felt there must be something wrong with her. We had many conversations, and I suggested she look to other classes for the "right person," but she had her mind set on what she wanted, and nothing else would do. However, in high school she was able to be more philosophical about the situation and found rich relationships with those who had common interests.

Both Paula and Jamie rejected superficial images of what girls should be like. They defined themselves differently from the expected image of sexualized girls, and they struggled to find appreciation for their uniqueness, and especially to find a soul mate.

I pondered this situation many times over my decades of teaching middle and high school students. The expectations that are set by television and movie imagery can't always be fulfilled. Real people do not always live happily ever after as in fairy tales. Because girls are so focused on relationships, they are particularly vulnerable to feeling rejected and lonely. When we add the conflicted expectations to the situation, we can understand why girls today are so vulnerable and at risk.

CHAPTER 8

The Transformation of the Feeling Life

As middle-schoolers travel the path from eleven to fourteen, their feeling life is expressed in phases. Each youngster has a unique way of moving through these phases as their emotional life develops from self-involvement to relating to others.

ELEVEN- TO TWELVE-YEAR-OLDS

The changes that arise in 11–12-year-olds (girls 11–12 and boys 13–14) are destabilizing. It is as if the youngsters woke up in an alien body. This stressful situation leads to problems sleeping when in fact, they need more sleep. The hormonal brain changes are shifting their energy. This results in extreme emotionality. Everything takes more time—studying, organizing their room, remembering what was told to them. The social life becomes challenging also, and they don't yet have the coping skills of the adolescent.

Parents ask, "What happened to the golden years when my child was sunny and bright?" "Why don't I know my child anymore?"

Parents set rules, but their children continually challenge them. On one hand, middle-schoolers want to be respected and treated like adolescents even though they are not there yet. They are moody and changeable like the younger children they once were. As they live in the storm of feelings, they aren't sure what they feel, and the adults are often just as uncertain. This is a time for adults to count to ten and develop a sense of humor, knowing that this, too, will change.

One teacher called this time a time of "contracts toward increasing responsibility." In other words, a parent or teacher can state, "Get your work done and you can then discuss what it is you want." Or a parent can ask, "Why don't you finish cleaning your room as you said you would and then we can talk."

Some youngsters sail through this time, but as they approach age twelve, they begin to experience restlessness and moodiness. This is one of the most tender, fragile times in human life. We can look at them and remark, "Oh, there are those wacky sixth-graders. They are funny, they are sad; they can't control their arms and legs which move around like on a disjointed puppet. They take risks, jump off bridges, run across busy streets, cry for unknown reasons, and giggle without stopping.

They have occasional glimmerings that something is happening in their bodies over which they have no control. New feelings come and go. They are on unsettled ground, looking for something to count on. Until now, they had experienced themselves unconsciously, but in the stirrings of a newly birthing soul, they begin to notice what they had not noticed before. They don't understand any of it yet, and it is puzzling.

Although 11–12-year-olds may be regarded as a little unpredictable and confused, that is only the outer impression. Inside there is a tender soul, just waking up to this new world. Something precious is stirring. Their feelings rule what they like and don't like, what they want, what they desire. They don't like to be stopped from getting their needs met. They don't want to have to wait. Why can't they have it or do it now? Doesn't this sound like a two-year-old? There are good reasons for this similarity. Life is all about them, as they feel themselves to be the center of their world.

As cause-and-effect thinking begins to arise, it is difficult for them to see beyond the immediate experience. As an example, when I was in sixth grade, I had the following experience. We returned from summer vacation ready for the new year. Classmates were whispering about summer sexual experiences. I had spent the summer learning to swim, bicycle, and participate in a children's opera in day camp. Yet I wanted to be included in the conversation. I wrote a note to one of my friends sitting further down the row. I used words I had heard but had no idea of their meaning. I would blush today to read that note. One of the boys intercepted it and threatened to show it to my mother. I was horrified at the thought and told him it was not going to happen. He replied, "Then give me your entire stamp collection, and I won't show her the note." I had been collecting stamps for several years and was proud of how thick the album had become. The next day, I handed the album to him, and my mother never knew about it.

Cause-and-effect thinking? The cause was that the boy took my note. The effect was that he would tell my mother unless I gave him my stamps. I couldn't see any other solution. However, what would have happened if I had challenged him and said, "Go ahead." Or if I had said, "I don't care if you do because my mother will believe me." Or "I'm going to tell our teacher what you are threatening to do." But I could not get past my immediate panic to consider other possibilities. There was only one effect: He threatened me, and I gave him what he wanted.

Perhaps an adult could have helped by setting up a conversation between the boy and me. The conversation might have begun like this. "Why do you want Betty's stamp album? Are you interested in stamps?"

Such a conversation might have led to understanding what this boy's intentions were beyond blackmail. It might have helped him understand his motivations and explore options. Both of us would have benefited.

Emotions and intellect share a common origin and happen together with the changing sense of self, identity, and conscience. According to neuropsychologist Stanley Greenspan, "The mind's most important faculties are rooted in emotional experiences from very early in life—before even the earliest awareness of symbols, conscious or unconscious." (Greenspan, p. 40)

Whenever a child faces a new task, the emotions that he or she feels when learning it rise to the surface again and again. A feeling of frustration, accomplishment, or failure comes with the attempt at the skill and it influences how successful he or she is. During this 11–12 phase, such emotions rise up when new math concepts are taught or even when the teams are chosen during recess. Feelings of inadequacy and rejection are powerful reminders of previous hurt feelings and rejection.

Here's another one of my sixth-grade experiences: Our teacher decided to have us make physics boards in which one wire was attached to a paper with a question, and another wire was connected to a paper with an answer. If you connected the correct question wire with the correct answer wire, two bulbs lit up. At the same time, she also wanted us to learn about the Russian revolution. So she divided the class into two groups. I was in the group that would research the Russian revolution. In my sixth-grade mind, I figured that I had been chosen to be in the history team because she knew I couldn't do physics. I dealt with that feeling of inadequacy for years, and it rose up in high school physics classes and became a stumbling block that I had to overcome.

Emotional development involves middle-schoolers' recognizing their own feelings and the feelings of others. Often, they have a feeling but can't express what it is. We can help by suggesting different feelings until they become clearer on what it is they are feeling. Once they recognize their feelings, they have to learn how to manage them. "What do I do when someone tattles on me or betrays my trust?" As middle-schoolers expand their relationships, they encounter new situations, and have to figure out how to cope with new and unfamiliar issues.

One of the strongest aspects of emotional development is for middle-schoolers to recognize their strengths and weaknesses, to realize that everyone has challenges, to be flexible, and to develop healthy self-esteem. Youngsters have different temperaments in the way they respond to these issues. One middle-schooler feels excited at the prospect of moving to a new school; another is devastated at the loss of familiar places and friends. Another is ready to tackle the challenges that will come and can hardly wait to show her skills, and another seems unfazed by the news. All middle-schoolers, regardless of temperament, need to feel the support and encouragement from adults. As long as the youngster feels loved and valued, there is a good possibility of a successful transition to adolescence.

Changes in body and brain can make feelings more intense, causing early adolescents to react more strongly, as they have a hard time controlling their feelings. Moods change very quickly so that a choice they make one moment will be different in the next. Love, hate, crying, laughing, freezing up, silliness, feeling out of control—how can they handle the changing emotions? How can they navigate this turmoil? They cry over little things, slam the door or yell for no apparent reason. They are overly sensitive to what people say to them. Yet they are not sensitive to what they say to others. Their extreme feelings lead to power struggles, exaggerations, and feelings of rejection when they are corrected.

Yet it is important for adults to point out inappropriate behavior and to give them guidelines as to how they can express themselves appropriately. They may begin to understand puns and more subtle jokes, and they struggle to differentiate vulgarity, sick jokes, and acceptable slang. Playing with words is their way of dueling, arguing is their logical way to get what they want. These behaviors will wear out the adult while empowering the youngster.

Eleven- and twelve-year-olds become more aware of their bodies, compare themselves with others, feel insecure, and look to popular culture as models of how to be and what to wear. The acceleration of teenage life down to the 12-year phase is furthered by images from magazines, television, movies, and now social media. Often this makes girls look like hookers. Boys more often dress like sports stars and wear the names of their favorite teams on their shirts, although others are attempting to act smooth in the way they have seen older boys in the movies do. Imitating bodily gestures and facial expressions before they have the maturity to understand what they are doing causes them to look like caricatures of teenagers. Just spend a Saturday afternoon at the mall and you will see what I mean. These youngsters are the cash cows for department stores that follow each trend very carefully to create styles for them to purchase and part with their dollars.

THIRTEEN- TO FOURTEEN-YEAR-OLDS

From 13 to 14 years, young people express their confusion by being irritable, easily excited, more likely to explode than succeed in controlling their emotions, feeling uncertain, unhappy, and sensitive. They are withdrawn, spending a lot of time alone, needing privacy, and convinced everyone else is watching and judging. This is a lot for a youngster to handle.

At this 13- to-14-year age, these young people are very concerned with body image, and their self-esteem is at a low ebb. They are not sociable with adults, but more focused on friendship groups. They are exploring themselves horizontally with peers rather than vertically in relationship to authority. Parents may feel out of the loop with their children whose main interest is focused on other middle-schoolers. Their sensitivity to acceptance or rejection is heightened.

Out of their inner life, something new emerges. Changes in thinking wake them up. Rather than being swept up in their emotions, they begin to see that thinking is a tool they can use. They recognize their feeling impulses and try to gain control. Sitting in on eighth- and ninth-grade classes is a good way to observe the range of emotional maturity 13- and 14-year-olds display.

It is helpful if they can have conversations with adults who help them figure out ways to handle difficult situations such as bullying, feeling left out, how to invite only particular classmates to a birthday celebration, or how to handle stressful family obligations. Problem-solving discussions help them begin to gain insight into other people's feelings and help them feel empowered to imagine other possibilities of behavior.

They are beginning to wonder who they are, what kind of person they are becoming or want to become. What are their interests? They are moving into new territory, facing the unknown. This period of instability can be confusing, but they are looking at ways to traverse the seas, looking for a compass to guide their actions.

They also have deep feelings that need times of quiet to absorb what is happening, to be alone with themselves. They are responsible and irresponsible, funny and angry, pushing away their parents and relying on their parents to support them, moving away from their family and spending more time with friends. They will push limits and demand freedom, but they need boundaries and resist boundaries at the same time.

Around 14, they are becoming more stable, are generally happy, easy-going, and aware of their own strengths and weaknesses. They find many faults with their parents and are embarrassed by them. They like to be busy and involved in many extracurricular activities. Their social circle is large and varied. They have friends of both genders, are anxious to be liked, and have a stronger interest in the opposite sex.

PERSONAL FABLE, IMAGINARY AUDIENCE, AND STRESS

Thanks to David Elkind, who introduced the concept of the personal fable and the imaginary audience, we can have access to the middle-schooler's sense of self.

Personal fable—Middle-schoolers carry the assumption of specialness. "Other people will grow up and die, but I won't." "I can get away with copying someone else's homework, and I won't get caught." "I can take my father's car out for a little spin, and he won't ever know about it." This feeling of special power stays with us for the rest of our lives and may lead immature adults to behave in a risky manner. "I will be famous. Everyone will think about me." They feel protected by a shield of invulnerability that gives them hope. Each one feels that his or her experience is unique and special.

With the recent spate of killings by adolescents, we have seen that the criminal is stuck in this phase of personal fable. They want to be known by everyone. Many television news anchors, not wanting to call attention to the criminal, will withhold the name of a murderer so that it doesn't inspire another unstable adult who is still acting out the personal fable of a middle school child.

Imaginary audience—Middle-schoolers become self-centered, caught up in their own changes and feel they are on stage. When they get dressed in the morning, they are sure everyone will look at them. They are the center. When they walk into the classroom, they are looking at their classmates' responses to their latest outfit or stride. Are they getting the attention from their world out there?

They are sensitive to any mistake or shortcoming because they feel it will be noticed by everyone. This can be devastating to some middle-schoolers who feel there is no place for them to be safe, no cave to hide in.

The combination of the personal fable and the imaginary audience can work in both positive and negative ways. When they believe they are special in an undesirable way, they are concerned that everybody knows what is going on. At the same time, they feel they are the only ones concerned about their bodies and assume their pain is theirs uniquely. Other students are able to cope better, but they don't understand what is going on. They feel that they are the only ones who feel lonely. No one else ever had it so bad or so good. The misery will never end. They resent adults who tell them, "This will pass, and you will feel better one day."

Stress is one of the strongest influences on emotional development of middle-schoolers. David Elkind pointed out that there are two kinds of stresses. One kind is predictable and can be planned for, such as knowing for weeks that there will be a test on a particular date. Of course, it is stressful, but adults can help middle-schoolers plan for the event by studying along the way rather than leaving it till the last minute. The other kind of stress is unpredictable and cannot be planned for. This includes unexpected illness or death, natural disasters, or war. Adults can help middle-schoolers through this stress by recognizing how problematic it is and supporting them in as many ways as possible.

Most of all, as with little children, middle-schoolers also need to feel safe. However, what makes them feel safe is knowing what is expected, knowing they are not alone, and knowing that if they make mistakes, they will still have support. Some middle-schoolers are willing to take more or greater risks than others. Practice in problem-solving situations may help them figure out strategies for how to cope with the stress of risk-taking. For example, a shy student wanted to try out for a part in a class play but was fearful of rejection. A supportive adult can help the student think through how they might handle rejection by realizing it is not based on their self-worth, but on skill or experience.

In the middle school years, physical appearance has a strong influence on a girl's self-esteem, while for boys it may be physical strength. No matter what it is that determines their self-esteem during this time, adults can help them face the problem rather than avoiding it.

Daniel Goleman in 1994 drew attention to the importance of emotional development, *emotional intelligence*. Whereas earlier, the IQ determined someone's success, he pointed out that EI (Emotional Intelligence) was actually a stronger indicator of success. Being able to get along with people, to recognize and manage your emotions, act cooperatively with others in teams, and feeling comfortable with who you are are skills that middle-schoolers need to develop.

Some schools designate a teacher to develop a program of social-emotional learning for the middle school classes. Here they play-act different situations, discussing options of ways to respond. They may be able to identify what the stressors are and make a game plan for how to handle those situations. They may come to see that if and when a friendship breaks up, it is a mighty blow, but it isn't the end of the world. Having a friend makes life tolerable, even wonderful, but having no friend is the most traumatic experience for a middle-schooler.

As middle-schoolers shift from the family to friends, it is still the closeness of the family that helps them meet situations that are disappointing, frightening or just plain miserable.

Having appropriate activities for middle-schoolers to receive the attention and appreciation by the community is important. Drama, sports, academic recognition, buddies between classes, service projects—all are celebrations that allow youngsters to enjoy the spotlight in appropriate ways. They feed the youngsters' sense of achievement and help expand their growing sense of identity.

AFTER FOURTEEN

After 14, they often become unstable again. At 15, they may be quarrelsome, reluctant to communicate, express a strong desire for independence, and want to be free of family. Their relationship with siblings may be better than with parents. Friendship is more important, with one or two "best" friends. Dating and romantic relationships are commonplace.

Fifteen-year-olds try harder to cover up their feelings and are more apt to be moody and withdrawn. They have many social challenges. They begin to think abstractly, to think about and understand consequences; they can reason and explore options: What if? These kinds of conversations at home and at school go a long way to helping youngsters develop their civilizing mind.

CHAPTER 9
Thinking in the Middle School Years

How do children think? In the past, researchers assumed that children think the way adults think. Children were then assessed and judged on when they reached adult cognitive capacities. Psychologist Jean Piaget's research led him to see that there are four different stages of cognition. One stage needs to be accomplished before the next stage could occur. Piaget's child-centered approach transformed education.

My university psychology professor tasked me with researching how children think by asking if they identified form or shape first. After months of poring through research studies, I had no conclusive answer.

When I attended a lecture by Francis Edmunds, director of a Waldorf teacher-education program in England, I asked him that same question. Drawing on the work of Rudolf Steiner, he replied that children think in pictures. The development of children's thinking is a more complex process than that brief answer, yet he was bringing a new perspective that stimulated my own thinking. It was this experience that led me to become a Waldorf teacher.

Rudolf Steiner's approach is based on developmental stages of the child similar in some respects to Piaget's understanding, but is broader and includes spiritual and soul development as well as physical and emotional development. This approach has led teachers to engage in developing their understanding of child development and serving children in many different cultures, with over a thousand Waldorf or Steiner schools around the world since 1919.

DEVELOPMENTAL PATTERNS

Steiner's approach is a holistic one based on three key developmental aspects that follow a pattern from early childhood through adolescence:

0–7:   Thinking through movement and the senses:
        movement-thinking
7–14:   Thinking through imaginative pictures: feeling-thinking
14–21: Thinking through concepts leading to independent
        judgment: abstract-thinking

The growth spurt of neurons around eleven coincides with new thinking capacities. Rudolf Steiner spoke of cause-and-effect thinking as a way children of middle school age begin to organize their world. Jean Piaget spoke of the beginning of formal operational thinking. Both researchers describe a new capacity of mind in which 11–12-year-olds stand outside their instinctual behavior and "operate" on it or "organize" it. They begin to notice patterns in the physical world as well as in their own behavior. They don't yet have the capacity to understand what they see or experience, but they have taken the first step. This is the beginning of being able to reflect on their actions.

The big shift in understanding how children think occurred in the 1990s when psychologists began to record their observations and gather the results from neuroscience, allowing us to understand the development of the brain, the interconnections between the different parts, and how particular activities stimulate brain development. This is a very complicated process that is still being investigated and much is still not understood. The use of such techniques as fMRIs and CT scans have helped us to understand that the brain is not static, but is constantly undergoing change and development as the person has different experiences. The term used is "plasticity," meaning the brain can be changed by experience.

Most researchers agree that the prefrontal cortex has a significant influence on thinking. The brain develops from back to front, and the prefrontal cortex is the last position of the brain to fully develop. It is already present at birth and develops in critical growth spurts of neurons. As each neural spurt of brain cells occurs, it presents an opportunity for learning, and then the energy shifts to the next opportunity. These windows of opportunity rely on experience and connection with an adult model for new capacities to develop. This is why it is so problematic for children in the early adolescent years to be guided by teenagers rather than by adults.

When the prefrontal cortex matures, it makes it possible to do higher-level thinking and to express higher virtues such as compassion and empathy. Executive function, the capacity to develop complex decision-making and planning, takes place later in adolescent development. Adolescents and young adults become self-aware and assess risks and dangers. Working with this new capacity, they are able to strengthen their inner spark that until now has been tended by adults.

THE FIRST SEVEN YEARS

The key experiences that form the foundation for thinking in the middle school years are set down in the first seven years. The vehicle of these key learning experiences is primarily imitation. These experiences include a rich life of sensory stimulation, a healthy emotional relationship with an adult to imitate, communication through the languages of speech and music, opportunities for rich imitation, symbolism, and, finally, play.

Through imaginative play the child thinks about situations and acts them out, thus developing concrete skills. Thinking through movement, the senses, and feelings occurs before verbal ability. If we force a child to learn to read and to work with verbal materials (preschool and kindergarten), we are like a builder who is too eager to see results and fails to put in the foundation before beginning to erect the walls. Thinking is not isolated but is interconnected with feelings and actions.

111

FROM SEVEN TO ELEVEN

As the child begins formal learning in grade school, the experiences gathered earlier become more conscious and are now filled with feeling and thinking working together.

The child begins by imitating the teacher in writing, reading, movement exercises, and playing music. Then gradually, around age 8 or 9, he or she gains more independence and initiates these experiences out of himself.

THREE ASPECTS OF THINKING

Rudolf Steiner described three key aspects of the child's thinking at this stage as learning through rhythm, artistic activities, and imaginative pictures. These provide the key elements of the Waldorf approach.

Learning through rhythm and repetition

If we look back in history we find that before the advent of reading and writing, people learned and remembered through rhythm. They sang songs that accompanied their work, songs that helped them saw wood or work the forge, march in formation, or rock babies to sleep. Rhythm is experienced in language, particularly in poetry and song. It is also experienced by doing things in the same way at the same time of the day or week, and by celebrating the seasons year in and year out. Learning in rhythm develops memory.

We are often in awe at the capacity of children to memorize scenes from a play or poem because it was taught with accent on the rhythm that relates to the breathing and heartbeat of the child. Walking in rhythm helps us remember lines in poetry; clapping the rhythm helps us remember songs. In commercials, information on products is put into a song or jingle. Once we memorize something with rhythm, it stays with us, and later on we can then think about it.

Learning through artistic activities

Each artistic genre awakens a path of experiencing the world in a different way, involving the body and the soul. From the earliest time of history, human beings have connected with nature, each other, and the higher worlds through song, chanting, drumming, dance, painting designs on their homes and bodies, shaping their buildings, shaping their vessels, weaving cloth, and etching wood. Each artistic experience gives the child a new perspective that leads to connecting and understanding.

Through participating in the visual arts—painting, drawing, sculpting, and modeling—the child is able to transform a thought through the materials of pencil, paint, or clay.

Through participating in the time arts—movement, singing, instrument playing, dance, eurythmy, poetry, story, and drama—the child explores through the body and voice.

Through the practical arts—crafts and handwork—the child transforms wool, cotton, cloth, and wood into something practical and beautiful. Children love to make things with their hands. Through imitation, using simple tools, they are stimulated to understand work. Once children make something, they have a skill for life that integrates an idea, measurement, and purpose. One of my favorite gifts was a child's finger-knitted flat circle hanging on an upright dowel. "What is it?" I asked. My foster-son answered, "An apple warmer."

Matti Bergström, Finnish professor and neurophysiologist, had this to say on the importance of handwork for children:

> The brain discovers what the fingers explore. The density
> of nerve endings in our fingertips is enormous. Their
> discrimination is almost as good as that of our eyes. If we don't
> use our fingers, if in childhood and youth we become "finger-
> blind," this rich network of nerves is impoverished—that
> represents a huge loss to the brain and thwarts the individual's
> all-around development. Such damage may be likened to
> blindness itself. Perhaps worse, while a blind person may simply
> not be able to find this or that object, the finger-blind cannot
> understand its inner meaning and value.

If we neglect to develop and train our children's fingers and the creative form-building capacity of their hand muscles, then we neglect to develop their understanding of the unity of things; we thwart their aesthetic and creative powers. (Ikea, 1994, Swedish Handicraft exhibition, New Jersey)

Learning through imaginative pictures

When children listen to richly described images, they create their own images in their mind's eye. They move out of the present moment and into their minds where they can organize their thoughts and make predictions as to what will happen next. When a child reflects on stories, this awakens the understanding of the structure and sequence of stories as well as the understanding that words have meaning. Because the story is told without visual pictures, the child has to activate thinking inwardly to consider what is happening, how it feels, where it's going next.

Alexander Luria, "a renowned neuropsychologist fascinated by the workings of growing brains, insisted that language physically builds the brain's higher reasoning centers. He claimed that, without language, humans would not have developed abstract, categorical thinking." (Healy quoting Luria from *Language and Cognition*, New York: Wiley, 1982)

Language, in the course of social history, became the decisive instrument that helped humans transcend the boundaries of sensory experience, assign symbols, and formulate certain generalizations and categories. When the child names something, pronouncing, for example, "That is a steam engine," he begins to *understand* that in the movement of the machine named, steam plays a role and that it moves other objects. In mastering words and using them, the child *analyzes and synthesizes* the phenomena of the external world, using not only his personal experiences but the experiences of mankind. He classifies objects, he begins to perceive them differently and, with this, to remember them differently. [italics added] (Healy citing Vocate, D.

The Theory of A.R. Luria, Hillsdale, NJ: Lawrence Erlbaum Associates, 1987, p. 29)

Developing visual thinking through listening, representing information graphically by drawing, or holding it in their inner eye helps children experience, remember, and gain new understanding. Being able to see patterns sets the groundwork for understanding mathematics and spatial relationships. Imagining oneself in different scenes or as an historical character strengthens problem-solving and a feeling of inner connection with what is being experienced. All forms of artistic work strengthen this capacity to connect what is being learned with feelings.

Children have different strengths in learning based on their sense experiences—some learn best by hearing, seeing, through touch or through their bodily movement, by working together or working alone. The more sense experiences the children have access to, the more able they are to connect with what is being learned. This multisensory approach provides skills for problem-solving as well as providing an outlet for creativity.

> Language is not only a means of generalization; it is at the same time the source of thought. When the child masters language, he gains the potentiality to organize anew his perceptions, his memory; he masters more complex forms of reflection of objects in the external world; he gains the capacity to draw conclusions from his observations, to make deductions, the potentiality of thinking. (Healy quoting Luria from *Educational Psychology in the USSR*, Stanford: Stanford University Press, 1968, p. 85)

For example, learning the geography and history of California by modeling the physical aspects of the state with clay, beeswax, or papier mâché, singing songs of the early settlers, painting and drawing scenes, role playing early characters in California history, visiting Sutter's Fort and observing the different craftspeople at work, using a forge to shape a nail, imagining oneself as a member of the Donner party, and so on all awaken thought that children can more easily remember than if they were only reading about it.

Through listening and seeing, children begin to differentiate patterns in language, reading, and grammar. Rich images evoke strong feelings that make it easier to remember and think about what they are learning. This is also a key time for learning other languages.

THINKING AND THE MIDDLE SCHOOL CHILD

What had been for them a balanced period of their thinking, feeling, and willing in grades four and five, eleven–twelve-year-olds now experience a new brain spurt, ushering in a period of instability. The brain and the body are growing at a fast rate, and their equilibrium is thrown off balance. They begin to separate their thinking from their feeling and will and are easily upset and frustrated. "Why can't things work anymore? Why does the teacher say I was talking? I wasn't talking." Impulsivity propels them, and they can't figure out what the problem is. They feel they are being singled out.

Around age eleven, children think about their actions and express themselves verbally. Increased connectivity in the brain cells takes place during this time with changes in thinking. The greatest pace of brain growth since age two to three occurs around age eleven. This is also the time of the greatest intensity of hormonal activity and will take two years to consolidate before the next big spurt. Patience is needed.

"Twice in our lives, the temporal lobe purges information it deems unnecessary so it can make room for new information, roughly at age two and eleven." (Icard, p. 32)

Eleven-year-olds have a similar challenge to two-year-olds. Both ages are coming to terms with a new body, a new identity, emotions, desires, and intellectual thoughts. Both are going through momentous brain growth. Rich opportunities are awakening.

This alteration is referred to as myelination. Which information will be cleaned out to make room for new knowledge? What is used least must go first. If the youngster stops practicing a certain skill, that skill will be pruned, flushed out to make room for something else. This is why it is so important for middle school children to continue practicing their musical instruments or other skills and not quit when they are eleven. They should stay with it until after age thirteen, although it would be ideal to continue until age 15/16. Then if they want to stop, there is always the possibility of picking it up again without too much difficulty. This is also true of learning another language.

"The brain is only about halfway developed during the middle school years. The girl's brain reaches full biological maturity at age 22; the boy's brain at 28." (Icard, p. 24)

This means that for the rest of early and then later adolescence, middle-schoolers do not have full capacity for thinking and responsible action. The more often we recall what we learn, the more we will remember what was presented. Middle school children need to be repeatedly reminded to remember what they are told. Let's remember this when we become frustrated with our youngsters.

The difference between eleven years of age and fifteen was exemplified by my granddaughter. When Louisa was eleven, she treasured her American Girl doll. When I asked her what she would like for Christmas, she took out the catalog and pointed to some clothes. Horrified by the price, I found two sets of clothes to fit her doll from another company. When I called to wish her a Merry Christmas, I asked her if she had received the outfits. She blurted out, "But Grandma, they weren't in the catalog." When Louisa was fifteen, I visited her family. I asked her if she remembered that experience. She was embarrassed and said, "Oh, Grandma, I was so stupid then. Thank you for sending them."

CHANGES IN THINKING

Around 12- to 14-years-old, middle-schoolers begin to move from the life of dreamy feelings and rhythmical response to head thinking, where their conscience will be guided by ideals. They begin to see purpose in what is happening at first within their own thoughts, and then outside in their social relationships. Everything that has happened before begins to be understood by logical concepts. They will continue to use logical thinking and become more skillful with it.

A new capacity to think causally changes children's relations to others. They are able to manipulate words to see what effect they will have on others. They are able to identify a soft spot in the adult, and they argue, challenge, and test the adult's reason for doing something.

They can use this same tool of thinking in practicing objectivity with the laws of the physical world. In the study of physics—optics, acoustics, heat, electricity, and magnetism—they can set up a hypothesis. What happens if I look at the prism from above? From below? What happens when I do it repeatedly during the week? They begin to observe consistent facts. This leads them to question why this is the case. They come to see that there is order in the physical world, and they can begin to make predictions. They are using their perception and their objectivity. It is not a matter of guessing a right answer, but trusting their observations. There is a sense of security in knowing that physical laws can be counted on.

A similar kind of thinking can be used in humanities classes. If they are studying the rise and fall of the Roman Empire, they can begin to understand that if a country becomes too large and has to depend on slaves, the people become soft and decadent, and this weakens them to being conquered by an enemy. Students can begin to entertain "what if" questions. What would have happened *if* Caesar had not crossed the Rubicon? They begin to think abstractly, but if they feel stressed, they can easily lose the thread and have a difficult time answering the question. Then they become concrete thinkers again.

Middle-schoolers like to master things—to collect baseball cards, trade with each other, collect stamps, keep statistics of their favorite teams. This kind of activity feels good because they feel competitive, but they don't have to answer difficult thought questions, mainly simple answers to who, what, where, and when.

Their hearts open up and they take in the world. They want to change things for the better, but that is very difficult. They have lots of ideas, but some of them are irrational. Two mothers of sixth-graders were shaking their heads as they shared the following with me:

James, a sixth-grader, told his mother: I want to work at United Air Lines when I grow up.
Mother: Why not Southwest? Why do you want to work for United?
James: Because they have classes.
Mother: What kind?
James: You know, first and second class.

Or sixth-grader Ronald said: "When I grow up, I want to work in a cubicle." He liked to visit his mother at work. He would go from cubicle to cubicle, chatting with people. That seemed to him an interesting way to work.

The sixth-grader is trying to make sense of the world with limited information. There is so much noise going on inside their minds that they respond to whatever captures their attention. They are trying to figure it out. They will think about the people who are close to them as well as popular figures, and they will choose their own role models.

This is a key time to help them prepare for executive function by helping them plan things, identify the hindrances, problem-solve, and control their impulses. Although executive function will not be fully mature until adulthood, this is a key time to work on it. Because middle-schoolers tend to process things emotionally, this kind of planning helps them cool down the heat. They have difficulty doing this on their own, but with adult help, they can assess situations without being impulsive. Without this help, they may prefer risk-taking and daring challenges.

With this change in thinking, they can begin to see possibilities in the future. This is just at the beginning stage, and until executive function matures, they are unable to see the consequences, both negative and positive, that may come from particular behavior.

In addition to their academic skills, their decision-making skills in their daily behavior will improve. They will begin to strengthen their conscience by differentiating right from wrong and by anticipating the consequences of different options.

CHANGES IN LANGUAGE USAGE

The period before twelve years of age is a time of growth in the language centers of the brain. This is the critical period for learning world languages and beginning to understand metaphors. For example, what is an idiom? "It's raining cats and dogs." We know the meaning is not literal, so what does it mean? They can also begin to detect sarcasm and feel power in manipulating words.

Language is a new tool that can be used for good or ill. The sixth-graders gain a sense of power through the words that they choose. However, they don't have the emotional maturity to take responsibility for what they say. Adults need to guide them by being very direct.

Working with grammar, syntax, and structure allows the youngster to move beyond the physical world into the mind where cause-and-effect rule. Building vocabulary, tracing Greek or Latin roots of words, synonyms and antonyms, and using language to compare and contrast all raise the level of thinking. This takes time and practice.

In writing exercises, they experiment with active and passive voices. They can write business letters in which they objectively inquire about a product, thank a business for sending the product, or explain why a product is not working. These kinds of exercises help them express themselves in appropriate ways. They can express an opinion and back it up with facts. Another way to help them with objectivity in writing is self-editing or peer editing.

They begin to separate fact from fiction as they learn about different genres of literature. When they do research, they learn to evaluate the credibility of various printed media and internet sources of information.

As they move into eighth grade, their attention span increases. They are able to focus and stay longer with a problem. When they choose their own role models, they will imitate behavior. The quality of the model will affect how young teens are able to take hold of impulses and govern their behavior. It will depend on the quality of the coach, the teacher, the neighborhood leader, sports star or Hollywood icon whether they are able to exert self-discipline or whether they emulate antisocial behavior. Because thinking is in the midst of rebuilding, their decision-making is weak, they struggle with controlling impulses, and they are trying to think critically. But this is all part of a mix, and despite middle-schoolers being smart and respectful, they don't have it all together. They are in the process of reconstruction.

ARTISTIC AND PRACTICAL EXPERIENCES

The areas for understanding spatial relations have reached their peak of growth by thirteen. Geometric drawing, movement in space, and three-dimensional model building can be learned more easily during this time.

During one geology class, we were studying volcanoes. Earlier we had done geometric drawing, a great favorite of the sixth-graders. We sculpted a volcano out of papier mâché, inserted a can of dried ice and ink into the center, and watched the bubbles emerge from the center as a volcanic eruption. A gasp of wonder went through the class, "Look, the bubbles are all hexagons." This was an example of art and science supporting each other.

Painting and sculpting strengthen their senses of color and spatial relations. They can grasp an idea and begin to put it into practice. More and more able to handle the materials, they feel a sense of accomplishment.

They learn to use tools safely and with skill. Guiding chisels, rasps, files, and sandpaper, they learn to follow the right direction and not split the wood. They find branches and begin whittling them. Through carving they need to guide the tool with appropriate pressure and direction. If they have been knitting before, this is a good time for them to challenge themselves with complicated patterns that require focus.

Many schools these days are discontinuing arts and practical activities. In the pressure to focus on scores, these subjects disappear. This is a huge loss to a child's learning, sense of joy and empowerment.

For over ten years I developed a program for juvenile delinquents in a community school and juvenile hall. These youngsters had either been trouble-makers or dropped out silently while sitting unengaged in the back of the room. The arts were a central part of the curriculum.

One boy described how he recited Robert Frost's poem to himself as he rode his bike and didn't need to throw rocks at squirrels. Others delighted at playing musical instruments rather than being disruptive. Whereas they had usually become disruptive and chaotic on Friday afternoons, anxious to be freed from school, they now began to have music festivals and applaud each other's accomplishments. They illustrated their work pages, painted and drew, relishing good-quality materials that they had been previously denied to them. Many of them had talent that would have been used primarily in graffiti, but now they had multiple options for expressing themselves.

Frank Wilson, neurologist and hand surgeon, conducted significant research on the use of the hand in human evolution. He showed that having the opportunity to manipulate objects leads to acquisition of language and cognitive skills. Movement connected with music awakens both cognitive skills and emotions. He spoke of how juggling is a good use of the hands because not only is it a skill, but it has an emotional element in the way of predicting where your hands need to be to catch the ball. "Whatever you can do with your hands gives you a small world that you can actually cope with, as opposed to the big world, where perhaps you can't." (Wilson, p. 219)

When I taught sixth grade, we were cutting geometric figures out of balsa wood. At the same time, we were studying sound and deafness, sight and blindness. Out of discussions with the children, we decided to visit the Easter Seals Center and help blind children cut designs out of wood. Armed with coping saws, the sixth-graders shared their skill with others, connecting the intellectual learning about physics with a social gesture. Craft work is often cross-disciplinary. Using mathematics and measurement, aesthetics, practical usefulness, exploring historical artifacts, etc., help children come to understanding and learning.

Through the complex changes that middle-schoolers experience from the ages of eleven to fourteen, their sense of identity is affected. In the first stage, they respond to each situation as final. They can't think ahead or have an overview. They can only take each concrete situation as the totality of who they are. Being able to think beyond this comes later in adolescence when they can reflect on themselves. In the second stage, they begin to recognize different aspects of themselves and define themselves differently. "I am a struggling student." "I like to go skating." "I don't like asparagus." "I don't like to go to my grandmother's house." In the third stage, they begin to understand they are more complex, incorporating varied aspects, struggling with some things, achieving well with others. They are not one way or the other. As long as they have consistency, they begin to see their strengths and areas of weakness without being devastated. For example, "I am struggling with spelling, but I try hard. Some things are harder than others." They move beyond the narrow identity such as, "I'll be a baseball player because I've been playing Little League since I was seven."

WHAT'S NEXT?

The first fourteen years are preparation for the mid-adolescent period (15–17). Prefrontal growth allows children to go beyond the limitations and constraints of the earlier neural system. During this time, the teen has made great strides in critical thinking, impulse control, and moderating social behavior. This concludes the first stage of prefrontal development. All parts of the brain other than the prefrontal myelinate or stabilize, making permanent what has been achieved up to that time. The rest of the brain has matured.

Now comes the most significant event which signals a second phase of development—the secondary growth spurt of the prefrontal— from fifteen to eighteen years, referred to as middle adolescence.

Through using their prefrontal cortex, they now are able to incorporate their instincts and transform them. The teenager is developing executive function and with practice is beginning to make careful, thoughtful, and informed decisions. They tend to speed up their thinking, and we have to help them slow down and consider what they are saying or doing. But we need to know that this a new stage and will take until the twenties to stabilize.

In his TED talk, "Self-Regulation in Schools" (2015), Daniel Siegel speaks of the need to differentiate between the brain and the mind. The three Rs are reflection, relationships, and resilience. These are the kinds of things you can do in your mind-awareness, as this helps you regulate and communicate. He calls *reflection* "time in." The prefrontal cortex connects to all parts of the brain, lets you pick up in your cortex what's happening in your body and links everything. This is integration.

It is during these high school years that the teenager turns to the outer world, to figure out how it works, and then to the inner world, striving toward truth, developing independent judgment. It is in the last phase, from eighteen to twenty-one, that they can be more self-directed, more analytical, and more aware of themselves. Whether that actually happens in each case remains to be seen.

CHAPTER 10

Inside the Schoolhouse

DEVELOPING IDENTITY

Each child expresses individuality through body type, temperament, and interests. In everyday life, parents recognize how different each child in the family is, how each responds to parents and grandparents, how each connects with nature, especially with their pets, and how each deals with challenge and disappointment. In the classroom, the teachers also are concerned with the individualities of the children they teach. By careful observation and learning about childhood temperaments, teachers appreciate each child's uniqueness and strive to acknowledge and support them.

Children are not usually aware of their own identity in the classroom. They are much more aware of how they feel, who is friendly and nice, who is annoying, who leaves them out of activities, who tries to be first. As they begin to experience themselves individually, they start to see and value differences.

By the time they reach middle school, children are becoming conscious of this dynamic in the classroom, trying to figure out their relationship to the group, and what their own values and opinions are. Through listening to their peers, they consider ideas they would not have thought of by themselves such as trying out for a part in a play, participating in after-school sports, or volunteering to make a presentation in class. Each decision may create anxiety, but with an adult's encouragement, they may gain courage and perseverance. Social interaction is one of the main influences in forming identity as middle-schoolers become aware of themselves as individuals.

For example, middle-schoolers may experience group pressure to become popular by behaving in a way contrary to what they are comfortable with. If they want to be liked, they may have to act in ways that contradict their own values. Working on becoming an individual requires middle-schoolers to reflect on their actions. They have to be outside and inside themselves at the same time. This is very challenging for eleven- or twelve-year-olds. Teachers can help them in this process by organizing discussion time in class, sometimes with the whole class, at other times in small groups or in pairs.

They can gain insight through discussing characters in a book. What kind of choices does the character make? Are they wise choices? What else could they have done? It is easier for middle-schoolers to objectively discuss a character in a book than to put the focus on themselves. They are still very fragile and in the process of growth and development.

Writing exercises can be done in class in which middle-schoolers describe their interests and what they would like to learn more about.

Middle-schoolers need to be respected for their individuality. They are trying to shape their identity within their family, within their class or school, and within other groups. Relationships within the class community, school community, and neighborhood community help them establish their identity and learn to help others as well.

Part of the process of becoming an individual during the middle school years is the erratic quality of their behavior. One day they are bold, another day timid; one day they want to be different, another day they just want to fit in. Each of these is a separate, concrete experience that over time transforms into an overall sense of "who I am."

By eighth grade, middle-schoolers, begin to define themselves. "I'm a science nerd," "I'm an athlete," "I'm a musician" or "I'm a rock climber." Over time we see that these identities change as new interests emerge, and middle-schoolers expand their sense of self. It is important in this respect for adults not to limit their perception of the middle-schooler, but to keep open the possibilities of expanded self-awareness.

RELATIONSHIPS WITH TEACHERS

Teachers become key helpful figures in relationships with middle-schoolers, and it is important not to betray that trust. Does the student feel seen, heard, valued? Middle-schoolers want their teachers to respect them and recognize that they are not children any more. They want to be treated seriously, with interest in their thoughts and feelings.

As students come into the later middle school years, it is helpful to have other teachers in addition to ones they have had for a long time. They are interested in who the teachers are, how differently they teach, and if the teachers respond well to them. They appreciate teachers who have enthusiasm for their subject and who find ways to involve students in exploring it. Middle-schoolers love to work together in teams, and with the teacher's clear instructions and guidance, they can enter into the subject and make progress.

I have heard teachers say that they find it difficult to inspire middle-schoolers academically because they are so emotional and willful. This might be an unnecessarily limited point of view. Middle-schoolers are open to the world, interested in everything going on around them, but they need teachers to model that interest and understand how their students learn best. They need their teachers to be firm, but loving, as well as humorous or serious at the appropriate moments. They need their teachers to be creative, imaginative, and always ready for a joke.

Once a teacher becomes (or appears to become) punitive, middle-schoolers label the teacher as "mean" and find it difficult to relate to him or her. Emotions affect their perceptions. They will still do their work for the teacher, but then it may be motivated by fear or pressure. Such feelings prevent them from participating in their learning process in the best way.

It is not always easy for teachers to remain warm and humorous as middle-schoolers can be rude as they figure out appropriate responses. These youngsters need to be corrected and guided at the same time. It helps to discuss any problems with a student on the next day when things have calmed down so the student can reflect on the situation, what he or she said or did and how the response could have been different.

Teachers who have taken their class from the early grades into fifth, sixth, or seventh grade have contacted me, nervously asking, "What happened? In fifth grade I was still the authority, but now in sixth grade, they are a tribe, powerfully uniting against me. Their energy is intimidating." If teachers can dip into inner resources of humor and patience and develop a broader perspective, they will find that getting through sixth grade can bring smooth sailing into seventh and eighth grades—not easier, but able to ride the waves instead of being smacked by them.

Teaching middle-schoolers is not every teacher's strength. The teacher has to know when to take things personally and when to ignore behavior. It is a fine art that successful teachers demonstrate very effectively. It is essential for teachers to recognize that because middle-schoolers are observing everything the teacher does, their attitude and enthusiasm can change a youngster's life. Middle-schoolers watch their teachers' gestures and voice, feel a positive connection with them or feel rejected by them. They are hyper-sensitive to the teachers' responses. Because they feel that everything revolves around them, they interpret their teachers' actions as directed specifically at them.

In middle school, my family moved to Hollywood, Florida, a small town where teachers and students often live in the same neighborhood. During eighth grade, I had two experiences that were memorable in my relationship with my teachers.

One day I was walking along the side of the road in my neighborhood. My physics teacher stopped and offered me a lift. Her husband was driving, and she was in the passenger seat. I sat behind him. At one point, he put his arm around his wife's shoulder and tenderly twisted a curl of hair. I was infuriated. I thought. "She is my teacher. Get your hands off her." Was I making sense? Of course not, but it illustrates the example of the middle-schooler's sense of personal fable. Everything is all about me.

During that year, I lost my algebra textbook, and I didn't have money to buy a new one. My math teacher offered me the opportunity to do an hour of weeding in her yard, and in exchange she would replace the book. I was happy to do that and from then on remained grateful to her and felt that teachers could be my friends.

We had crushes on our teachers, male and female. We loved to talk about them in our little groups. We analyzed every detail of their responses, and we longed for connections with them.

In small schools there are many opportunities for students to connect with teachers, not only in class, but on field trips. This is especially true on camping trips. Everyone gets to experience each other in new ways, outside the structured classroom, on hikes, sleeping outside on tarps, cooking meals, and washing dishes.

It is heartening when I see a teacher walking around the school yard in conversation with a middle-schooler, not because there has been a problem, but because of sincere interest. The more students can feel recognized and affirmed by their teachers, the better they learn and the better they mature.

RELATIONSHIPS WITH CLASSMATES

Classroom relationships are key in the development of middle-schoolers. Let's remember that eight hours a day in school every weekday is more time than middle-schoolers spend awake at home. What happens between them offers possibilities for warmth, frustration, cooperation, misunderstandings, and new reflections of themselves. It is the real laboratory of middle school emotional development, and what happens there has effects on their self-esteem that last for decades.

Some teachers have a box with a slot through which students can write a note to the teacher, perhaps noticing bullying or experiencing bullying, pointing out something positive that a classmate has done, or mentioning a conflict between classmates. The teacher can use these messages for classroom discussion. Feeling safe in class helps middle-schoolers express their concerns and feel seen. Recognition is also a positive result of this approach to questions and discussion.

From the moment students enter class until they leave for home, the classroom is stage for a daily drama. They size each other up, make internal judgments about what they see, who is wearing what, who is going where, and how that impacts them.

The social scene provides opportunities for friendships made and lost, of fun, of working together in teams, in learning together, in testing limits both personally and as a group. The social scene is terrifying for some children who don't know what to do or how to behave. Even with those who are not terrified, they are nervous. "Will I fit in?" "Will I be liked?" "Will I be chosen?" There is no other time in our lives when we are as emotionally fragile as in middle school.

New students are challenged to find ways to connect within a group that had been together for many years. This is not an easy task. Belonging is a chief need for middle-schoolers, and making their way into a new group is very challenging. The teacher can be helpful in supporting the integration of new students.

When I moved to a new school in seventh grade, I became friends with a very shy girl. She did not have many friends, and she reached out to me. We got together at each other's houses, made up games, developed make-believe clubs, and enjoyed being together. This continued throughout the year, but because I joined Girl Scouts, I made other friends as well. When we moved into high school (eighth–twelfth grades), our seventh-grade friendship did not continue. There was no big event that happened, but we both moved on to other relationships. The new group I connected with became the center of my eighth- to eleventh-grade social and academic life until I moved away to finish high school in New York. Sixty-three years later I am still very close friends with one of those eighth-graders. Moving in and out of friendships is part of the middle school experience.

Certain middle-schoolers take on the role of greeting new students, being extremely helpful while showing them around. Because these students tend to feel lonely, they don't already have strong friendships in the class, and they try to get to know a new classmate, hoping it will turn into a solid friendship. However, often the friendship does not last, as the new student begins to get to know other students and, in time, finds soulmates. There are exceptions where these new connections become long-time friends, each very happy to have found the other.

CURRICULUM—MOVING FROM CONCRETE TO ABSTRACT THINKING

The choice of subjects can heighten middle-schoolers' preparation for the civilizing mind. Sixth-graders gain a sense of confidence by using their thinking to understand cause-and-effect in science. Thinking becomes a tool that they are able to consciously use as it undergoes transformation over the next years. In seventh grade, their thinking expands as they begin to see themselves in a new way. By studying the great figures of the Renaissance, they can imagine that each person has many different possibilities. This feeling cultivates imagination of what their lives can be. In eighth grade, they are ready to focus on contemporary life—current history, breakthroughs in science and technology, mathematics, geography, political and social life. In this way, they become citizens of their country and their time. If the teacher understands how the curriculum is a pathway toward self-development, the journey through the middle school years can be a deeply powerful meeting between teacher and students. I experienced this three-year transformation over and over again in my teaching career and each time expressed my gratitude to Rudolf Steiner for his brilliant insight.

In this particular stage of development, middle-schoolers are more often engaged with their school subjects when they involve connection with the real world—real machines, real equipment, real people from different countries, real children who have special needs whom they can help. When schools offer connections with the real world through experiential methods in which their senses are engaged, middle-schoolers thrive.

Their feelings are enriched as they are awed by the power of a machine, feel tenderness toward helping younger children on the playground, feel accomplishment when threading a real loom, enjoy working in the garden with real vegetables that will be harvested and sold at the school market, or put on a hat or garment of a visitor from Africa, Latin America, or Asia. Their thinking is engaged by following these experiences with quiet reflection, problem solving, and research. Middle-schoolers want to meet the real world, not fake exercises or kits with already prepared parts.

Middle-schoolers like to collect things or facts, recite the capitals of all the states, memorize the major rivers of Africa, discuss baseball players' statistics, collect cards and bugs and anything else that piques their interest. While sixth-graders' black-and-white thinking results in concrete responses, seventh- and eighth-graders move beyond concrete thinking to larger issues that require abstraction. For example, having learned the capitals, they might discuss why capitals are seldom the largest city in the state. This requires that they consider different reasons, evaluate them, and arrive at new ideas.

Science experiments offer the opportunity for middle-schoolers to participate, develop scientific method, and come to their own conclusions. For example, in studying astronomy, they become aware of the night sky, following the moon and the constellations. Although they can find out about them on the internet, it is a completely different experience to observe them night after night, tracking movement, and coming to their own conclusion. I took my seventh-grade camping during our astronomy study. I woke them up every hour so they could draw the stars moving around the North Star. In one night, these changes reflect what is happening over the course of a year. Despite their annoyance at my waking them, they learned something out of direct experience that was easier to remember than what they read in a book.

Physics offers so many opportunities to build, to work with machines, learn about mechanical advantage, and become objective observers. Integrating science with social studies and arts offers a multisensory experience in which students benefit from different perspectives.

In one sixth-grade class, the study of optics included learning about blindness, practicing Braille, and hearing visitors describe changes in the lives of blind people. Reading the life of Helen Keller and acting out scenes brought empathy with her struggles. In a similar way, the study of acoustics could include learning about how people deal with deafness.

In one sixth-grade math class, students developed a fundraising project to sell tee shirts to raise money for their class trip, with a percentage being donated to a worthy charity. They designed the shirt, ordered the shirts, silkscreened the design, worked out the costs and the selling price, divided the class into teams, sold the shirts, and so on. This project offered them opportunities to think through each stage of the project, work together in teams, sharpen their business math skills, and consider which charity they would support and why. There were times they had to decide what to do if a class member was not following through on the task. A project like this needs the teacher to hold a balance between having the students learn from their decisions (and mistakes) and solving problems for them.

One of the most humorous moments was in a seventh-grade mechanics class. The teacher had fastened a pulley to the ceiling, and students were pulling each other up and figuring out mechanical advantage. One time they hoisted him up very close to the ceiling. With delightful shouts they yelled, "Goodbye Mr. X. We're going out for break."

In another situation, students were hoisting each other up to the branches of a large tree, and then they pleaded to be able to hoist their teacher up as well. Once he was up, they laughingly told him they couldn't take him down. However, they felt sorry for him and hoisted up some snacks. After a little while, they brought him down, feeling he was such a good sport. His positive attitude went a long way in helping the students trust him and enjoy learning. It is these experiences of warmth and humor that can keep middle-schoolers involved in their studies.

Seventh grade and eighth grade are opportunities to study physiology, as students become acquainted with their bodies and health issues. It is important to be factual and at the same time not to treat the body as a machine. Students of this age need information to be able to make decisions about how to treat their own bodies as well as how to treat others with respect. Middle-schoolers have many false ideas of how their body works, and they are empowered when they understand it correctly. Learning about the brain and its functions also sets a background for how to protect their minds from effects of addictions of many kinds, including from cell phones.

Health issues are significant ways to connect middle-schoolers with the world around them. They learn about the foods they eat: what constitutes a healthy diet, how food is grown and distributed, and what is included in labels on packaged foods. Keeping a daily diary of what they eat gives them concrete information. Understanding the effects of preservatives, GMOs, etc., leads them into more abstract thinking as they decide what changes they can make in their daily habits. Health issues also include smoking, alcohol, and drugs. This study can easily expand into questions about relationships and sexuality.

Deciding how much detail to go into depends on the school's policies and on the attitudes of teachers, parents, and students. Some would argue that this class should already happen in sixth, maybe even fifth grade. In some schools, this class would be taught by the teacher as part of biology; in others it is taught by a different teacher who focuses on social and emotional skills, or has sections with a separate male teacher or female teacher holding question and answer sessions. The Campaign to Prevent Teen Pregnancy, now called Power to Decide, has all kinds of helpful information available for the classroom.

This is also a time to teach seventh- and eighth-graders about consumer issues. Learning to become critical viewers of whatever they take into their bodies, feelings, and minds empowers them. Consumer education would include the role of advertising, the power of imagery, and knowledge to guide their decision-making in how to spend their money. Discussions about the effect of commercials, propaganda, and buying power help guide them at this time when they are being affected by marketing media.

In eighth grade as they study the industrial revolution in history, they should move on to the electronic revolution and all the changes that have come about with the development of the computer. Being able to construct a simple computer takes away the mystique and helps them understand what is involved.

Middle-schoolers need to work on their writing, developing their thoughts so that they are clear and sequential. When they strengthen their writing skills, they discover they have a voice with which they can share their perspective. Various styles of writing open up windows of opportunity. Reading different forms of literature, sharing thoughts on books, writing reports, alternative endings, and book reviews all strengthen their writing and reading skills.

Based on a book they are reading, they can speak from a character's perspective, discovering the difference between first person or the more objective third-person's view. Poetry writing offers opportunity to bring imagination into their thoughts and allows for feelings to emerge on topics that are usually difficult to understand.

They can develop a class or middle school newspaper or newsletter, dividing up responsibilities for interviewing, writing up reports, coming up with enjoyable games, producing it, and working with social situations that arise from working together.

Some students feel that since there are so many problems in the world, they want to reject it. It is easier to turn their backs on it and find refuge in imaginary worlds, science fiction, chapter books of other worlds, or video games. There is nothing wrong with that, but we need to stimulate their interest in this world and how they are part of it. Teachers can challenge middle-schoolers to connect to what is happening in their community where they can make a difference, feel that what they are doing has purpose, and realize it is worth paying attention to local needs.

We never know when an area of the curriculum rises to become a life-changing experience years later. In one sixth-grade class, students spoke the words of "The Rune of St. Patrick" during their study of medieval history. Many years later, during the Persian Gulf War, one sixth-grader had become a commander of his ship. He stood on the deck looking at smoke on the mainland. As he wrote his mother, he told her the words that came to him during that moment were those he had recited in sixth grade:

> At Tara today in this fateful hour
> I place all Heaven with its power,
> And the sun with its brightness,
> And the snow with its whiteness.
> And fire with all the strength it hath,
> And lightning with its rapid wrath,
> And the winds with their swiftness along their path,
> And the sea with its deepness,
> And the rocks with its steepness,
> And the earth with its starkness,
>   All these I place,
>   By God's almighty help and grace,
> Between myself and the powers of darkness.

ROLE MODELS, STORY, AND SERVICE

Earlier in the book three important experiences for middle-schoolers were cited: role models, the importance of story, and service projects. In this chapter different ways in which teachers serve as role models has been emphasized. The three experiences are intertwined, as a person acting as a role model often has a story to tell, or the role model may be involved in service to others.

Inviting visitors to the classroom may serve all three experiences at once. For example, a visitor could be a local person who has done something important for others, perhaps a volunteer running the food bank for the homeless, a social worker helping children with special needs, or an ecologist setting up a wetland area near the school. These real people act as role models. The description of the problem, what was needed, how the person went about solving it, and how it turned out is a story that can inspire middle-schoolers. The service that is being offered in the community shows middle-schoolers that they too can work together to help others.

Storytelling comes in many forms. Drama is a way to interest middle-schoolers in their subjects. As with so many projects described, putting on scenes or a full-length play is a challenge for students and teachers. Many opportunities arise in putting on a play—choosing a play or writing one as a class; casting the parts; working on gestures and blocking, costumes and set; supporting students who have difficulty memorizing and challenging those who find that easy. Often, older students and teachers will look back at their middle school years and remember the plays they performed and the trips they took as their happiest memories.

Different classes require different plays, and a sensitive teacher can often choose just the right play to solve a social situation or to highlight a shy student's capacities. One unforgettable experience with my own class was with the sixth-grade play, *Daughters of the Grachii*. Set in ancient Rome, it describes an aristocratic family whose two brothers take on the challenge of overcoming corruption. Both are assassinated. We were due to perform it for parents in June 1968, but we postponed because of the assassination of Robert Kennedy. It was as if the play had become real, and this current tragedy opened up profound conversations with these youngsters who had put their hearts and souls into the play. They could empathize with the Kennedy family and the grief of a nation in a way they could not have done without the play and their own dawning capacities of judgment.

In seventh grade we did two dramatic offerings. The students acted out scenes from King Arthur, complete with staging in a wooded area with a real horse. The only problem was that our leading man, King Arthur, had not told his parents he had the key role, and since they lived on the far side of town, they arrived late, and we had to do some creative improvising. As the teacher, I learned the lesson of informing parents of their children's participation and not relying on the youngsters to communicate the information. It might seem strange that his parents didn't realize how important it was for him to arrive early to get into his costume and be prepared for the opening scene. But this cannot be taken for granted, especially when parents are busy working full time, or are from other cultures where English isn't their first language.

The other dramatic experience was the class's original scenes from the Renaissance. One of the strong girls played Michelangelo, and I can still hear her powerful voice as she said, "I'm a sculptor. It is what I was born for." Michelangelo's competitive relationship with Leonardo da Vinci was played out between two rival girls who were able to focus their differences as to whether painting or sculpture was the perfect art.

By the end of eighth grade, these youngsters had matured significantly, and we tackled Shakespeare's *As You Like It*. Of course, I had learned from experience and communicated regularly with the parents about their children's roles and responsibilities.

Some years later, when I taught a different class (this time for seventh and eighth grades), we put on scenes from *1776* to dramatize the dilemmas of the newly forming United States, displaying the tensions between Thomas Jefferson, John Adams, and Benjamin Franklin. These were not sophisticated productions, but the students approached their performances as if they would be performing on Broadway.

For their eighth-grade play, we chose to do something quite different. We were going to travel to British Columbia by train and bus for our eighth-grade trip, and we wanted to perform our play for the schools who would host us along the way. We decided to take a legend they had loved in second grade, *The King of Ireland's Son*, and write the scenes together as a class. Taking a trunk with costumes and props on the train was no simple feat, but it all worked out well, and they were excited to be on tour.

I mention these experiences because I am not a drama specialist, but it is amazing how much one can accomplish with enthusiasm and interest in the subject. In high school, they can have "real drama teachers," but one of the challenges of being a Waldorf teacher or any teacher who has the experience of teaching youngsters over several years is that we keep on learning and stretching ourselves, being supported by colleagues and parents who offer their advice. It might not be as easy to do this with high school students who want their teachers to have expertise in their subject, but middle school students are open to all kinds of possibilities. It makes teaching these grades an adventure.

Today, however, teaching middle school has its particular challenges today. With the advent of video games, teachers of elementary grades experience that many boys lack motivation to exert effort, resist reading required books, avoid work on arithmetic problems, and often do not complete classroom tasks. These students can either become hostile or they give up entirely. They want to disappear into the excitement of their video games. This continues in early adolescence with the deepened situation in which some boys don't want to compete with the girls and pretend they could really do well if they chose to exert the effort.

Through some video games, they play with partners in other communities in virtual online combat. After your son has spent two hours leading a squad of fighters in a raid on terrorist headquarters, issuing commands through his headset-mounted microphone to his online comrades, and racing through a hail of virtual bullets to destroy the enemy power generator, well, studying Spanish grammar from a textbook can seem hopelessly dull. The virtual world is fast-moving, interactive, collaborative, and fun. (Sax *Boys Adrift*, p. 79)

Motivating them involves finding other activities that challenge the boys' will to power, to be in charge, to engage in constant action, to compete with each other, to win.

139

Our task as teachers is to find ways boys can be heroes, and drama is a very effective way to meet this situation. It has moments of hard work, frustration, risk, challenge, and thrill.

SERVICE

What does it mean to be involved in a service project? Rather than feeling disconnected with other people's challenges, middle-schoolers feel empowered when they can help others. Or they can engage in a service project that helps the earth or animals. The main ingredient in a service project is that it brings good to others through our efforts. For these to be meaningful, teachers have to be well-organized, engaged, and enthusiastic.

Service includes integrating our thinking, feeling, and willing. We identify an issue, discuss what we could do to help, share our feelings about it, and set about doing something over and over that will make a difference. Doing something one time is like icing on the cake. Doing something repeatedly has substance to it. We have to be careful not to do something just so we can feel good about ourselves, although that certainly can be a byproduct of our activity.

Some service projects involve fundraising, for example sending money to a school for needy children, either within our own country or elsewhere. It is not enough to focus on the money aspect, but on learning about the issues. Where is the school located? What are the issues that impact the children? Can we make a relationship with the school, with the children through being penpals, writing letters, or Skyping with them?

Other service projects are labor-intensive such as cleaning trails, collecting recyclables, or planting a garden. Expanding the project through photography or writing a journal expands the learning that comes out of the experience. Making friendship bracelets for children with cancer brings together craft activities, understanding of childhood illnesses, and feeling happy to bring a smile to a child's face. The project that stands out in my own life was filling Christmas stockings for soldiers after the end of WWII. We realized how important it was for them to receive small things from home—soap, shaving cream, and a chocolate bar.

Some service projects are about cultivating relations. One school sent their seventh grade to the nearby senior center every Thursday afternoon. The students knitted with the elderly, chatting away while they got to know one another. This helped them get beyond being afraid of being around old people and, instead, getting to enjoy them. That especially happened when they started singing old songs that both groups knew.

Involving middle-schoolers in service projects and experiential learning stimulates their interest and motivates them to learn something new, follow through on their responsibility, and experience the pleasure of offering it to the community. There are many different kinds of projects, and there are many exciting ideas that can be found in teacher conferences, libraries and websites, and in speaking with seasoned middle school teachers.

STRUCTURES OF SCHOOLS

When a child finishes fifth grade, something new is coming. It shows itself in different ways: frustration, confusion, excitement, fear, challenge, hiding, and so on. What is the next step in school? That depends. At the time when so many changes are happening and the Vulnerability Gap is looming, changes in schools can be challenging. What is the next step? That depends on the structure of schools. Each school structure has its own strengths and challenges in supporting middle-schoolers. Some examples follow.

1. Some schools are kindergarten through eighth grade. The eighth-graders are the senior students and are guided to be models for the younger children. Without high school students as a constant presence, middle-schoolers seem younger than if they were modeling older teenagers, yet older as they take on responsibilities toward their younger friends. They are given more time to mature. I have been at

141

school board meetings where parents have requested to have more K–8 schools because they want their children to be part of a school community where teachers and students get to know each other well. They would give up fancy labs with high-tech equipment in favor of giving their children more time to grow up. In such schools, there may be differences for middle school classes such as having a team of subject teachers who work together to meet the special needs of this age group. Yet middle-schoolers are embedded in an environment that is familiar but also has aspects that are new and exciting.

Are the classes self-contained in which one teacher teaches all subjects or are there different situations where specialty teachers augment the work of the main teacher, perhaps in mathematics, science, English, music, art, or physical education? There are many different versions of how the middle school classes can be organized.

2. Some schools are separate middle schools, usually sixth through eighth grades. In these cases, the teachers may be specially equipped to work with middle school children. These schools tend to have a larger number of students so that there can be differentiated classes in math and English, as well as electives. Yet, it is as if they are plucked out of a stream of child development, with neither younger ones for them to care for or older ones for them to emulate.

Everything is new. Is it exciting? Is it scary? How do I find my way around? What if I don't make friends? What if I want to make new friends? Is this a school where the eighth-graders welcome new students or where they put them through a hazing experience? It is not easy to find one's way.

3. Some schools are kindergarten through twelfth grade. These tend to be small public schools or private schools. The positive aspect is that there is a school community of children experiencing the various stages of development. There are opportunities for high school students to tutor or do service projects with younger students. The middle school students are embedded in the school with attention given to

142

their needs, yet they are not carrying the responsibility of being the oldest. They have the advantage of looking at what is coming ahead, and yet they are not there. In such schools, there is often a separate area of the campus for middle school and high school.

No matter what the structure of the school, there are individual differences in what the teacher is expected to teach and how much they are expected to be involved in extracurricular activities. In some schools, there are specialists who teach music, art, physical education, and some academic subjects, while in others the teacher has a fully self-contained classroom.

Regardless of the structure, children and parents need to acclimate themselves to the new reality. Orientation to the structure is necessary for both. Parents who tend to be overprotective may find it difficult to connect with many different teachers when they were used to communicating with one. Children discover that teachers have different styles of teaching and different expectations.

There is no right way to structure the school. It is a constantly evolving process in which teachers in communication with parents should be the significant shapers of the form, always keeping in mind the questions: Who are middle-schoolers today? What do they need? What is the best way our community can meet them? What are our resources? It takes courage and vision to tackle these questions and choose the form that works in this particular time and place.

CHAPTER 11

Technology and Middle School

Technology has always been a presence in our lives. Whenever knowledge is put into practical use to solve problems or invent useful tools, we rely on technology. With the industrial revolution, technology incorporated machines, while in the digital age technology includes devices that connect to the internet and can be used to access information and solve problems. While technology has always been the purview of adults, digital technology has become a powerful force in children's and adolescents' lives.

Everywhere one goes the scene is the same: Children, teenagers, and adults are looking down at their phones. One person commented that it looks as if they are playing cards, each one looking at his own deck. But, no, no one is looking at another. Each is in an isolated world connected through the device. Children's recreational use of screens and smartphones is now the dominant activity in their lives. Each of us has our own experiences with the smartphone and can cite examples of its use for good as well as for its dangers. As we consider the use by middle school children, it becomes necessary to realize that this is a habit that, once developed, is difficult to break.

There are no rules for middle-schoolers on how to behave in this new social-media landscape, no guides for how to respond to the way others are behaving or treating them. "They were social media pioneers, but it was as if they were commanding their covered wagons without any maps or sextants." (Sales, p. 371)

Every writer considers certain questions essential for communication—who, what, where, when, how, and why. What is the impact of technology on middle-schoolers? In previous decades, movies and television were our concern as both parents and teachers. Who was in control, what was the content, where was it being experienced, at what or how many hours, how was it affecting neurological development, and why was it being used in the first place? Parents were in control because they usually controlled what movies were seen, or the only television in the house was where parents could control its use. Over time that has changed: additional televisions in other rooms, the ability to record programs for later use, the advent of VHS copies of movies all gave parents more freedom. However, the bottom line was that control depended on where the machine was located.

In the past, I characterized television as a stranger who enters the house and competes with the parents, bringing in different values and influences. When children are young, they imitate those around them unconsciously, but middle-schoolers imitate teenagers and chosen adults intentionally. The impact of television is mild compared to what the computer has brought into the home.

The questions have shifted. Who is in control now? Parents no longer have complete control over content although they can put limits on it. Middle-schoolers have more freedom in deciding what they want to access, as well as when and where. The laptop can be carried to other places outside the home, and the smartphones can be used anywhere there is a wifi connection. When middle-schoolers have their smartphones or computers in their bedrooms, they have control of their use away from their parents. They can justify use of devices for communication, information, and entertainment, but they do not have the capacity to understand how much is enough. Most of all, they do not consider the effects on their neurological development when the dangerous tendency toward addiction sets in.

Television is mostly passive viewing. What the computer and smartphone offer which television does not is interaction with others. Being able to connect with others either near or far away in a video game is very exciting; it stimulates competition and collaboration. Some video games provide what games have always provided—working in teams or solo to reach a goal that can be used for social or anti-social purposes, to compete with others and win. The process includes strategizing the steps in the game and experiencing anticipation and excitement. The problem with video games for middle-schoolers is how we answer the key questions—What is the content? What is the purpose? Who is in control? When is it being played? How is it affecting neurological development?

While children have always been tempted to do what parents forbid—sneaking sexy magazines into their rooms and hiding them under the mattresses, or imitating the beauty, bodily gestures, and sexy poses of movie stars or body builders—parents today have little or no access to what is flooding the minds of their eleven- and twelve-year-olds through digital devices. In addition, the world of YouTube opens up a secret candy store of information streaming into the mind of the child without any adult guidance, pouring distorted guidance of pornography, violence, and commercialization. It also offers access to information on how to build, create, and make all manner of things in an accessible and timely way.

While middle school boys tend to use technology for video gaming to enjoy the competitive, aggressive experience of power over others, girls tend to use technology for social media to connect with others, to satisfy their desire to be included, liked, appreciated, admired, become famous, or look like a celebrity.

The monster in the media is the prevalence of pornography that has become a shadow overlaying the understanding and experience of sexuality. It has colored many boys' images of sexual relations, infused their comments in texting and the way they speak about girls and speak to them, and impacting how they act with girls. Under the influence of these images and messages, boys consider their own and others' bodies as objects purely for their own satisfaction. Pornography has also snuck in to the images of how girls regard their own bodies, how they dress and portray themselves on social media by modeling themselves after celebrities who are actually porn stars.

Kaiser Family Foundation research indicates that children 8–18 years old spend on average an astounding 5½ hours every day indulging in various entertainment screen technologies including video games, social networks, online videos, and TV. High-school-age students spend on average an additional 2½ hours each day texting and talking on their phones—more time than they spend in school. We need to be concerned and attentive.

Middle school children are likely targets of overuse of all this entertainment technology. At this crucial time in their development, they are affected in four areas—family life, social life, school, and their brain development. I will deal with technology in school in a separate chapter.

FAMILY LIFE

Face-to-face communication and relationships are essential for healthy development.

> Much of what is conveyed between parent and teen is nonverbal—through facial expressions, eye contact, hugs, and tone of voice. The human mind is specially attuned to these unspoken cues. They trigger dopamine, oxytocin, and other "feel-good" brain chemicals that foster and maintain attachment, including the one between parents and teens. (Freed, *Wired Child*, p. 170)

Attachment to parents is one of the most significant experiences in child development. Playing online games greatly decreases time with family. Using technology for homework and research is not the only issue. The bigger issue is that children need parental involvement to develop executive function.

Kids with healthy parent attachment regulate their emotions better, score higher intellectually and academically, and have higher self-esteem than kids without a healthy bond. Attachment remains vital into the teen years. (Freed, *Wired Child*, p. 20)

Parents are very busy and have less time to supervise their children. They are overwhelmed by companies advertising that all the use of digital technology is normal and poses little risk of addiction. The reality is that children are wired, and parents themselves are caught up in constant use of the smartphone or the internet. Science is beginning to describe the problems that the overuse of technology is causing in children's development.

On average, parents are on screens 6½ hours a day between television, computer, mobile phones, and other screen time. The result is that individuals in the family are all going their own ways with little time for communicating, problem solving, planning, or enjoying doing things together. They may be in the same room, but their minds are elsewhere.

Lynn & Johnson, in *Breaking the Trance,* claim that parents are also in a trance that includes the ideas and beliefs they have swallowed about what it means to be a good parent, including such thoughts as "This is the way it is now;" "My kids should like me;" "I can't make my kids do anything they don't want to." Parents have to create a new set of beliefs including their own commitment to relationships with people rather than virtual ones, facing the challenges, recognizing that strict parents can also be loving parents, and changing children's behavior.

However, regular video game use works like a drug, causing dopamine, a powerful reward-based neurotransmitter, to flood into the brain. Each time the boy plays an electronic game, he feels pleasure and wants to play it more. As time goes on, he needs to play more often to get the same amount of pleasure. Meanwhile, nothing else he could do will give him that rush of pleasure, so why even try. He will defend the use of the video game with all of his middle school self-righteousness.

Dr. Sax quotes Prof. Anderson's recommendation (p. 88, see #28) that the parent play the video game or watch it being played. He suggests questions for the parent to ask:

1. Does the game involve some characters trying to harm others?
2. Does this happen frequently, more than once or twice in 30 minutes?
3. Is the harm rewarded in any way?
4. Is the harm portrayed as humorous?
5. Are nonviolent solutions absent or less "fun" than the violent ones?
6. Are realistic consequences of violence included or absent from the game?

A common family situation finds the middle-schooler closed up in his or her room, lost in the haze of the screen. Parents don't know what is being experienced, who the contacts are, how much time should be allowed for this, or what this isolation is doing to family life. What can parents do?

1. Know what your children are watching. Look at some of it with them. Put limits on what they can connect with.

2. Set times when no one is on a screen. This includes family meals and family discussions.

3. Limit access to computers by having them in a common area where parents can see what is being accessed. Keep the smartphone out of the bedroom during sleep.

4. Work together with other parents in your school or neighborhood. Join parent action groups such as "Wait until Eighth Grade Pledge" before letting children have smartphones. If parents need to have immediate contact with their children for safety reasons or other serious concerns, give them a basic phone that only calls and texts.

5. Guide middle-schoolers to participate in outdoor activities, reading, participating in family activities or following a hobby or particular interest that does not rely on screen use. Don't wait until the children are in middle school, begin earlier to support their interests.

6. Look at your own use of technology. Are you present with your child or are you also constantly distracted by the phone or screen?

Freed quotes Sherry Turkle, who found in her research that

> children often named the same three examples of being emotionally hurt and not wanting to show it when their parent was using a device rather than paying attention to them: at meals, during pickup either after school or an extracurricular activity, or during sporting events. (Quoted by Freed, *Wired Child*, p. 25. Turkle, *Alone Together: Why We Expect More from Technology and Less from Each Other*. New York: Basic Books, p. 267)

Because texting makes it possible for children to contact their parents quickly and often, middle-schoolers may put off solving their problems on their own. Instead, there is a constant flow between parent and child so that middle-schoolers can immediately share their problems and get a quick fix. Parents often regard this constant interaction as a proof that their child loves and relies on them. But this poses the question of how much should the middle-schooler face issues and try to figure out what to do without relying on their parents for solutions. How much help is too much? Middle-schoolers need time to reflect on what is happening, time to discuss the situation, and opportunities to experience support. Reacting immediately often short-circuits conversations in which the youngster can figure out themselves ways to reply to a situation. Is there something being lost here?

Melinda Gates, who has spent her career in technology, writes:

> Still, as a mother who wants to make sure her children are safe and happy, I worry. And I think back to how I might have

done things differently. Parents should decide for themselves what works for their family, but I probably would have waited longer before putting a computer in my children's pockets. Phones and apps aren't good or bad by themselves, but for adolescents who don't yet have the emotional tools to navigate life's complications and confusions, they can exacerbate the difficulties of growing up: learning how to be kind, coping with feelings of exclusion, taking advantage of freedom while exercising self-control. It's more important than ever to teach empathy from the very beginning, because our kids are going to need it. (*On Parenting Perspective*, August 24, courtesy of the Gates Archive)

Family life forms the foundation of a child's life. What is missing cannot easily be made up.

FRIENDS AND SOCIAL LIFE

"The social world of middle school is incredibly important to a child's development and should be treated with respect." (Icard)

The way the middle-schoolers think about themselves sets the foundation for what they will think in high school. Their views can be fixed and even stuck.

Peers are everything—what do they say, wear, listen to, watch, and eat. Because middle-schoolers are separating from their parents as a way to develop their own identity, the authority of their friends takes the place of their parents, at least for a while.

Middle school students are developing their social networks. As they become aware of themselves within a social group, they are extremely vulnerable to what people say or think about them. They do not yet have the self-confidence to recognize that you can't please everyone. When friends comment about each other on social media, they take things literally and hard.

Part of the vulnerability of this age group is that they are affected by what comes at them. They take comments that are casually or thoughtlessly made to be the truth. So much of what they are awakening to is the complexity of group behavior. They struggle to know what it takes to be liked, to be popular, to be accepted. If they hear that you have to do certain things to be popular, they will believe that and do their best to conform. Their sense of self is frail, just beginning to come to birth, and they need time, support, and human connections as they make their way along the path of development.

Networking or texting is the primary use of smartphones. Middle school students are vulnerable to social connections, either longing to be accepted or feeling left out. The ways in which smartphones affect social popularity place a heavy burden on young adolescents. They use internet platforms such as Facebook, Instagram, etc., as a way of measuring how others see them. How many "likes" does their picture receive? Are they seeing photos of a party they were not invited to attend? Because their emotions are leading them, they respond erratically in social situations. They don't understand the consequences of what they say publicly, even when they are saying something hurtful about a classmate. They lack judgment about the consequences of their actions.

CHAPTER 12
Middle-Schoolers Love Their Devices

TECHNOLOGY IN SCHOOL

Schools have different policies for the use of technology in middle- school classrooms. Some schools use technology every day, connecting white boards to computers, projectors, and laptops. Students may use computers and phones for research, for projects with schools across the world, or for calculators or dictionary usage.

Other schools choose to use it only where necessary, and they prefer to use simpler means of communicating information: They prefer black or green boards on which they can draw detailed illustrations and graphs. They emphasize mental mathematics before relying on calculators and require that middle-schoolers use dictionaries and other reference books. They are not against technology, but they want students to know how to access information in multiple ways before relying on computers. When power is turned off, or they find themselves in more primitive situations, it is helpful to know how to solve problems using their own capacities. It has been reported that some students have temper tantrums because a teacher would not let them use calculators for fairly simple math problems.

Schools have different rules regarding cell phone usage. No matter the rule, this is challenging in any circumstances. Some schools require cell phones to be turned in at the beginning of class and used only in emergencies. Others allow cell phone usage during breaks or lunchtime. Some allow students to listen to music on their cell phones while doing math problems or writing. There are as many variations on the use of cell phones in class as there are people's imaginations.

France is considering ruling out all use of cell phones in schools. One of the objections to the no-cellphone-rule is by parents who want to access their children at all times. Schools let the parents know they can contact the school office if they must speak to their child.

The greatest issue of technology in schools is how to respond when students' use of digital devices in antisocial ways such as bullying and harassment. Some schools are using Cyber Civics, a three-year program for middle schools that includes lessons in digital citizenship, information literacy, and media literacy. Diana Graber (dgraber@ cybercivics.com), founder of Cyber Civics, supports parents with information on her website on ways to handle home situations around cell phones. I attended one of her workshops and found the program to be a very helpful way to offer middle-schoolers support and involve them in thinking through issues that arise out of cell phone usage.

Of course, this kind of attention on cell phone use holds the potential of encouraging children to use them, albeit responsibly. Given the research on the highly addictive nature of electronics, especially with the young, this might be considered before introducing an actual course on how to use any electronic means of living, working, and communicating.

As with other issues, adults are the models. If cell phone usage is restricted in school, teachers have to curb their usage as well, at least when they are on the yard during recess duty. They can go into the faculty room or elsewhere to use them. This is more challenging than it seems at first as I discovered when I was observing classes. The temptation to check our phone is just as powerful for adults as for children, perhaps more so.

MIDDLE SCHOOL GIRLS AND TECHNOLOGY

Girls, focused on relationship, already have a tendency to project themselves into the social scene. They long to have close friends, and they will cooperate with others to attain a group goal. At the same time, they are supersensitive to how members of a group regard each other. If a girl feels betrayed by another girl she thought was a friend, the result is devastating. Because of this sensitivity, some girls are overwhelmed by the social jungle that middle school can be and will withdraw to avoid the social pain that is caused by constant judgment by other girls or by boys. This isolates these girls socially and often causes lifelong scars.

It is fun to take photos of each other, and it is a way girls may bond during sleepovers. Most of the time it is harmless. However, lacking any sense of boundaries, they can be seduced by the power of what they have seen in magazines or on YouTube videos. They study the way a particular model or makeup company or pop star is showing them how to purse their lips or push out their breasts. Without thinking, they post pictures of themselves, hoping to collect a phenomenal number of "likes." Not content with how they look, they often photoshop their images so that they look like the star they are imitating. Popular culture defines the standard of beauty, and these middle-schoolers are doing their best to meet that standard.

Girls who have interests such as gymnastics, horseback riding, animal care, religious activities, community service, drama, sports, or other clubs group with others who have similar interests, giving them a kind of protection from the onslaught of popular cultural influences. Others have a strong enough home life and involvement with parents that allows them a balance between family life and social life.

What is the real concern here? The main point is that during the middle school years girls develop a sense of self: who they are and who they will become. If the girl is focused on a superficial view based mainly on her looks or commercial focuses, then these influences plus interaction with other girls in the social scene become the primary ways for her to know who she is. The early identification of beauty and sexuality creates behavior that becomes internalized over time and will affect her high school years, often overshadowing more subtle aspects of her personality.

Girls use social media platforms to show each other who they are, who they are with, what they are doing—without understanding the cost to themselves. Because of what other girls post, it becomes easy to feel that others are way ahead of the game, and they need to make up time, have sexual experiences, provide oral sex for boys, dress provocatively. And, at the same time, they feel everyone is watching them. According to many girls, seventh grade is when this kind of communication increases. It seems strange to even write this, and it would be easy for parents to be in denial that such thoughts or activities are going on. In many cases, it is mostly talk, but girls at this age have no way of knowing what is true and what is boastful projection.

Girls want attention from boys; often they want to have boys as friends, but this wish is often misunderstood. Depending on the social framework in which the girl lives, she is at the mercy of what others say about her. What are the social interactions of the girl's life? Does she have a best friend? Is she in a popular clique? Is she isolated?

When girls post their thoughts, they may be trying to entertain their friends, consider certain actions, share deep thoughts, or comment on others without realizing the impact of their words. There is an enormous difference between what they post on the internet and what they would have written into a note or in their diary.

When I taught sixth grade, one day I picked up a note from the floor. It was vulgar, and, after being surprised by its detail, I chose to tear it up and throw it away. The girl who wrote it later became a nun, and I am sure she would be very embarrassed to know I had read it. Girls of this age do not censor what they say or write; they try on language like the latest outfit and never mean for it to be permanent. But once it is on social media, it is there to go out, give false impressions, painfully hurt others, and fix a girl's view of herself. Just as a girl can hurt others, she can also be hurt by others.

Girls have a tendency to want to be perfect in whatever area they decide perfection should rule—their looks, their social behavior, their academic performance. There is so much learning at this time and so many paths to choose, how can they know which is the right one? We know that girls have a tendency to show disdain for their own bodies and even their own capacities, never feeling good enough. We know that this follows us into adult life as well. But middle school girls do not yet have the mental development to look objectively and realize that everyone has good points and aspects that could use improvement, that no one is perfect.

Since we are concerned in this chapter with technology, we recognize that social media has changed the scene of girls' lives. Each generation of girls has its own way in which social media affects their self-image. These generations do not last thirty years as used to be the rule. Now everything has speeded up, and keeping up with the latest social media platform, game, musical star, or what is "hot" is challenging. This is not the world their parents grew up in, nor even the one older siblings grew up in. The social scene is intense, colored by pornography—nasty and degrading. It is pressured, lacking in self-respect, vulgar, and virtual. If a girl rejects it, she may be labeled a "prude," "scared," or accused of "slut-shaming" other girls.

Why are they spending so much time on social media? Girls have always valued being seen as pretty or nice, but when they receive dozens of "likes" for a particular pose, the reward centers in their brains light up, affecting their hormones so that they are flooded with a sense of pleasure. But when they are ignored, attacked, or ridiculed, they are devastated. Worst of all, they have been publicly shamed. Their self-esteem is threatened, and anxiety and depression can lead to mental health problems.

The social scene is not benign. An American Psychological Association (APA) study in 2007 found girls are being sexualized or treated as

> objects of sexual desire ... as things rather than as people with legitimate sexual feelings of their own—in virtually every form of media, including movies, television, music videos and lyrics, video games and the internet, advertising, cartoons, clothing, and toys.... The APA surveyed multiple studies which found links between sexualization of girls and a wide range of mental health issues, including low self-esteem, anxiety, depression,

eating disorders, cutting, even cognitive dysfunction…. Chronic attention to physical appearance leaves fewer cognitive resources available for other mental and physical activities. (Sales, p. 14)

The prevalence of pornography on internet sites has been traced to affect attitudes about how boys and girls treat each other in a sexual context, both on and off social media, with violence against women through verbal insults, demands for sexual performance, and physical abuse.

If parents want to have a view into this world, they can look at Kim Kardashian's book, *Selfish*, which came out in 2015. It is hard to believe that she is considered one of the most famous women in the world, the social media's biggest star, with many millions of followers of her site. She is listed on Wikipedia as an American reality television personality, socialite, actress, businesswoman, and model. Her job is herself—doing whatever she wants, wearing whatever she wants, posing in seductive poses, including comments from her husband, musician Kanye West. She has a game app in which players can spend real money to purchase virtual clothing that teens can order using their parents' credit cards. From Kardashian's point of view, the parents are the ones with the problem if they are not monitoring the parental controls of their children. She says:

> There's nothing wrong with the premise of a game that encourages youngsters to aspire to superstardom full of material wealth…. In the game you definitely see that it's just fun and it's not really serious. You pick your friends and you pick your clothes. (*Pop Culture*, "Kim Kardashian defends her popular Hollywood app: Parents must 'be responsible.'" Eun Kyung Kim, *Today*, Aug. 12, 2014)

These are the images middle school girls are looking at, this is what they are shown to emulate, and, as they try to be cool, they are at the mercy of other girls' judgments.

What about the boys? How are they experiencing technology in their social life? Boys want to be part of a tribe, physically active, checking their own behavior with what other boys are doing. Competing within the tribe is common. What other boys think is a much stronger motivator than what girls or adults think about them.

How does their focus on video games affect their social life? Everything is in perspective. There are video games and there are video games. Which ones they focus on and how often they engage has an impact on their social behavior.

While girls are more connected to their feelings, boys identify with their physical activity. They love taking risks, being part of a team that takes on challenges, and they live on the edge of knowing whether or not they will be successful. Anyone who has raised boys knows they can turn anything into a competition, including who can pee the furthest or the most accurately into a toilet. This was certainly my experience as a parent of sons.

Boys who are good friends can play their hardest against each other on separate teams, trying their best to win. After the game, they can laugh and return to being good friends. In contrast, girls often take things deeply personally.

Most middle school boys are not as interested as girls in social media, but video games instead. By high school, they do much more texting than in sixth to eighth grades. Boys not only love competing, but they want to feel in charge, make up their own rules when necessary, and lead the fight. Video games are perfect to meet their need for power.

Boys can be very creative in their use of video games:

> Today, any boy with a high-speed internet connection can play in real time against another gamer across town or on the other side of the planet. Sophisticated headsets allow boys to engage in simulated online combat in teams, arranging coordinated ambushes of enemy fighters using high-tech virtual weaponry. (Sax, *Boys Adrift*, p. 79)

What does this mean for a boy in his social setting? The activities in his social life often seem pale in comparison to video games, and he would prefer the isolation of his room, engaged in the midst of battle rather than having to interact with others. Dr. Sax cites the following studies in *Boys Adrift*, p. 83. "The more realistic the violence, the bigger the effects." (Sax quoting Bartlett and Rodeheffer, *Aggressive Behavior*, volume 35, pp. 213–224, 2009)

> Young people who play violent video games change their brains, becoming desensitized to violence in ways not seen in young people who play nonviolent video games. (Sax quoting Bartholow, *Journal of Experimental Social Psychology*, vol. 42, pp. 532–539, 2006)

Because video games are so seductive, boys are less involved with the real world of friends unless their friends are also involved in the game. The dangers are in their looking at classmates and friends as objects and acting in a more aggressive way.

A pattern that begins slowly in seventh and eighth grades will be in full bloom by ninth grade. Boys begin playing video games, mostly alone in their rooms, and don't want to join the family for meals. They begin to resent their parents for demanding this, and they get testy and angry. Their room becomes a refuge from the social demands of interacting with others. They downplay the importance of their school work and claim they could do better if they really tried, but it isn't important. Even those who were once active in sports start to lose interest as they're too much work. They withdraw from friends who are not gamers, and then they either stop doing schoolwork or begin skipping school to play video games. The next step is that they want to be home-schooled rather than have to go to class where they are experiencing failure from lack of trying. Parents are desperately trying to wean them from the games, but the combination of early adolescent erratic behavior and frustration with adults trying to control them leads to their being sent to psychologists to deal with addiction.

There are three areas where boys are affected in their social life through technology. As described above, being addicted to video games results in antisocial behavior of isolation. The second temptation arises from their exposure to pornography, and the third to cyber-bullying.

PORNOGRAPHY

Pornography is everywhere. It can be accessed directly or it may surprisingly show up by surprise when boys may be searching for something else. There are many sites on the internet as well as on YouTube which show images of sexual interaction that include violence against women and acts of sex demeaning the other person. Watching porn changes the way boys look at girls, to view them as sex objects, there to be violently abused and degraded. It has changed the language boys use toward girls, and this is regularly heard in YouTube lyrics where women are called "bitches," "cunts," etc. They see girls on a scale of who is hottest and what they can do for them.

Pornography has seeped into movies, cable television, rap songs, magazine photos, fashion modeling, and books. What used to be clearly defined as porn now appears as part of public discourse. Young adolescents then accept it as part of normal behavior, and it becomes a model for how to relate to each other. Coarseness in language and behavior that were been unacceptable in the past are now considered part of everyday communication. The more unconscious adults are about this, the more youngsters consider it to be what everybody accepts.

PORN VIDEOS

Watching porn videos affects boys' ability to interact with girls. Often it is easier to masturbate to a video than to develop intimacy in a relationship.

Some boys are intimidated by the images shown in porn and don't know how to connect them to a real-life relationship. Boys are often scared of the kind of social interaction that requires listening, responding, finding areas of common interest, allowing feelings to erupt, and caring for another human being.

Can you imagine how porn videos affect the way a boy thinks about a girl he has a crush on? He doesn't know how to relate to her in a respectful way. Instead, he has images of violently abusing women. What is he to do with these images that crowd his mind?

Although it is mostly boys who are watching porn videos, some girls also watch them as a way to learn about sexy behavior. The boys then feel they have to deliver on what the girls expects. Coarse language, behavior, and expectations have colored the world of sex.

CYBER-BULLYING

Boys are going through significant changes in their physical bodies as well as in their psychological makeup. With their emotions charging their energy, they lack brakes on their impulses. Within the social life of a school or neighborhood, a boy who has been influenced by porn may express this by sending pictures of his penis (referred to as a "dick pic") or collecting nude photos of girls and sending them around.

Heavy users of porn may take photos of girls in uncompromising positions and use them as blackmail unless a girl does what he wants, which is usually oral sex. The sad thing is that often the girl has no emotional relationship to the boy, and it is a mechanical act. Both the boys and the girls suffer from unhealthy emotional relationships in such cases, and it affects the way they develop intimacy in their tender adolescent awakening.

> Cyber-bullying is more common among tech-heavy kids because children's tech time is spent almost entirely in entertainment domains, including social networks and online games, where mean things are easier said than in real life because kids don't have to face the target of their comments. (Freed, *Wired Child*, p. 21)

While girls use cyber-bullying as a way of emotional manipulation, boys more often use it to satisfy their physical needs.

TECHNOLOGY WITHIN THE SCHOOLHOUSE

As the 21st century began, the nation's schools, vulnerable as they've always been to academic fads, have been reshaped again and again by another wave of promising cures. "… In this fevered world, technology has become the ultimate innovation, the device that will let schools get closer to their academic dreams no matter what the goals may be. Or so the theory goes." (Oppenheimer, p. xiv)

Visiting schools is an eye-opener. As visitors enter a kindergarten, a third-grade class, or a high school biology class, they see computers everywhere. Education has been transformed so that classroom activities, presentations, homework, and group projects fit into what the computer can accommodate. PowerPoint presentations have become the norm in many classrooms so that students are copying the text from the screen rather than transforming the teacher's tone of voice, facial expression, and information into notes, an important process for thinking.

This is not to say that computers should be eliminated from classrooms, particularly in high school, but we need to observe the effect they have on students' learning as well as on their health.

One of the biggest downsides to having technology in the classroom is the amount of money that is being spent, not just on the devices themselves, but on the networks, servers, telecommunication wires, and constant upgrades. This does not even address the issue of whether the effect of wired classrooms is healthy for children.

Curriculum is written by media companies, often supplying cartoon-like games to teach reading, writing, and arithmetic. Students are writing on computers in the classroom, as well as doing mathematics, science, and social studies in elementary school. Again, there may be a place for some of this, but the exorbitant costs of equipping the school and classroom with internet access often takes money from spending on books, art supplies, and science equipment. Sixth-graders may appear very sophisticated in their knowledge of marine biology because they have interacted with a video program rather than being asked to record what they see in tide pools, but it is not the same level of thinking.

Middle school classrooms can easily come to depend on technology rather than on human interaction. It is not a matter of being old-fashioned or wanting to return to a past time in history. It is a matter of looking at the essential aspects of education just at this time in the child's development. Computers may make some children feel they are doing something grownup or sophisticated, but they may not be helping them in the long run.

Middle-schoolers need opportunities to build self-reliance and self-confidence, to develop critical thinking and problem solving skills.

EFFECTS ON BRAIN DEVELOPMENT

One of the clearest descriptions of the effect of technology on the brain was given by Laurence Steinberg, psychology professor at Temple University and author of *Age of Opportunity*. He describes two different competing brain systems: one having to do with seeking reward and excitement and the other putting the brakes on impulses. (Freed, *Boys Adrift*, p. 163)

If sensation-seeking is at its peak between fifteen and seventeen, it is obvious that the older middle-schoolers and those beginning high school are struggling to bring impulses under control. As they move into their secondary growth spurt around the age of sixteen, they start to exercise more control and hold back their desire for thrills. Yet it is only the beginning.

In *Wired Child*, Richard Freed points out that brain imaging techniques such as fMRI and PET scans reveal video gaming impacts the mind in a way similar to drugs and alcohol. "Video gaming triggers the release of dopamine at levels comparable to an intravenous injection of amphetamine, a powerful and addictive psychostimulant." (p. 77)

Not only do the problems show up in a dumbing down of compassion and concentration, but there are actual changes in the brain. This addiction stimulates the sense of pleasure in the brain and affects areas related to motivation, insight, self-control, and decision-making.

When used repeatedly for long hours, video games and social media have similar results—changes in the reward center of the brain. The hunger for constant sensory stimulation creates a craving for more screen time. Both keep the children on edge, feeling they need their fix, nervously awaiting the answer to a text, or the next installment of a game, or how their friends respond to their latest photo.

It is clear to me that boys are at risk, and parents need to step in and step up to take charge. Are parents helpless? No, but they may feel there is nothing more they can do. But what parents would stand by while their children were drinking poison?

Parents have the capacity to break the video-gaming habit since most of the video game watching happens at home. They need to take the situation seriously and recognize that they still have a chance to change their son's habits while they are in middle school. As happens with drug addiction, boys will be in denial that there is any problem with their gaming. They will accuse their parents of making a big deal over nothing. After all, their friends are doing this, and they're just fine. But they are not fine, and some youngsters are more susceptible than others—more allergic.

Despite the advertising and money spent on trying to convince parents and teachers that their video-game programs can make children more imaginative and creative, this is not the case. The gains are virtual, not real. In *Breaking the Trance*, Lynn and Johnson remind us that

> a child's nervous system needs to be put in situations in which he has to use his mind and talents to overcome *real*, not *virtual* *obstacles*. This process begins with boredom. Deprived of access to recreational screen media, the child becomes bored and deals with the boredom by finding things to do. The child's brain needs this type of boredom because without it, it cannot exercise the neurons that are part of the imagining process. This is how all of us develop the skills and wisdom to grow up—by

imagining our lives and finding resourceful ways to bring that imagination into reality. (p. 13)

All the time spent on video games on smartphone or computer is time in which the middle school boys are avoiding boredom. They need to engage with the real world, be curious about it, begin to pay attention to what is around them, what they find in nature or in problems of history and culture. To do this, they need to focus, take time, and activate their thinking. If they are constantly entertained by the screen, they will not exercise their own thinking and imagination.

The program Lynn and Johnson offer parents to develop screen control through seven steps is impressive. I recommend parents read their book, *Breaking the Trance,* and make a plan.

What happens to the middle school boys if they do not change their habits? What kind of future can we imagine?

Researcher Jean Twenge, psychology professor and author, has been researching young people for twenty-five years and has come to some shocking conclusions. "The iPhone's ubiquity has led to 'iGen' as being on the brink of the worst mental health crisis in decades." (*Sacramento Bee,* Oct. 3, 2017) She traces this specifically to the constant use of the iPhone, especially when it is used for more than two hours a day.

Twenge's concern is particularly strong when she references the changes in older adolescents and adults since 2007, the year the iPhone was introduced. Her research indicates that those who have been using the iPhone for over two hours a day for years have developed certain behavioral patterns that create a different kind of generation. If we can be aware of the dangers, this may give us enough incentive to do something about the way we guide our children and young adolescents while we still have a chance.

Twenge refers to nine symptoms that are radically different from other generations. Adolescents are spending less time with their friends. The percentage of young people who go out on a date, have a driver's license, have a part-time job, have ever had sex, are getting pregnant, or drink alcohol is lower. A higher percentage are sleep-deprived, and a higher percentage report feeling lonely.

Now, what about the girls? Are they escaping problems in their brain development? Some girls do game, but in general, they game less than boys and tend to read more. They tend to do better in school than boys and are more likely to attend college. However, some girls are just as addicted to the screen, using it for social networking and talking or texting on their phone.

Girls also are caught in the tension between reward and impulse control just as the boys are. They are more likely to be affected in their social development. While the boys feel connected to their gaming pals, the girls are affected by being judged by their peers. Disappearing into cyberspace deprives them of relationships with their family and face-to-face relationships with their friends.

Boys and girls in middle school would benefit from boundaries that sharply limit their daily time on cell phones as well as engaging in digital literacy programs. In this way they learn how to avoid shaming or hurting others and how to respond to requests for embarrassing photos. They learn about social pressure through technology and how to withstand it, how to reclaim their own time so that they do not have to be available all the time for the latest text. When digital education is shared in the classroom, students learn how they are being manipulated and how this will affect them. Students will have more time to connect in after-school activities, whether they are sports or drama, tutoring younger children or caring for an animal. The will have time to experience new interests that will help them develop their capacities for a brighter future. They learn about real relationships that help them develop intimacy and friendship, deal with the challenges that occur when youngsters have to speak to each other to clear up misunderstandings, and find the satisfaction of deep friendship.

Even before they get to middle school, children are using screens for games. Many have already developed the habit of relying on screen devices to fill their time. When children say they are bored, parents become anxious and often offer screen entertainment or games. They parents may have used them as baby sitters or ways to hold their attention when they were cranky or parents were busy.

This is not to say that all technology is bad, but it is a matter of balance. Middle school children are not yet able to establish balance on their own, and they need the guidance of adults to set boundaries.

Our society is facing dire consequences if we do not protect the brains of middle-schoolers. Clear thinking, compassion, the ability to strategize and reflect on our behavior are necessary skills for a healthy society. We cannot risk the loss of these capacities in our children and adolescents.

CHAPTER 13
Middle-Schoolers as Consumers

During the middle school years when youngsters are shaping their individuality, they are absorbing ads that draw on narcissism, entitlement, and dissatisfaction. Their identities are being defined by their consumer habits. Middle-schoolers want to be accepted. They don't want to be deprived of what everyone else has because if everybody else has it, it's cool.

Marketing of merchandise has moved down into the preschool age. At this age, children have difficulty differentiating advertising from reality in ads, as well as between a program and commercials. They believe that advertising is true and that everything that is presented actually happens. Around the age of 12, with their new cause-and-effect thinking, they begin to understand the differences, and yet they are still influenced by whatever they think will make them cool. By the time they are age 12, middle-schoolers have become brand loyal.

Why is consumerism a problem? The forces behind consumerism —whether through ads, billboards, television, the internet or other media—have one goal and that is to make big money for companies. Consumer society's main message is that human beings exist to get jobs, earn money, and buy stuff. Buying the right stuff will make us feel good, make us more attractive, help us get friends and partners, and give meaning to our life. This is a moral problem in contrast and competition with the long-held values of family life and society—be honest, work hard, and share with others.

Since electronics are much more powerful and seductive than face-to-face speech, and children are exposed to media for more hours than to their parents' teachings and modeling, the combination of electronics with advertising has led to consumerism becoming a new "religion." The adult world is modeling the same weakness. It was not surprising that after 9/11, President George Bush's advice was that people should help the country by going shopping.

Consumerism has imposed itself into children's lives from infancy on, stealing their childhood, giving the impression that through buying they will have a good life. It has led to corruption of society, emphasizing greed and selfishness. It has changed everyone's priorities. Consumerism tells children they need things that they don't really need, in fact, in many cases unhealthy for them, e.g., sugar cereals, soft drinks, or gadgets that often break. These products become symbols of power and acceptance, whether it is a particular sports jacket or an expensive backpack. Children become envious of those who have the best logos on their possessions, even motivating them to steal.

Consumerism fills the gap of being connected with others. Since adolescents fear being alone, commercial images of people laughing together creates the impression that if you buy the right product, you will have friends and be accepted.

Brian Swimme, PhD, in his article, "How do our kids get so caught up in consumerism?" put it very clearly:

The image of the ideal human is also deeply set in our minds by the unending preachments of the ad. The ideal is not Jesus or Socrates. Forget all about Rachel Carson or Confucius or Martin Luther King, Jr., and all their suffering and love and wisdom. In the propaganda of the ad the ideal people, the fully human humans, are relaxed and carefree—drinking Pepsis around a pool—unencumbered by powerful ideas concerning the nature of goodness, undisturbed by visions of suffering that could be alleviated if human were committed to justice. None of that ever appears. In the religion of the ad the task of civilizations is much simpler. The ultimate meaning for human existence is getting all this stuff. That's paradise. And the meaning of the Earth? Premanufactured consumer stuff.

THE POWER OF ADVERTISING

Professional designers with brain power and sophisticated electronic gadgets have tons of money to hire sports stars and movie stars to promote their products. They create a dissatisfaction with our lives, our bodies, and our relationships, and create a craving for a consumer product to fill the need or insecurity. This is emotional manipulation.

> Comparing the marketing of today with the marketing of yesteryear is like comparing a BB gun to a smart bomb. Modern marketing is enhanced by technology, focused by child psychologists, and fueled by billions of dollars. (Susan Linn, *Consuming Kids*)

Children have no protection against the onslaught.

How did this start? A major event occurred in 1929 in a report issued by the White House Conference on Child Health and Protection. In their report, "The Home and the Child," children are viewed as independent beings with particular concerns of their own.

> Parents should give children their own rooms, furniture, playrooms, toys, etc. They should take them shopping and let them pick the things out for themselves. This gives the child a feeling of pride in ownership and eventually teaches him that his personality can be expressed through things. 1931. (quoted in Richard Robbins, *Global Problem and the Culture of Capitalism*, Allyn and Bacon, 1999, pp. 24–25)

In just the past ninety years, children's lives in America have changed dramatically with the consumer economy fueled by economic power rivaling that of adults.

What children watch affects them. Programs come and go, but advertising continues to get stronger and more sophisticated in order to hold attention. The difference between virtual and reality worlds becomes fuzzier. Commercials have become more clever and faster paced, which confuses one's ability to think. The commercials during previews at the movies contain subliminal messages to make our mouths water as we crave popcorn and soft drinks. Meanwhile, the portions have become larger and larger, leading to obesity in children and adults.

Ads have to be more and more clever because artificial stimulation acts like a drug to gain the middle-schoolers' attention. This leads to overstimulation and addiction, or else they are easily bored. The brain isn't capable of differentiating and dealing at these speeds so middle-schoolers enter a zone of not thinking, just accepting what is promoted.

Advertisers target the concrete thinking of middle-schoolers: If the ad says something, it must be true. Side effects are presented only in advertisements for adult medicines, including even possibility of death. But in ads targeted to middle-schoolers and teens, the compelling image of a celebrity is a more potent authority than parents. They carry the message that you should look like them and buy what they advertise or there's something wrong with you. This gives rise to insecurity, self-loathing of body, eating disorders, and over-importance of bodily image.

Middle-schoolers and teenagers focus on appearances. Am I pretty enough? Sexy enough? Strong enough? While this is the appropriate time for them to be looking at themselves from outside, media and consumerism have pushed this concern to a much earlier age to the point that it defines the child's self-image and brings self-consciousness at a time when they do not have the cognitive skills to understand the power of manipulation. They emphasize that what you wear is more important than who you are, whether they show sexualizing of the girl's body or muscularizing of the boy's body.

However, it isn't only about outer appearances. It is also about values. If they can be accepted, recognized, and valued because they buy the right stuff, they will crave that acceptance. Their choice of goods represents how cool they are, not their true self-worth.

WHAT CAN WE DO?

For children in middle school to resist all the unhealthy messages coming toward them and overwhelm their fragile sense of self, they have to develop a healthy self-image, one that they are comfortable with. They have to hold off. This is not easy.

How do middle-schoolers do that? We have to start by getting advertisers to change the images in their ads:

- Show images where scenes of beauty are connected with kindness and love rather than the image of beauty identified with sexy outfits.
- Show images of family meals with healthy food rather than images of fast food being cool.
- Show images of water or juice rather than highly caffeinated soft drinks.
- Show images of healthy snacks rather than fast food commercials during children's programming.
- Get sponsors of fast food to make changes.
- Show images where people are speaking about the qualities of their friends, not the designer labels on their friends' clothes.
- Show images of families resolving conflict peacefully rather than through violence and aggression.
- Monitor television watching, video games, buying of brand items.
- Offer other activities: crafts, being in nature, participating in plays, playing outdoors.
- Refuse to buy clothes that are advertising brands. Explain to middle-schoolers why you are doing this.
- Make presents, cut down on how many gifts, giving a gift to someone less fortunate, focus on giving experiences rather than things.

- Give simple chores in the household (countering the "I am entitled" and "I want" attitudes).
- Spend time together rather than spend money.

The biggest issues are: Buy less, make more. Simplify life. Focus on family life.

It is time for parents to take action and tell corporations and advertisers to keep their hands off our children. Give middle-schoolers your time. Build up their sense of accomplishment and self-worth. Strengthen the imagination so that they can hold off media images that fill them with escapist fantasy, false needs, and negative values. The sense of a separate self with inner space that is one's own does not develop in this situation. It creates youngsters who are so filled up that they feel empty. This sounds like a contradiction, but it is not. When they are filled up with outer images, there is no sense of an inner space, a place for reflection. It is like keeping ourselves so busy, we have no time to think.

We can counter the need for media images with experiences that allow them to become interested in other people, other cultures. We can create situations, alternative experiences that help others and lead to middle-schoolers feeling that this, too, is cool. For example, when the "popular" students consider volunteering to be cool, that catches on to others who hold those students higher in the social scale. Teachers can be particularly effective in creating such a situation in their classes.

We can support a shift in social standing when the "new cool" is based on values that have to do with integrity, sharing, creativity, etc. For example, when achieving success in drama, martial arts, and service projects such as building a kindergarten for homeless children, etc., is regarded as cool, then it becomes attractive to others.

Media images can fuel feelings of self-loathing and body-hatred. Middle-schoolers can never be skinny enough or sexy enough or strong enough. This creates insecurity just at the time when in their psychological development they are overwhelmed by messages from outside. They are looking for models they want to emulate and pattern their lives on. The power of sports stars and movies and music stars presented in expensive slick ads with the stars using or wearing the product is compelling. Middle-schoolers are more apt to imitate these models even when teenagers are becoming suspicious of how they are being manipulated. However, to penetrate this awareness is difficult for most teenagers until they are older.

While teenagers receive most of their information on sex and products from the media, studies show they still value their parents' attitudes. This tells us that we have a responsibility to start early in the middle school age to speak about these issues, letting them understand what is considered healthy sexuality and how to manage media. These conversations can be casual without pressure. The last thing middle-schoolers want is to be preached at by their parents. They are more likely to take it seriously if it is mentioned by a teacher they admire or a school counselor. Often they are amazed to discover that their teacher or counselor says the same things their parents are saying. Imagine that!

What is happening inwardly to strengthen children? This is where parents and teachers are so critical. We have to create an inner wall to stave off the environmental pollution that surrounds us. Adults can laugh about ads and grasp how the advertisers are trying to hook us to buy the item, but children cannot. Even young teens cannot.

CONSUMER EDUCATION

Having a class in consumer education helps middle-schoolers understand the power of marketing. They can make a list of things they need and things they want, and then discuss how this list would affect what they would buy. Understanding the difference helps them become critical thinkers.

Can they see through the images in commercials? How do they relate to funny icons that speak? Can they pick out what the intention of the advertiser is? Eighth-graders can make reports in which they figure out why advertisers show products in particular ways. What is the intention? What is the influence of having a celebrity describe a favorite product? What does it mean to be influenced?

Such consumer education goes a long way to helping middle-schoolers wake up and develop critical thinking skills. Such skills can also be developed in their classes on technology, cell phone and computer usage, social media, and the models in TV, magazine, and billboard ads.

For example, a class of middle-schoolers can choose an item such as a bicycle. They could do research, compare it with similar bicycles made by a different company, assess the prices, features, and included extras, and then decide whether they would want to buy this product. Terms such as conspicuous consumption, holiday shopping, Black Friday, etc., would be discussed. They would take pride in sharing this kind of information with their parents. Since middle-schoolers have an effect on what parents buy through "pester power," having such clarity could inform what they learn about clothing brands, electronic gadgets, even appliances for the home.

With middle-schoolers having access to income either through their allowances, birthday gifts, odd jobs, or other, they would be surprised to realize how much influence they have on shops in the mall. Where the marketing forces want to direct how middle-schoolers use their own or their parents' money, becoming educated consumers can protect them from these forces and help them decide for themselves what they need and want.

Although middle-schoolers are more likely to listen to ads that include teenagers as models instead of adults, they are still influenced by their parents' buying habits. The focus on being skinny is one of the causes for the increase of girls' smoking during this time. We know from studies that if a child forms a brand loyalty to cigarettes around age thirteen, this will probably be their choice in adulthood.

Middle-schoolers as educated consumers can be discerning about what they buy or crave. If middle-schoolers can become partners in exploring the effect of advertising, they may feel empowered to be pioneers. By working together in groups, they can gain strength in making difficult decisions and feeling powerful. With guidance, videos that show what goes on behind the scenes, and involving them in researching consumerism, these young people can begin to make careful choices.

CHAPTER 14

Parents Are People Too

Being a parent is very challenging because it is a major part of the whole life-system in which we are engaged. Yet, I am convinced it is the most sacred work we do. In addition to the stresses that have always been there, the stresses around parenting have changed radically. That sounds counter-intuitive because we have so many energy-saving appliances. But life is faster, more complex, more unknowing. Past conventions that held society together have loosened.

On the whole, parents have lost confidence in their ability to be an authority with their children, and the children are ruling the roost. Children need parents who are willing to be adult, set boundaries, and have reasonable expectations. Having been a teacher and a parent of middle school students, I can empathize with the challenges parents of children in my class had as well as reflect on experiences with my own three children, a foster child, and several exchange students. We all need help, especially when our children reach middle school and begin to have a mind of their own, as well as language to communicate their wishes and demands.

The family is the image of human society. What children learn in their family gives them the model for what life is all about, how people relate to each other, what each is willing to give to the other, and how each one's strengths and weaknesses affect everyone else. For some children, the family experience is a gift that will shape their lives positively. For others, it is something to avoid.

When our children reach the middle school years, we are confronted with our own fears, anxieties, and dreams. We want to protect them from growing up too soon, and yet sometimes we want to join in with them and become teens ourselves. Regardless, the most important task is to guide them.

> I strongly believe that ALL parents (and I include myself here) are still psychologically stuck in one or some of the many phases of normal teen development. [She considers the teen years as 13–18.] When our teenage children reach the stages (ages) where we have our own significant unresolved hurt or pain, we become caught in emotions and confusion that we don't understand. We may try to enforce rigid control over our teens, rather than offering guidance and limits. We may go unconscious about the very things we ourselves did or didn't do as a teen and hesitate to see the problem as ours. We may be slow to get outside help, finding out from the police, school, friends, other parents, or relatives that our teen has a secret life that we knew nothing about. (Elium, *Raising a Teenager*, pp. 6–7)

One of the most important things in working with middle-schoolers is finding time to talk with them. The past generation of parents told their children to go out and play. Parents today have many worries—strangers, violence, injuries, falls, and bullying. So, on one hand, the children have everything, and on another, they are lacking critical experiences.

PARENTAL DYNAMICS

As the middle school years are one of the most fragile, everything that goes on around the youngsters affects them in ways they don't understand. Their reasoning skills are not there yet, so they experience each situation as all there is, but they lack context. For example, a parent says, "You'll get over these feelings of loneliness. One day you will look back and appreciate that you have friends and family who love you." The child can't imagine that, they can't think of themselves looking back. All they know is what they feel right in the moment.

Because middle school students are going through so much internal change, they need to be able to count on their parents. Although they may outwardly reject them, they rely on them and listen to them even when it doesn't seem so.

In cases where parents are at odds with each other, the youngsters pay the price. To get what they want, middle-schoolers learn how to manipulate adults, playing them against each other, or cleverly have them think the place to go or the thing to do was really the parent's idea when it was what the youngster wanted all the time. At times the results do not benefit the youngster in the long run, but the enjoyment of temporary success increases the sense of power. The parent has given in, and peace and quiet can resume.

Our family shared Monday evening dinners with our relatives next door. These were tense situations in which the cousins' behavior was enough to make you want to dig a hole and hide. Their parents disagreed on discipline and how much backtalk they would tolerate. Everyone was stressed. When we would eat next door, the children sat at a separate table from the adults. When the two families had dinner at our house, we mixed the children with the adults. We found that parent conversation was a model that the early teens could learn from and they could contribute to. One evening after we returned home, my son said, "You'd never let us speak to you like that." It was clear that he wanted to be sure that we'd never tolerate such behavior.

Middle-schoolers look for stability, and the lack of it adds to confusion. They need adults who are adults. When the parents turn to the child for approval or rely on the child for making big decisions, this incorrect placement of authority destabilizes the youngster. Although confrontation may be avoided in the short run, there is an eroding of healthy authority. There are ways to include youngsters in group decisions. In fact, it is important to do so, as long as everyone is clear who is making the final decision. Creative ideas can emerge when youngsters are included and respected in conversations.

Parents under stress become self-centered, just trying to get through each day. They may lose sight of their children's needs and focus only on their own. Children are left to make their own meals, arrange rides, spend a lot of time without supervision, and receive little supervision of their homework. Some latchkey kids who come home to an empty house have hours alone before parents return, and can fill the time with video games, unapproved visits with classmates, internet porn, or other inappropriate behavior. Justifying the child's long hours alone by saying their children are flexible and will do just fine may be delusional.

Parents who have to work long hours often try to keep connected with their children by calling every hour to remind them what they should be doing and letting them know when the parent will return. This helps the youngster feel the parent's presence. Having a neighbor or grandparent available to help out by actually being in the house or by having the middle-schooler spend time in the friend's or grandparent's home can be a lifesaver.

Single parents have the added stress of managing the home and the relationship with the child(ren) on their own. Their intentions are often very good, and they want to be an involved parent, attending their children's activities and supporting their son or daughter's interests, but it is hard to do everything. It is a question of balance—how to fulfill expectations at work and how to fulfill needs at home.

With several children in the family, the parents' task is more complicated. It becomes important to build a strong support network of friends and extended family that can offer ongoing love and commitment: help with appointments, provide a sensitive listening ear, and occasionally give the parent a break. Financial pressures, medical issues, house repairs, and school vacation schedules all add to the single parent's stress.

Where parents share a healthy relationship with each other, the parenting of a middle-schooler is a shared experience with times of warmth and companionship, humor, stability, and even adventure.

The child is embedded in the "home and hearth." But no relationship is perfect, and parents will still experience problems and struggle to maintain balance. If they are able to remember that their middle-schooler is affected by tension, they may be able to assure them that things will be all right. Children can tolerate a lot as long as they don't feel their life is on the verge of collapsing.

I remember my parents fighting with each other and the way it turned my stomach. I would hide in my bedroom and promise myself that when I grew up I would never fight with my husband. It would have been healthier for me as a child to understand that parents do have times when they disagree with each other; they will work it out, and the world isn't going to come to an end. I would have benefited from their explaining to us that although they disagreed, they still loved each other. Unfortunately, my parents' generation was not as aware of the psychological effects of their behavior on their children.

My adult son is aware of how sensitive I am about parental fighting. During the Christmas holidays, I was visiting him and his wife. They were disagreeing about where the Christmas tree nursery was. Although it wasn't loud or angry, I could feel my stomach beginning to knot (a carryover from childhood). My son turned to me and said, "Don't worry, Mom, we are not arguing, we just have a difference of opinion." It turned out that both of them were correct about the nursery address because there was one on both opposite sides of town. We all began laughing. It was a reminder how experiences in childhood stay with us as triggers in our adult years. Parents are people too!

When children of middle schoolage get into difficulty because of bad behavior, parents have to be careful not to identify so closely that they protect their children from the repercussions. An example:

Sixth-grader Susannah was the treasurer of her class. After a fundraiser, Susannah collected the money and turned it in. However, she kept back $25. The money was found in Susannah's wallet in her backpack. Her mother accused the teacher of being unfair because her daughter would never take money. The whole issue then became focused on, "My child would not...," as if the child's actions were a reflection of the adult. Because the parent was not able to accept this as an opportunity to help her daughter work through the issue, give back the money, and write an apology, the mother withdrew the child from the school.

CAUGHT IN THE MIDDLE

Each situation is different, but children are often caught in the middle of marital problems, divorce, and loss. Children are expected to tough it out and keep going. But middle-schoolchildren are fragile. They know enough to know their parents are having a hard time but do not understand (and shouldn't have to) the complexity of adult relationships. An example:

Twelve-year-old Peter sat with his head down, away from his classmates. His father had just moved out, and Peter had been asked to help carry boxes of his dad's stuff to the car. He was filled with such mixed emotions as he sat there, almost paralyzed in sadness. Maybe life would be quieter at home, maybe he would still see his father on weekends, maybe he would have to become the man in the house, whatever that might mean, maybe he would have to help with his younger siblings, maybe, maybe, maybe. He didn't know who to blame, but he felt that maybe he had done something to cause his father to leave. "Maybe if I had been more helpful, maybe if I had not beaten him at chess, maybe if I had cleaned my room." He felt guilty, but he didn't know why. He just felt rotten.

Being caught in the middle of a custody battle is devastating to a middle-schooler. Without the ability to understand adult relationships, the child's whole sense of survival is threatened. Russell said he felt he was in the middle of a war. It didn't really matter who was wrong and who was right. He hated the whole thing. If he indicated any interest in being with his father, his mother accused him of being disloyal, and at times she even threatened to hurt herself. Russell had to back his mother since he lived with her. Occasionally, he would say something, but mostly he was quiet. He just wanted the whole situation to go back to the way it had been before. There was no way he could understand what either parent was feeling. He just wanted to get through each week. As soon as he turned eighteen, he joined the army.

One thirteen-year-old dealt with tension between her parents by climbing out of her window and going off to smoke pot with other young teens. She was furious with her father for leaving and did not want to hear his point of view. She resented her mother, but felt loyal to her and absorbed her mother's view of the relationship. Earlier, she had been a delightful child, eager to learn, and full of adventure. The rough experience of the family's breaking apart resulted in a very angry teenager who chose a hard and fast life, taking decades to come back to balance.

Seventh-grader John didn't ask questions when his father moved out. He became quiet and moody. One night as his mother and sisters were having dinner, John pounded his fist on the table and demanded, "I just want to know what is going on around here."

Divorced parents feel tempted to share their feelings with their children, confiding in them about their own personal life, often even asking their child's opinion about a new "friend." It is stressful when one parent makes comments about the former partner's taste in girlfriends or boyfriends or involves the children in new arrangements. "Won't it be nice? We will all go to the mountains for the weekend." The word "all" includes the parent, the parent's new friend, and that new friend's children. What is the middle-schooler supposed to do? Pretend everything is fine? Who are these people? Is he/she moving in to the house? What about his/her kids?

When parents go through divorce, each child's experiences is depends on what stage of development he or she is in. For example, in one family, the oldest child had had a stable childhood, and she was in eleventh grade when her parents separated. She was upset with them, but her personality was already formed so she wasn't emotionally traumatized.

Her brother was in seventh grade when he experienced a stressful household: His father had left. His mother was struggling to care for the family, work full time, and he was confused about his role. Whereas he had been the middle child focused on himself, on adventures, fort building, and ice skating, now he had to take more responsibility, and the worst of it was that his father was not there. As he was beginning to shape his identity, the situation was unsettling. The middle-schooler does not have the capacity to understand the feelings of each adult and is just trying to go with the flow.

His younger sister was in fourth grade, and she was affected differently. She had been very close to her father, felt that she was his favorite, and now he was gone. Her mother was struggling, and she felt it, but didn't know what to do. When the possibility of her mother seeing another man arose, she was very upset because it upset her fantasy of believing her parents would come back together one day. She carried the feeling of abandonment into her adult years and only then she could begin to understand an adult's feelings.

Middle-schoolers respond to these situations with their feelings first—anger, sadness, fury, withdrawal.

INDIVIDUALS WITHIN THE FAMILY

The pathway to becoming an individual has many twists and turns. Sixth-graders are like buds, delicate yet full of promise. Eighth-graders are like blossoms, becoming strong and multicolored. They will come more fully into their selves as they flower in high school. As children go through middle school, they have opportunities to explore areas of interest, try out different roles, relate to success and failure, reach out to adults, decide on friendships, feel happy, lonely, determined, and unsure as they find their way through social dramas. Each of these experiences helps to shape the youngster's sense of identity and individuality.

Parents need to determine how involved they will be in their middle-schooler's experience. Helpfulness is good, but too much helpfulness hinders the child from figuring for themselves what to do. Part of their challenge is to manage separation from parents, and as painful as this can seem at times, it is necessary. Taking small steps along the way prepares for the bigger shift that will happen after high school.

Of course, they have started making these steps when they were younger: deciding what to do, wear, choose games to play, or visit friends. If they constantly feel too timid to make some of these decisions, they may be overly dependent on their parents. Naturally, parents should make decisions regarding safety and appropriateness in certain situations, yet allowing for areas of independent choices.

Some of the areas in which the middle-schooler takes these steps include the decoration of their room, the clothes they wear, the electives they take, the after-school activities and games they join. Certain decisions need discussion—whether or not the youngster goes along with the family to visit grandparents, whether a friend can come along on a vacation or road trip, choosing a different diet from the rest of the family, and many others.

There are also experiences that middle-schoolers choose which are secret, or at least parents don't learn about them for a long time. Eighth-graders might choose to attend a party with high school students and not tell their parents about it. Depending on the parents' attitude, this can lead to many difficult conversations. Other eighth-graders make poor decisions regarding alcohol and sex. The more common decisions today have to do with social media.

All of these experiences are opportunities for growth. They allow for conversation with parents as to how to deal with the decision they made, what else they could have done differently, and how to deal with the results. No matter how poor the decision is, parents need to let their children know that they are there to support them and help them take responsibility for their actions.

WHO IS IN CHARGE?

With their newly acquired thinking skills, the middle-schoolers sharpen their verbal capacity by arguing with their parents or figuring out which one is most malleable. The difficulty for the parent is that when their children sharpen their arguing skills, there is no end to the encounter. The child has the energy to keep on going without any conclusion. If they don't get their way, they continue arguing the next day. The parent is exhausted and often gives in to the request even though it is not a desirable stance to take. The middle-schooler knows the parent's weak spots and twists the sword in, causing frustration and sometimes, despair. A few hours later, the parent is still feeling upset while the youngster has gone along on his or her merry way.

For many years I taught a class to twelfth-graders during which they looked back at their family life. A common theme was "I hated my mother when she wouldn't let me go to that concert, but now I'm grateful for her guidance." By the time they are 17 or 18 years old, they look back and recognize how much they thought they knew and how little they actually did know. But it wouldn't have helped to have told them that when they were in the midst of a middle school funk.

There is no easy way to survive this stage of life. The warm feelings of love toward a baby or toddler do not carry over so easily to a middle-schooler who is challenging every statement. We have to develop skills to engage the youngster in a conversation in which each person's view is heard and respected.

Despite the fact that middle-schoolers will argue about family arrangements, they do want to know an adult is in charge. If there is a choice of a family vacation, the children need to be listened to for their ideas, but it has to be clear who is making the final decision. Sometimes suggesting they bring a friend along can ease the decision. On the other hand, having the middle-schooler and his/her friend hunkered down in the bedroom playing video games is not the best idea of a family vacation.

Often the decision of which parent the child will spend a vacation with is decided by the divorce arrangements. At least, in that case, it is clear. Yet there will still be times when the divorced parents will need to negotiate visitation because of commitments that interfere with the agreed-upon arrangements. If they can work this out without too much stress, the child wins. If the child feels battered by the conversation, it is a nightmare.

I recall with affection visiting a friend's family. The eighth-grade son did not want to continue playing the violin. His mother was very strong willed and just kept at him to practice. As I watched this, I was thinking she was going too far. But she knew her son, and after his many protests, she made some jokes, but she did not give in. By the time he finished practice, he was smiling. In high school, he was allowed to change instruments if he wanted, and he enthusiastically took up the guitar.

If parents get too caught up in the difficult aspect of raising middle-schoolers, they can miss the wonderful creative moments when their children have very good ideas, excitement, idealism, and spontaneity. This experience is not to be missed!

SEEKING MORE INDEPENDENCE

Middle-schoolers have an unrealistic sense of their own capacities to handle independence. They want to be allowed to try new experiences, go further away from home, or hang out with different groups of friends. They feel they have good judgment, and their parents should be comfortable with that. At the same time, they want their parents to help them out with rides and money, and they will count on their parents to rescue them if needed. They do need to begin the process that in the future will result in the child moving away from home. It is a process that goes through many stages.

A boy doesn't want his mother to be affectionate in front of his friends. As he shifts his loyalty from parents to friends, he uses his peers in this struggle for freedom. "Everyone has a cell phone." "Everyone gets to stay out late." "Everyone gets to choose where to go in the summer."

Here are a couple of ways a conversation can go:

Boy: Everyone has an iPhone but me.
Parent: Everyone? Every single person has an iPhone?

Boy: Yes, and I'm treated like a baby because you won't get me one. You don't trust me just because other students use theirs in bad ways, I'm mature enough to use it well.

Or

Boy: You don't trust me. You never let me do anything I want or have anything I want. I hate you.

Or

Boy: Everyone in my class has an iPhone, except me.
Parent: Well, maybe that's true or maybe not. However, you do not need an iPhone. When you go to high school, we will consider it.

I had the good fortune of sharing a workshop with David Elkind, noted psychologist and author of *The Hurried Child* and *All Grown up and No Place to Go*. He described how he insisted to his grandmother that he wanted something that everyone else had. His grandmother put her hands around his face in a loving way and said, "David, I know that you want it, but what do you need?" The difference between wanting and needing is an important one for a middle school child to wrestle with.

A boy takes on the battle for independence first within the family and then outside. He spends more time away from home, usually with male friends, and he works hard to prove his masculinity either with other boys, with girlfriends, and by taking on jobs outside of home. A parent says, "Mike will not lift a finger to help in the yard, but he earned $180 weeding, mowing the lawn, and watering plants for neighbors. They remark how responsible he is, but we can't get him to do anything at home."

Part of gaining independence is the keeping of secrets. They want to have their own sense of power, choosing how to spend their time and with whom. Sixth-grade Annette confided in me, "When I go home this afternoon, I'll spend two hours on my favorite video game. My mother won't know. She'll think I'm doing my homework."

189

Diaries, secret languages, codes, and hand gestures, whispering, sneaking—all are part of the keeping of secrets. It is only when our children become adults do we find out some of the many secretive things they did.

Girls also want to become independent, but they do it in a different way. They are conflicted between leaning on their mothers for advice and pushing them away. They will borrow their mother's clothes, and then say that she is old-fashioned. They are constant complainers because they are caught between seeing their mothers as models and wanting to separate from them. Going shopping with a middle school daughter is an unforgettable experience. Mother says the outfit looks good, the girl decides her mother has no taste. The mother says an outfit does not look good on her, the girl decides to buy it.

Even obedient children find ways to be independent. Lana was a very respectful girl, interested in everything going around her, and not given to rebelliousness. Her family was stationed in Asia where her father was teaching. Everywhere they went, people wanted to take group photos. Lana hated all that fuss. She wasn't going to embarrass her parents by refusing to be in the group pictures, but as the photographs showed, she crossed her eyes each time. Everyone finds their own way to say, "I will decide what to do."

The tug-of-war between freedom and responsibility in the path to independence is felt by both parents and middle-schoolers. How much responsibility is too much or too little?

A girl experiences her relationship with her father in a different way. Depending on how he treats her, she may cultivate her own relationship with him—sitting on his lap, going to the market with him, sharing secrets—and leaving her mother out. How her father treats her may have an effect on her feeling of femininity. Does he tell her she looks attractive, does he tell her she is starting to get a little pudgy, does he tell her he doesn't want her to grow up too quickly, does he criticize her attempts to dress like a teenager? She is supersensitive and takes his comments very deeply. After all, he is the first man in her life, and her relationship with him will affect her later relationships with men.

Girls are more able to turn to her father or mother for help when they are facing a problem without losing face. Because they are more connected with their emotional life, they value support when they ask for it. Boys are less likely to share their difficulty and feel they have to handle it themselves. This leaves boys out in the cold when they really need the warmth of their parents' love.

Middle-schoolers try to exercise independence, especially as they get to eighth grade, by expressing whether they will join family gatherings or participate in religious practices. Often, the religious rite of passage of confirmation or bar and bat mitzvahs serves as a turning point. After that, youngsters can make his/her own choices. They also want to be free to choose their own friends regardless of their parents' opinions.

CHOICE AND FREEDOM

How much freedom is okay? How involved should adults be? Planning is one of the tough skills for middle-schoolers. They can hardly remember where they left their backpacks, yet they want to be trusted to go off on an adventure. What will they do, where will they go, how will they travel, where will they sleep, how will they eat, etc. Here is how the parents can be helpful in the planning stage. Instead of taking over the planning, they can discuss the situation. What kind of adventure will work? Is the adventure going off on your bicycle for the rest of the day or is it going overnight? How much freedom can a 12-, 13-, or 14-year-old have without adult supervision? In some parts of the country it is normal for middle-schoolers to be gone all day on their own; in other places, no. What would be acceptable for two or three youngsters going off on their own? A trip to the mall? Why? What for? What will they do there? A bike ride and picnic along the trail to the state park? It is very common in Europe for youngsters to take trains by themselves to visit friends or family members many hours away. This is much less so in the U.S. where there is more concern about safety.

It may be that the adventure would be a group activity away from the family, with a class, a club, or another family. For example, if middle-schoolers are going on a camping trip with a club, the Y, a Scout group, or the class, the adult can help them plan what is needed by going through the list, but letting them figure out what they have and what they need to get. They are not on their own the way high school students would be. If middle-schoolers are left on their own to do this, the results can be devastating. "I couldn't find my poncho." "I didn't bring the extra pair of shoes that was required, and now I'm soaking wet. I'm miserable. I hate this. I'm never going to do this again."

Every opportunity should be used to help middle-schoolers organize their lives without completely making the decisions for them.

HOW MUCH IS TOO MUCH?

The tendency, especially for middle-class parents, is to give their children too many experiences. They fill their after-school hours with music lessons, sports activities, dance, and going from one thing to another, having a quick dinner snack along the way, coming home late, still having some homework, and not getting enough sleep. Parents need to ask themselves how much is enough? Are they doing this because they want to, or is it to please me?

Saturdays are often filled with required games or rehearsals. Parents either drop off the child at the event or stay and observe. These experiences place middle-schoolers in constant comparison with others. Are parents going to criticize how the game went or what the youngster should have done better? I live across the street from a playing field that is filled every Saturday morning with teams. Sometimes it is not clear whether the children or the parents are emotionally involved in what is happening. Cheering is one thing, but yelling corrections or judgments is another.

When organized activities fill up the non-school time, they take away from family time, whether it involves working together in the yard, taking the dog for a walk, or going on a picnic. Once children are in middle school, time becomes very precious.

The middle-schooler's new sense of cause-and-effect thinking plays out in the family dynamics. If the adults overly praise and call a lot of attention to middle-schoolers' accomplishments—ballet, baseball, tech savvy, etc., they assume that is their identity. Then they may be reluctant to try new things or give up the old ones as those have become their identity. It helps if parents find positive things to say about a number of skills or talents so that middle-schoolers don't limit their identity to a narrow one.

At the same time, if the parents overly praise someone else's child because of a particular talent, or compare it unfavorably with their own child, the youngster may feel "I'm not good at anything, a total failure." Middle-schoolers are very concrete, taking each example as the total assessment.

Parents reading this may feel they can never win, that no matter what they say, it can be taken incorrectly by the middle-schooler. This is true. What parents can do to make the best of the situation is to say something like, "You've worked very hard to improve your spelling. Sometimes you may feel you aren't making much progress, but it won't be perfect overnight. Let's see if you can improve a little each time you do the spelling test."

Or "I really enjoyed your classmate Jill's performance in the play. She must have put a lot of effort into learning all those lines. What do you think?" That leaves the conversation open, even if the answer is "I don't know." And "Remember when you were the knight or the shepherd in that play in fourth grade? This play was so much harder."

Concrete thinking can lead to assumptions. When I was in seventh grade, the class was planning to go on a glass-bottom boat in the canal. It would cost $1.00. I didn't feel I could ask my parents for the money because I had overheard them speaking about money being tight. I had no perspective what that meant, so I didn't tell my parents about the trip, but I stayed back at school when the class left. Years later when my mother heard about it, she said, "We would have found the money. Why didn't you ask?" What does "tight" mean? I assumed in my seventh-grade mind that tight meant they couldn't give me $1.00. Indeed, middle-schoolers are trying to figure out the world, and it is difficult with only half their brain mature.

Middle-schoolers often see the world in terms of "never," "always," and "everyone else." Zack played soccer in middle school. His parents were both working long hours, but they made an effort to catch at least one game in the season. When Zack was a twelfth-grader, he told me his parents never supported him, never came to observe him especially that day he had made the winning goal. The fact that his parents had come to one game didn't change his sense of loss while seeing other parents there regularly. When we discussed it, and I asked whether they had attended even one game, he responded that maybe they did, but he didn't think so. It was hard, even with his greater ability to figure things out, for him to overcome the conclusion he had reached in eighth grade.

HEALTHY AND UNHEALTHY ATTACHMENTS

The adult–child bonding and nurturing in their early years, as well as play, set the foundation of healthy attachment. Without those experiences, especially in the first three years, the child lacks the trust in the people and the environment. The gestures made toward them during their childhood are imprinted on them; those of aggression, of kindness, of gently holding, of disinterest—all sit like an undigested meal. It will take the next few years for them to work through these experiences as they begin to build their own identity. Am I what I have been before? A third daughter, a sad, orphaned boy, a happy-go-lucky boy, a jealous sister? A neglected child? A loved child? Or am I something different, something more?

Young children have demonstrated that they have certain moral instincts toward others, loving, generous, and kind. During childhood, they imitated the adults in language and movement. They turned to those authority figures who guided them, listened to what they were told, and followed their directions. They accept the rules and conventions of life—don't be rude to your parents, be quiet in class, don't steal candy from the store, help your grandmother load the groceries, brush your teeth twice a day, don't take your classmate's lunch, and so on.

However, around age 11 or 12, they realize that there are different kinds of rules. They can affirm some by their own inner compass, and they make sense. They recognize that other rules were made by people and are different in different families and in different schools. Which rules are necessary for a moral life and which are purely made by adults? They do not yet understand the reasons behind the conventional rules and begin to test them, to use new thinking skills to see what happens when they don't behave according to custom. As they respond to authority in a new way, they argue and negotiate.

"I don't have to do what you tell me."

"Why do I have to sit with the family at dinner?"

"Why do I have to go to church or synagogue?"

"Why do I have to go to Aunt Lily's? I hate that. There's nothing for me to do."

"Why can't I just be with my friends?"

"Why can't I have a cell phone?"

"Why do we have to sit in assigned seats?"

In these situations, parents need to practice self-respect and not accept being spoken to in a harsh and vulgar way.

Remember that these times will pass, and although the bonds between parents and middle-schoolers are tested, there are brighter days ahead.

Closing Words

The duty of parents and teachers working with middle-schoolers is tending the spark—the spark of goodness, beauty, and truth—that lives within the hearts of young people.

Parents have the daily experience of meeting life with their middle-schoolers, modeling the way they keep their own spark alive. It is challenging, and it is essential. Only later do children realize what their parents have given them and then they express appreciation and gratitude.

Teachers have the task of relating to middle-schoolers with enthusiasm, respect, and integrity, opening their minds, hearts, and limbs to understand and care for others, to feel purpose in their lives, and to gather these treasures for future understanding.

A sixth-grade class spent the year reciting "If" by Rudyard Kipling. They discussed the situations described in the poem and how it referred to their own experience. When they spoke it together, they stood upright with firm voices. It was as if the words gave them backbone to face decisions. The poem ends,

> If you can talk with crowds and keep your virtue,
>   Or walk with Kings—nor lose the common touch,
> If neither foes nor loving friends can hurt you,
>   If all men count with you, but none too much;
> If you can fill the unforgiving minute
>   With sixty seconds' worth of distance run,
> Yours is the Earth and everything that's in it,
>   And—which is more—you'll be a Man, my son!

Girls could grasp that these words were meant for them, too, despite the limiting use of the words "Man" and "son".

In Waldorf schools a verse written by Rudolf Steiner is often spoken during assemblies.

> To wonder at beauty,
> Stand guard over truth,
> Look up to the noble,
> Resolve on the good,
> This leadeth us truly
> To purpose in living,
> To right in our doing,
> To peace in our feeling,
> To light in our thinking,
> And teaches us trust
> In the working of God,
> In all that there is
> In the widths of the world,
> In the depths of the soul.

As with many words spoken during middle school, understanding does not come until later. It was interesting to find that former students now in their forties and fifties chose to post this verse on Facebook during the difficult days of 2017. Some of those who did so would have scoffed at these "feel good" phrases when they were in high school, but now they grasp their deeper meaning and are grateful to have them in their soul's treasure chest.

Despite the challenges in society, despite the powerful forces working on middle school children during their Vulnerability Gap, it is our task to help them through this time, as they prepare for the civilizing mind that will make all the difference in the society they will help to build.

Bibliography

Aeppli, Willi. *Rudolf Steiner Education and the Developing Child*. New York: Anthroposophic Press, 1986.

Anderson, Craig, et al. "Violent Video Game Effects on Aggression, Empathy, and Prosocial Behavior in Eastern and Western Countries: A Meta-Analytic Review," *Psychological Bulletin*, volume 136, pp. 151–173, 2010.

Baldwin Dancy, Rahima. *You Are Your Child's First Teacher*, third edition, Berkeley: Ten Speed Press, 2012.

Bartlett, Christopher and Christopher Rodeheffer. "Effects of Realism on Extended Violent and Nonviolent Video Game Play on Aggressive Thoughts, Feelings, and Physiological Arousal." *Aggressive Behavior*, volume 35, pp. 213–224, 2009.

Bartholow, Bruce, et al. "Chronic Violent Video Game Exposure and Desensitization to Violence: Behavioral and Event-Related Potential Data," *Journal of Experimental Social Psychology*, vol. 42, pp. 532–539, 2006.

Brizendine, Louann. *The Female Brain*, New York: Morgan Road Books, 2006.

Csikszentmihalyi, Mihaly and Reed Larson, *Being Adolescent: Conflict and Growth in the Teenage Years*, New York: Basic Books, 1984.

Damour, Lisa. *Untangled: Guiding Teenage Girls through the Seven Transitions into Adulthood*, New York: Ballantine Books, 2016.

Elium, Jeanne and Don. *Raising a Daughter*, Berkeley, CA: Celestial Arts, 1994.

_____. *Raising a Son*, Hillsboro, OR: Beyond Words Pub., 1992.

_____. *Raising a Teenager*, Berkeley, CA: Celestial Arts, 1999.

Elkind, David. *All Grown up and No Place to Go*, New York: Perseus Books, 1998.

_____. *The Hurried Child*, Reading, MA: Addison-Wesley, 1981.

_____, ed. *Jean Piaget: Six Psychological Studies*, Sussex, UK: The Harvester Press, 1980.

Freed, Richard. *Wired Child, Reclaiming Childhood in a Digital Age*, 2015.

Garbarino, James. *Lost Boys*, New York: Anchor Books, 2000.

Greenspan, Louise and Julianna Deardorff. *The New Puberty*, New York: Rodale, 2014.

Greenspan, Stanley. *The Growth of the Mind and the Endangered Origins of Intelligence*, New York: Addison-Wesley Pub. Co., 1997.

Gurian, Michael and Patricia Henley. *Boys and Girls Learn Differently*, San Francisco: Jossey-Bass, 2001.

Gurian, Michael. *A Fine Young Man*, New York: Jeremy Tarcher/Penguin, 1998.

Healy, Jane M. *Endangered Minds*, New York: Simon & Schuster, 1990.

Himowitz, Kay S. "Tween: Ten Going on Sixteen," article *Targeting Tweens*, July 29039, 2002, New York.

Hinshaw, Stephen. *ADHD, What Everyone Needs to Know*, New York: Oxford University Press, 2016.

Hinshaw, Stephen and Rachel Kranz. *The Triple Bind, Saving Our Teenage Girls from Today's Pressures and Conflicting Expectations*, New York: Ballantine Books Trade Paperbacks, 2009.

Icard, Michelle. *Middle School Makeover: Improving the Way You and Your Child Experience the Middle School Years*, Bibliomotion Mass, 2014.

Jensen, Frances E. and Amy Ellis Nutt. *The Teenage Brain, A Neuroscientist's Survival Guide to Raising Adolescents and Young Adults*, New York: Harper Collins, 2015.

Kahumoku, Jr. George. *A Hawaiian Life, Volume Two,* Lahaina, HI: Kealia Press, 2016.

Kessler, Rachael. *The Soul of Education,* ASCD (Association for Supervision and Curriculum Development), Alexandria, VA, 2000.

Lynn, George and Cynthia Johnson. *Breaking the Trance,* Las Vegas, NV: Central Recovery Press, 2016.

Miller, Derek. *The Age Between, Adolescence and Therapy,* NJ: Jason Aronson, Inc., 1983.

Miller, Edward and Joan Almon. *Crisis in the Kindergarten: Why Children Need to Play in School,* College Park, MD: Alliance for Childhood, 2009.

NPR. "Hidden World of Girls. Why Do Girls Love Horses, Unicorns, and Dolphins," Feb. 9, 2011 on *All Things Considered,* National Public Radio.

Olfman, Sharna, ed. *Childhood Lost, How American Culture Is Failing Our Kid,* CT: Praeger, 2005.

Oppenheimer, Todd. *The Flickering Mind, The False Promise of Technology in the Classroom and How Learning Can Be Saved,* New York: Random House, 2003.

Pearce, Joseph Chilton. *The Biology of Transcendence,* VT: Park Street Press, 2002.

Pollack, William S. *Real Boys' Voices,* New York: Random House, 2000.

Postman, Neil. *Amusing Ourselves to Death,* New York: Viking, 1985.

Sales, Nancy Jo. *American Girls, Social Media and the Secret Lives of Teenagers,* New York: Alfred A. Knopf, 2016.

Salter, Joan. *The Incarnating Child,* Glouchestershire, UK: Hawthorn Press, 1987.

Sax, Leonard. *Boys Adrift,* New York: Basic Books, 2016.

_____. *The Collapse of Parenting,* New York: Basic Books, 2016.

_____. *Girls on the Edge,* New York: Basic Books, 2010.

_____. *Why Gender Matters*, New York: Broadway Books, 2005.

Schoorel, Edmund. *The First Seven Years* Fair Oaks, CA: Rudolf Steiner College Press, 2004.

Siegel, Daniel J. *Brainstorm, The Power and Purpose of the Teenage Brain*, New York: Jeremy P. Tarcher/Penguin, 2015.

Smith, Sean. *Kim*, London: Harper Collins, 2015.

Staley, Betty. *Between Form and Freedom. Being a Teenager*, Glouchestershire, UK: Hawthorn Press, 2009.

_____. *Adolescence: The Sacred Passage, Inspired by the Legend of Parzival*, Fair Oaks, CA: Rudolf Steiner College Press, 2011.

Steiner, Rudolf. *The Child's Changing Consciousness and Waldorf Education*, Dornach, Switzerland: Anthroposophic Press, 1923.

_____. *Education for Adolescence*, Anthroposophic Press, 1996 translation of lectures given in 1921 in Stuttgart, Germany.

Swimme, Brian. "How Do Our Kids Get so Caught up in Consumerism?" https://prezi.com

Twenge, J. "iGen: Why Today's Super-Connected Kids Are Growing up Less Rebellious, More Tolerant, Less Happy—and Completely Unprepared for Adulthood—and What That Means for the Rest of Us," in *Sacramento Bee*, Tuesday, Oct. 3, 2017, p. 48.

Wilson, Frank R. *The Hand, How Its Use Shapes the Brain, Language, and Human Culture*, New York: Pantheon Books, 1998.

Wiseman, Rosalind, *Queen Bees & Wannabees: Helping Your Daughter Survive Cliques, Gossip, Boys, and the New Realities of the Girl World*, 3rd edition, New York: Harmony Books, 2016.

Wolfe, Naomi, *The Beauty Myth*, New York: W. Morrow, 1991.

Acknowledgments

I could not have written this book without the help of many people, most particularly the children I have come to know over the last fifty years. In addition to my own students, I have visited schools, observed middle school classes, spoken with teachers, principals, and psychologists and pondered the changes I was experiencing not only in American society, but in my visits to schools in Asia, East Africa, and Europe. Workshops with parents in these schools often brought up the same questions that I found close to home.

I want to thank the dozens of parents and teachers who kept encouraging me to write this book. I hope it is coming out in time to be helpful to them with their children.

I particularly want to thank Jeff Lough for his help in reading and commenting on the manuscript. Jeff's work as a school psychologist and contact with many middle-schoolers kept my writing current.

29539146R00113

Impulse spending, debt, and interest charges eat away at your money. Tips are provided on managing these items so they don't ruin your life.

We will also analyze whether going to university or college is worth it. Each person's situation will be different, but if you are seriously considering this route, options are presented on how you can pay for the tuition. If you have to take out a student loan, we will look at a budget example to see how this can be reasonably managed without causing long-term financial worry.

My parents, like many immigrants, came to Canada with nothing. They didn't have any money, and they didn't know any English. Yet, despite these substantial limitations, they managed to buy a restaurant, a house, and a car, raise seven children in Toronto, and become debt free using many of the strategies I'm going to share with you.

I am a Chartered Professional Accountant (CPA) from Canada. In 1997, I graduated from the business program at Toronto Metropolitan University (formerly known as Ryerson University). A few months after graduating, I got a job in an accounting firm and have worked as an accountant since then. I work with many different businesses and entrepreneurs. I started my accounting practice in 2012. I have two boys, a teen and a pre-teen.

As a parent, I started worrying about how my kids will be able to cope financially when they become adults. Then I started thinking about my nieces and nephews and wondered how they would be able to manage. What about my friends' kids? What about the whole younger generation? The gears in my head were spinning.

I've been teaching my kids a bit about money, but I felt I had to somehow share my finance knowledge to help others as well. At first, I wasn't quite sure how I would do this. However, through a series of events that followed shortly after coming up with my new goal, the idea of this book was born.

You're going to gain a wealth of knowledge on how to get more money in your bank account—based on my personal and professional experiences. I've spent many years learning the secrets and tips I'm going to share with you. To receive this knowledge, all you have to do is read this book in the comfort of your own home!

You *can* take control of your financial future! You don't want to miss any of this important information. I'll see you inside to start your personal finance journey . . .

Chapter 1
Money Basics and Scam Alerts

> "*The journey of a thousand miles begins with one step.*"
>
> — Lao Tzu

To begin your personal finance journey, we will start with a few basic topics. We'll discuss identification numbers, bank accounts, and the different forms of payment considered as money. We'll also talk about a few types of money scams, which I think are essential to be aware of as these have become so pervasive in our world. Everyone is looking for more money, including scammers, so we must understand how to protect our hard-earned money.

Identification numbers

One of the first things I would suggest doing is obtaining a social insurance number (SIN) or a Social Security Number (SSN).

In Canada, you will need to obtain a SIN from the government. The SIN is a unique nine-digit number that identifies you. You will need the SIN to work in Canada and access government benefits. As well, you will use the SIN to file your income taxes. Check with your parents to see if they have already applied for your SIN if you were born in Canada. If not, you can apply for it through a Service Canada office. Keep your SIN confidential and secure to avoid identity theft.

The Social Security Number (SSN) is the US equivalent to the SIN. As a US citizen or eligible US resident, you can apply online for this unique nine-digit number issued by the Social Security Administration. You will need your SSN to get a job. It's also used to determine if you can get Social Security benefits and be eligible for certain government programs. In addition, the Internal Revenue Service (IRS) uses it for tax matters, and you will need one to open a bank account.

Years ago, I was preparing a tax return for a taxpayer earning over $1 million as an investment manager. When the Canada Revenue Agency (CRA) checked his tax return, they sent a letter to the taxpayer saying that he forgot to report a few thousand dollars he had earned from another job. The taxpayer was confused as he only had one job. Why would he have another job earning a few thousand dollars when he already made over $1 million?

I called up the CRA to find out more about this. The CRA provided the name of an adult entertainment club with exotic dancers. The taxpayer then recalled that he had lost his wallet in this club. His wallet included his SIN, so someone must have used his SIN to get a job at the club. As a result, the taxpayer was responsible for paying the taxes on this extra income, even though he did not receive any of it.

TIP

You will not need to use your SIN or SSN every day, so just keep it at home in a safe place instead of carrying it around with you to avoid any loss or theft.

Open a bank account

The next thing I would suggest doing is opening a bank account. If you are under 18, your parents will need to help you open an account with both your names. Once you turn 18, the account can be just in your name. A bank account is where your money is stored. You probably have your birthday money or allowance in a drawer or a piggy bank right now. This is fine, but if you want your money to grow or increase, you can put it into a savings account.

A savings account is a place to save your money. The bank holds it for you until you decide to use it. The savings account will pay you a small amount of interest each month for keeping the money there. Interest is extra money the bank gives you, which is something you don't get if you just kept your money at home.

Look to open a high interest or high-yield savings account that doesn't have bank fees. The main purpose is for you to keep the money in the account with occasional withdrawals. You will open a chequing account if you need to use your money regularly.

Chequing accounts are used mainly for spending money. Money from your job can be deposited into this account, and then you can use the money to buy things. Chequing accounts do not usually pay interest. With chequing accounts, there are usually bank fees, which the bank takes out of your account each month to pay for having the account. The fees can be a few dollars each month.

When you open your bank account, you will receive a bank card which you will use to access your account. You will also need to set up a four-digit personal identification number (PIN) which is a four-digit code that only you know and must keep secret. This PIN tells the bank that you are taking money out or putting money into your account. If you lose your PIN or someone finds it out, they can use it to draw money from your account.

Scams

There are a lot of scammers out there who will try to get your personal and banking information to steal your identity and your money. The scam could be a phishing (pronounced "fishing") email or text *appearing* to be from your bank saying there is something wrong with your bank account. A scammer might say that your account has been frozen, and you need to click a link to unfreeze it.

Once you click that link, you will likely be asked to enter your name, address, personal information, bank card number, and PIN or online banking password. Once the thieves or scammers have this, they can take this information and hack your bank account to take your money. They will use this information to pretend to be you and might apply for a credit card under your name. Once they get the credit card, they will spend the money on the credit card, and you will be responsible for the charges unless you can prove that it wasn't you who spent the money.

Banks have introduced multi-factor authentication to reduce the chances of your account getting hacked. If you go into your online banking, in addition to asking for your password, they will ask for a unique code the bank will text you. You will then need the code texted to you to enter and access your online bank account. Thieves cannot access your account with multi-factor authentication, as they will not receive the code that was texted to your phone.

Another type of scam relating to bank cards and PINs is the taxi scam. Someone is posing as a taxi driver. They may have stolen a taxi cab and are using it to run a fake taxi business. The driver takes you to where you want to go, but at the end of the trip, they tell you they don't accept cash as payment, only debit cards, which is your bank card. They take your card, hand you the payment terminal, and watch you enter your PIN. Once completed, they quickly hand you back a different debit card, someone else's card they have previously stolen. If you are not carefully watching, you will not realize they have returned you a different card (Lev, 2022).

They now have your card and your PIN to purchase things. Once they have spent your money, they will pass this card on to the next unsuspecting victim.

I would recommend setting low daily withdrawal or spending limits of perhaps $100 on your account. If a scammer does get access to your account, your loss will be minimized as they will only be able to spend $100 each day, until you have the chance to contact the bank to stop any further unauthorized transactions. You can set the withdrawal limit to an amount you feel comfortable with as you will also be restricted by this spending limit.

TIPS

Here are some ways to protect your PIN:

- *When you set up your PIN, it should be something you can easily remember but difficult for others to guess.*
- *You shouldn't write down your PIN anywhere, as this will allow others to find and use it. If you do write it down, keep it in a secure place.*
- *Never hand your card to someone to make a payment, as you can tap or insert the card in the payment terminal yourself. If you do have to hand your card over, make sure you receive the same card back.*
- *When entering your PIN, use your other hand to shield your fingers so no one can see what you are entering.*

Another common scam is a text or email notifying you that your *"Amazon item could not be delivered."* Amazon is a huge e-commerce market with over 300 million active users worldwide (Flynn, 2022). There is a very good chance that someone, somewhere, could be waiting for a package from Amazon, so scammers use this knowledge and send out these fake messages. If you want to get your delivery, you will need to click a link to enter your Amazon account details to be able to resolve the delivery problem. Once the scammers have your Amazon information, they will use it to buy things on Amazon. They then have the opportunity to change the delivery address and your password for Amazon.

Other scams might tell you that you are eligible for free stuff or have won something. Again, you will need to enter your personal info to receive it. Of course, there isn't a free gift. Rarely anything is given for free without a catch, so don't get too excited about these messages.

TIPS

To help avoid identity theft and having your accounts hacked:

- *Pause and think before acting on a text, call, or email from an unknown person. Scammers are getting more and more creative. They target people in a rush, people who are vulnerable, easily scared, uninformed, and looking to make money quickly or get something for next to nothing. Scammers will use scare or worry tactics to make you act quickly without thinking.*
- *Don't click on links that look like they are from a bank*

or a vendor. Always directly enter the web address of the bank or vendor in your browser so that you know you are going to the correct website. Links can make it look like you're going to the official site but actually take you somewhere nefarious so they can steal your personal info. Alternatively, you can call the bank or vendor directly and ask them if they did send a message to you.

Different forms of payment

Money can come in many different forms for payment. Some of the ways you can pay for things are with cash, debit cards, Interac e-Transfer, credit cards, prepaid credit cards, gift cards, cheques, e-wallets, and PayPal.

Cash

Cash is a widely accepted method of payment in the form of paper bills and coins. There are several advantages to using cash. It's easy to use, and no fees are charged for using it. Cash also helps people manage their budgets better and reduce impulse spending. Once you pay for something in cash, you don't have to pay anything more for the item as the transaction is complete. Cash is limited to what you have in your bank account or in your hands. If you know you have $100 in your hands, you probably won't spend the full $100 right away on something you saw at the store. You know that once the $100 leaves your hands, you will not have any money left, which is not a good feeling. Using cash helps to control your spending. You do not need to rely on a wi-fi connection to pay in cash.

There are some disadvantages to using cash. Cash can be counterfeited, meaning it can be illegally copied and used. Usually, the bills are counterfeited rather than the coins, as the bills have more value. Printed bills have been given specific characteristics to help prove whether the money is real. If you are using cash, this is something to watch out for. If you unknowingly receive counterfeit cash and then try to spend it, you may not be able to use it if the person selling you the item realizes it is counterfeit. Report the counterfeit money to the bank or local authorities to help stop the distribution of the fake money.

When I was a teen, I worked as a cashier for a retail store called Canadian Tire (CT), a popular store in Canada that sells housewares, automotive goods (including tires), tools, and gardening items. CT has its own currency called CT money which, back then, was only paper bills. Each denomination of CT money had a different colour, and they came in denominations of $0.05, $0.10, $0.25, $0.50, and $1. They now also have electronic CT money, but paper bills still exist.

The CT money is given as a bonus for spending. For example, if you spend and pay with $200 cash, you would get back $0.80 in CT money. You could then use this CT money to spend in the store on your next purchase. Customers would save up their CT money and sometimes come in with $50 to even $200 in CT money. If you can believe it, there were instances where people would actually counterfeit the CT money! The counterfeit money was a slightly different colour, the size was a bit off, and the quality of the paper was a bit different. If you were in a rush, you probably wouldn't notice, but CT notified the cashiers of this counterfeit problem, so we would be on the lookout.

Other disadvantages of cash are that it is less convenient than carrying a card. Cash can get lost or stolen more easily, and it would be difficult to get it back. During the COVID-19 pandemic, stores didn't want to accept cash as they feared the virus would transfer onto the bills and coins. Using cash doesn't provide automatic record keeping of your transactions as you would see on a credit card statement. Also, you cannot buy anything online with cash.

There's been some talk that we may be entering a cashless society. Stores like the idea of operating on a cashless basis as it reduces the risk of getting robbed and the risk that employees mismanage the cash. The Bank of Canada, and the Federal Reserve, are exploring the idea of a central bank digital currency for the future (Bank of Canada, 2023) (Federal Reserve, 2022). However, some do not agree with this cashless society as there are lower income individuals who don't have a bank account or credit card, so they rely on cash to make their payments.

Credit card

A credit card is a plastic card issued by a bank or other financial institution. You have to fill out an application to get one, and you will need some income to qualify for a credit card. The card lets you buy things in person or online at any store that accepts credit card payments. The bank will loan you a certain amount that you can spend on the credit card. You will then need to pay the bank back for the items you purchased on the card with money from your bank account.

The advantages of using a credit card are that it is easy to use and carry. Depending on the card, you can earn points or rewards or get cash back for spending on the credit card.

The disadvantages of using a credit card are that you can quickly lose track of your spending and spend more than you can pay back to the bank on time. If you don't pay by the due date, you will be charged interest, which is extra money you have to pay. In addition, credit cards can be stolen and fraudulently used. Not all stores accept credit card payments as the store has to pay a fee when you use the credit card. There can be other fees associated with using a credit card.

Debit card

Debit cards, a.k.a. bank cards, are cards issued by the bank and linked to your bank account. Instead of going to the ATM to get cash, you can pay with a debit card. The money comes out of your account electronically, so you can see how much you have left in your account after spending. Not all online purchases can be made with a debit card. Also, depending on your account, you may or may not have fees charged for using the debit card.

Interac e-Transfer

Canadians can transfer money electronically to their friends, family, or small businesses to pay for goods and services using Interac e-Transfer. In your online banking, enter the recipient's name and email address or phone number. Enter the amount you want to send them and create a security question with a corresponding answer. The recipient will then receive an email or text with instructions on how to accept the funds. They must answer the security question correctly. Alternatively, the recipient can enable a feature called "Autodeposit", which automatically deposits funds from an Interac e-Transfer to their account without answering the security question. However, not all banks offer this feature.

Interac e-Transfers are secure and usually sent and received almost instantly, but sometimes there can be a little delay. They can be cancelled by the sender if the recipient hasn't accepted the funds yet. They will also expire after 30 days if not accepted. Each financial institution will limit how much can be transferred each day, which could be up to $2,000 or $3,000. There can be a nominal fee of $1 for sending each transfer but check with your financial institution to confirm the fees, if any.

Prepaid credit card

Prepaid credit cards can be purchased at stores. You don't have to fill out any application, and you don't have to have any income to buy the prepaid credit card. Once you pay for the card, the money is loaded onto it, and you can use it to buy something at a store that accepts credit cards. People typically get prepaid credit cards if they want to buy something online but don't have an actual credit card. Prepaid credit cards can also be given as gifts. Once the money on the prepaid credit card is spent, you will not be able to buy anything further on the card. You will need to pay a small fee of less than $10 when you purchase the prepaid credit card.

Gift cards

If you've received a gift card, someone purchased the card and loaded money onto it for you to spend. Gift cards can only be spent at the store that is shown on the card. For example, if someone gives you a Walmart gift card, you can only use that card at Walmart. There are no fees for buying gift cards. Once you have used all the money on the card, the card can no longer be used. Gift cards generally don't have an expiry date, but I would double check and try to use them sooner rather than later so you don't forget about them. Also, if you lose the gift card or it gets stolen, there is little you can do about it.

Cheque

Cheques or checks are documents that tell a bank to pay a specific amount of money from your bank account to the person holding the cheque. Cheques are rectangular pieces of paper with your bank account number on them. You have to order cheques from a company that is authorized to print cheques, as they come with certain security features. You will need to pay a fee for printing these cheques. You don't make cheques yourself.

If you want to pay someone with a cheque, you would write their name on the cheque, put the date for when you want to pay them, and write the amount you are paying them. You then need to sign the cheque, which shows you authorize the payment. Finally, you give the person the cheque, and they will take it to their bank to get the money from your account.

Cheques are easy to use, but not everyone accepts cheques as payment. The reason is that there is always the possibility that the person writing the cheque does not have money in their bank account to pay. You won't know if the person paying you has money in their account until the bank finishes processing the cheque, which could take a few days. Also, there is more chance of fraud with cheques as they can be easily duplicated, and signatures can be forged.

I worked for a company that used cheques to pay for everything. One day the bank called me and said they had a cheque from our company, payable to a particular individual. They wanted to confirm if we did, in fact, write the cheque. I looked into it and discovered that we didn't write that cheque! The bank stopped the transaction and did not take the money out of our account to pay the fraudster. Luckily, the bank was observant and noticed that the cheque was not authentic. Otherwise, we would have lost money and would never know who did it.

E-wallet

Google Pay and Apple Pay are examples of e-wallets. They are apps you can download on your smartphone. You store the details of your debit card and credit cards on the app so you can use them to pay for things. E-wallets can also store the details of loyalty or gift cards and help reduce the number of things you have to carry in your pocket or purse. It uses Bluetooth and wi-fi to securely transmit payment data (Kagan, Digital wallet explained: Types with examples and how it works, 2022).

E-wallets have some disadvantages. They aren't useful if there is an internet outage. Also, not all stores will have the technology to accept this kind of payment. Finally, if you lose your smartphone, there is the risk that someone could hack your phone to get your financial information (Kagan, Digital wallet explained: Types with examples and how it works, 2022).

PayPal

PayPal is an online platform that facilitates payments between individuals and businesses. PayPal customers need an email address to create a PayPal account and then connect it to their chequing account, a credit card, or both. Once PayPal has confirmed your identity, and you have money in your account, you can send or receive payments. Cash can be transferred to any email address or phone number, whether or not the recipient has a PayPal account. PayPal charges fees, however, there is no fee if you send money, in your home currency, to a friend or relative from your linked bank account. Millions of retailers online and around the world accept PayPal payments (Kagan, What is PayPal and how does it work?, 2022).

Caution

There are many types of scams. Personal information can be stolen very easily, but it's not so easy to get it back. It's very important that you guard your personal information like your SIN/SSN, PIN, address, and banking information. If someone gets a hold of it, they will use it to steal your identity, take your money, and spend and create debt under your name. It's tough to track down criminals, and it may be impossible to get your money back once they have taken it. Also, you will need to spend time and money to try to get your identity back and try to fix what the criminal has done. By protecting and safeguarding your personal information, you are helping to protect your money.

How do we get money? Getting a job is one option.

Chapter 2
Getting a Job – A Popular Way
To Make Money

"Opportunity is missed by most people because it is dressed in overalls and looks like work."

— Thomas Edison

G etting a job is a popular and easy way for teens to start making money. As a teenager with little to no work experience and perhaps no high school diploma, this process will feel overwhelming. To help reduce your anxiety, we'll go over the types of part-time jobs that are suitable for teens, how to find and get these jobs, and also talk about payroll taxes. With an open and positive mindset and some perseverance, you can definitely get a job.

Part-time jobs

Part-time jobs are flexible as you can work after school or on the weekends. Usually, you don't need a lot of experience, just a good attitude and work ethic.

Here is a list of possible jobs for teens (Indeed editorial team, 2022):

- Barista – prepares and serves coffee to customers in coffee shops
- Camp counselor – teaches and leads recreational camp activities
- Cashier
- Concession stand worker – sells snacks and drinks at festivals, cinemas, or fairs
- Library assistant – arranges books on the shelves and assists visitors with finding books or materials
- Lifeguard – needs to be an expert swimmer that is certified
- Pet sitter
- Baby sitter
- Restaurant server
- Retail sales associate – helps customers find and purchase products in retail stores
- Tutor – helps students to learn subject concepts and complete assignments
- Veterinary assistant – cares for animals and works under the supervision of a veterinarian

Benefits of having a job

While attending university, I worked some part-time jobs. As a cashier at CT, I started off earning minimum wage. I didn't make an enormous amount of money, but it did help to pay for some of my tuition and other things I wanted to buy.

Throughout my school years, I was very reserved, quiet, and shy. I barely spoke. If someone asked me a question, that was the only time I would respond to them. Otherwise, you wouldn't know I was around.

The cashier job helped me to improve my communication skills. In school, nobody minded if I didn't speak. However, part of the training in the store was to greet the customers, so I learned to do this. I also had to communicate with my co-workers and supervisors.

In addition, I learned how to manage my time, as I had school, homework, and a second part-time job.

My second job was at our family restaurant. I worked in a tiny, cramped, hot kitchen preparing vegetables, washing mountains of dishes, and serving hungry, impatient customers. On occasion, I went to pick up supplies and groceries. It was unpaid work, but I got free food and earned valuable experience in running a business, which has helped me to this day.

My experience at the restaurant actually helped me to get the cashier job. After my interview at CT, I found out that the hiring manager was a patron of our restaurant! She liked our food, giving me an edge over the other candidates applying for the job.

Never underestimate the benefits of volunteer work. Although you may not get monetary compensation, you get work experience, you're helping others, and you are able to make connections with different people that could eventually lead you to a paying job.

How to find a job

To find a job, besides looking online, just ask around. Ask friends, family, and neighbours if they know of any places that are hiring. Go around your neighbourhood and ask the retail stores, restaurants, coffee shops, grocery stores, or other places you might visit to see if they are hiring. Your school may also have part-time jobs posted.

Many jobs are not posted online as it costs businesses money to post jobs. Usually, business owners will ask around if they need some part-time help. If you are only looking online, you will miss out on many job opportunities.

Another option is to find out from your high school whether they offer a cooperative education (co-op) program. In Ontario, the co-op program gives Grade 11 and 12 students a chance to earn high school credits by completing a semester of unpaid work placement. You'll gain work experience and skills through the co-op program, which you can then put on your resume to help you get a paying job. It's also possible that the place where you did your co-op placement could decide to hire you at a later date (Settlement.org, 2019).

Resume

Once you've found the jobs you want to apply for, you will need to prepare your resume and cover letter to apply for the job. In some cases, you may also need to fill out an online job application form for the company you are applying to.

A resume is a document that lists your experience, education, and other activities that you may be involved in. It's usually written in bullet points to keep the information direct and easy to read. You can include the following in your resume:

- Highest level of education and relevant academic work. If you have already graduated from high school, you would mention this, and the year you graduated. In addition, you should note if you graduated with honours or received some awards. If you haven't graduated yet, you can mention your grade level and any school achievements.
- Student leadership positions – being a leader shows you have initiative and can work with others. Indicate where and what kind of leadership role you had and what you were able to accomplish as the leader.
- Volunteer and extracurricular activities – sharing some of your time with others shows you are helpful. Playing sports or music in a band can also show you are a team player and are able to learn other skills.
- If you have worked a part-time job before, you can also add details about this in your resume.

Cover letter

A cover letter is written to your potential employer, which tells them the position you are applying for, explains more about your qualifications, and explains why you want to work at their company. Cover letters are usually a page long. You do repeat some of the information in your resume, but the cover letter shows how you can communicate in writing.

The employer can also get a sense of your personality from reading the cover letter. Ensure it doesn't have spelling or grammatical errors, as this will make it look like you are sloppy or don't have attention to detail. If you are stating in your cover letter that you have good communication skills or are detail-oriented, it has to show in your writing!

You can find many online examples of how to write resumes and cover letters. Look for the ones geared more towards high school students or those with no prior work experience.

When I hired staff, I would first look at their resume to see if they had the education, experience, and skills we needed for the position being filled. If they met most of the criteria, I would then read the cover letter to see how well they wrote it. The letter also helped me to understand a bit more about them and why they wanted to work at our company. Finally, if they sounded enthusiastic and personable, I would consider them for an interview.

Job interview

Once you are invited for an interview, you will need to prepare for it. You will be nervous, but that is entirely normal. Preparing in advance will help to reduce anxiety, and you will have a greater chance of getting accepted for the job. Here are some tips for preparing for the interview (Indeed editorial team, 2022):

- Review the job description carefully and think about how your qualifications will be able to meet the job requirements.
- Research the business.
- Prepare answers to some common interview questions.
- Practice saying your responses out loud.
- Watch and adjust your body language as you are practicing your responses.
- Have some thoughtful questions ready to ask the interviewer.
- Print some hard copies of your resume to bring with you in case the interviewer didn't have time to print it.
- Plan your travel arrangements in advance.
- Be confident and speak positively of yourself. Explain your achievements or skills.

In interviews, when I'm hiring someone for a position, I like to ask candidates why they want to work for our company and why they think they can do the job. They may have already written this in their cover letter, but if they are able to tell me in the interview, I can then confirm that they did write that cover letter themselves.

I'll listen to how they respond and look at their body language to see if they are interested in working for our company. If they don't smile or sound as interested as they did in their cover letter, that's a concern. If they arrive late for the interview, that could indicate that they don't have good time management skills and could be coming to work late. On the other hand, if they ask questions about the business or the job itself, it shows they are interested and want to learn more. They're not showing up just to get a paycheque.

Candidates should also dress to impress.

Where to get help

All this will seem overwhelming if it's your first time applying for a job. However, if you complete each step one at a time, it will be very manageable and doable. You can also consult a trusted adult like parents or relatives and school guidance coun-sellors for assistance with these items. So don't worry or stress about this. There are people that can help. You just need to seek them out!

Your first paycheque

You've now been hired! Here are some things to keep in mind when getting your first paycheque:

- If given a choice between getting a physical cheque or direct deposit for your wages, it's best to ask for direct deposit so that you don't have to deposit the cheque yourself. The funds will just get automatically deposited on payday. Your employer will require your bank account information to set up the direct deposit.
- Your employer will also ask for your SIN or SSN as they need to report to the government how much wages

they have paid to you.

- Personal information such as your address will also be required for your employer's records.

- Employers can pay employees on a weekly, biweekly, semi-monthly, or monthly basis. If your employer pays on a biweekly basis, this means they pay all employees every two weeks. Let's say the employer pays on Friday the 2nd. Then the next payment would be on Friday the 16th. If you start work on Friday the 9th, you will get paid on the 16th, as that is when the next payday is for everyone in the company. Understanding when pay days fall is good, so you don't have to wonder when your money is coming!

Taxes

"The best way to teach your kids about taxes is by eating 30% of their ice cream."

— Bill Murray

You may have heard adults complain about "taxes." Once you start working, you will need to pay taxes as well.

Let's say your wage is $10 per hour. If you worked 10 hours, you would expect to be paid $100, right? Well, the $100 is what is called your gross pay. Your employer will need to deduct taxes from your pay, which is required by the government. The government uses this tax money to pay for various services they provide to the general public, like education and healthcare. Businesses like your employer will also need to pay a share of taxes, so don't feel like you are being targeted. The amount of tax can vary depending on where you live.

Taxes in Canada

In Canada, there are generally three things that will be deducted from your paycheque. There is a deduction for the Canada Pension Plan (CPP), Employment Insurance (EI), and income taxes. The gross pay less these deductions results in net pay, which is the amount that is deposited into your bank account.

Canada Pension Plan (CPP)

CPP is deducted if you are 18 years of age or older. This is a retirement pension that provides a monthly lifetime benefit to you when you retire. The amount of the benefit is based on your average earnings throughout your working life, your contributions to the CPP, and the age you decide to start receiving your CPP. Currently, you can apply to receive the CPP retirement pension when you are at least 60 years old. Essentially, you are saving for your retirement through the CPP (Government of Canada, 2023).

Each year the rates and maximum amounts required to contribute to the CPP change based on the rules set by the federal government. In 2022, you would contribute 5.70% of your employment income to the CPP up to an annual maximum of $3,499.80 (Government of Canada, 2022). You don't need to worry about calculating this, as your employer will calculate the amount of CPP you need to contribute on each paycheque, deduct it from your gross pay, and send the amount to the government on your behalf.

Employment insurance (EI)

EI is a federal government program that employees contribute to. If in the future, an employee loses their job through no fault of their own, they can apply to Service Canada to get EI benefits which are payments to help the individual until they are able to find new employment. There is no age limit for deducting EI premiums. The rates and maximum amounts for EI contributions vary each year depending on the rules set by the government. For 2022, you would contribute to EI 1.58% of your employment income up to an annual maximum of $952.74 (Government of Canada, 2022). Your employer will calculate and deduct the amount of EI you need to pay, and send it off to the government on your behalf.

Income tax

Income tax is a tax on the income you earn in a year. These taxes are used to help pay for various public facilities, programs, and services such as (Government of Canada, 2023):

- Education and schools
- Healthcare and hospitals
- Roads and bridges

- Police, ambulance, and fire services
- Libraries
- Parks and playgrounds, arenas, swimming pools
- Garbage and recycling collection
- Economic development
- Wildlife conservation
- National defence

The amount of income tax you pay depends on how much income you earn and the tax credits you claim. There will be federal and provincial/territorial taxes. A tax credit reduces the amount of tax you owe. Your employer will calculate the amount you need to pay in income taxes based on the federal TD1 personal tax credits form that you complete when you start your job. There is also a provincial/territorial TD1 form that has to be completed. Your employer will then deduct the income tax from your paycheque, and send it to the government on your behalf.

Generally speaking, if you earned less than $14,000 in income in 2022, you would not pay any federal income tax (Government of Canada, 2023).

T4

Once the year has ended, usually by the end of February of the following year, your employer would provide you with a summary of your employment income and the deductions for CPP, EI, and income taxes on a form called a T4. You would give this T4 to your accountant to file your annual income tax return. If you worked more than one part-time job in the year, you might receive multiple T4s, which you will also need to provide to your accountant.

The purpose of filing the annual income tax return is to determine if the correct amount of taxes have been paid to the government. In some instances, overpayments may have been made, which would result in a refund of the taxes to you. Other instances may result in additional taxes having to be paid if the government does not receive enough. Generally, for students, there is usually an overpayment of taxes, so it's best to file your income tax return to get a refund of the overpayment.

Taxes in the USA

In the US, federal income tax, social security, and Medicare taxes are required to be deducted from your employment income (United States Government, 2023).

Social security provides retirement income for adults age 62 and older (ADP, 2023). For 2022, it is calculated as 6.2% of gross wages (ADP, 2023). Medicare provides health coverage for adults over the age of 65 (ADP, 2023). For 2022 it is calculated as 1.45% of gross wages (ADP, 2023). The proportion of income taxes you have withheld depends on the deductions you claim when you are hired. For 2022, you wouldn't pay any income tax if your income was less than $12,550 (Freshbooks, 2023). In addition, some states and municipalities may have additional payroll taxes (ADP, 2023). Your employer will calculate these amounts for you and send them on your behalf to the government.

Why do we pay income taxes in the US?

Funds from income tax are used for the following (Kagan, Federal income tax, 2022):

- Build, repair, and maintain infrastructure
- Fund the pensions and benefits of government workers
- Fund Social Security programs
- Fund major health programs, including Medicare, Medicaid, CHIP, and marketplace subsidies
- Fund "safety net" programs to assist lower-income households
- Fund defence and international security programs
- Improve sectors such as education, health, agriculture, utilities, and public transportation
- Embark on new feats such as space exploration
- Provide emergency disaster relief

W-2

Once the year has ended, usually by the end of January of the following year, your employer would provide you with a summary of your employment income and the deductions for social security, Medicare, and income taxes on a form called a W-2 (The Investopedia team, 2022). You would give this W-2 to your accountant to file your annual income tax return. If you worked more than one part-time job in the year, you might receive multiple W-2s, which you will also need to provide to your accountant.

Key takeaways

There is some preparation to be done in order to get a job. Ask your family, friends, and neighbours about any job openings. Visit the local businesses to see if they are hiring. Have a trusted adult review your resume and cover letter to ensure it has no spelling or grammar mistakes. Once you get the interview, practice what you will say in advance to help calm your nerves. Be truthful and show that you are interested and willing to work.

In his younger years in Canada, my father worked various jobs delivering food, washing dishes, and cooking for the restaurants he worked at. These weren't glamorous jobs, but he paid close attention to everything in the restaurants and eventually took this knowledge to open his own restaurant.

Your employer will train you on various parts of your job as they understand you are a student with little experience. This is an opportunity to learn as much as possible about a business and also network with others. In addition, you can improve your communication and time management skills by working at a job. All these benefits will serve you well if you decide to start your own business or side hustle.

Chapter 3
Starting a Side Hustle Or Business

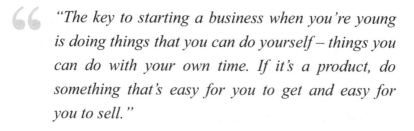 *"The key to starting a business when you're young is doing things that you can do yourself – things you can do with your own time. If it's a product, do something that's easy for you to get and easy for you to sell."*

— Mark Cuban

Starting your own "side hustle" or business is another way to earn income. There are many ads on YouTube where you will find people touting the ability to easily make millions of dollars in "passive income" without having to do much. If these claims were all true, we would be finding millionaires at every corner. In reality, "side hustles" or businesses take effort and time to build and generate income. Things do not happen overnight or in a matter of days.

In this chapter, we'll look at possible options for side hustles, how to find them, the advantages and disadvantages of owning a business, and the financial and tax matters you need to be aware of.

Side hustles

Side hustles are a way of earning additional income outside of your regular job. You might hear side hustles being referred to as freelance work or piecework. The work is small projects or tasks that can be done in your free time. Here are some side hustles you can consider:

- **Freelance writing** – if you like writing, there are quite a few magazines on the web offering payment to teens for their short stories and articles (Michaels, 2023).
- **Blogging** – if you are interested in a particular topic and would like to write about it, you can start a blog. Monetizing your blog takes time. It may take at least a year or two before you can make some money, but once it's started, you can make some consistent income (Michaels, 2023).
- **Social media manager** – this requires you to help other businesses manage their social media sites, such as Facebook, Pinterest, and Instagram, by posting to them daily and responding to questions and comments. You may also be creating content to help bring positive reviews and increase the site's popularity. This could be

a good side hustle if you like using social media (Michaels, 2023).

- **Caring for lawns** – for those who like to be outdoors, you can mow lawns in the summer, rake leaves in the fall, and shovel snow in the winter. In the spring, you can help get yards ready for gardening. You just have to learn how to operate equipment such as a lawn mower, trimmer, and other gardening tools (Michaels, 2023).

I had to take care of our lawn when I was a teen. My dad worked long hours at our family restaurant. He did not have time to take care of the lawn, so, as the eldest child in the family, I was assigned the task. He showed me how to use all the lawn equipment, and I took it from there. It was not difficult at all. The main thing I had to watch out for was to avoid mowing over the extension cord. The weeds were the most annoying to get rid of. You can probably get a lot of this work by asking your neighbours. I'm sure many of them would gladly hand it over to you for a reasonable fee.

- **Creating artwork or crafts** – teens can turn their hobbies into a business by selling crafts or artwork. Perhaps you know how to knit or crochet? Maybe you like to create digital art?

I read an article online about a young woman who created jewelry using vintage designer buttons. She sold these online and was making a surprisingly good amount of money.

I read another online article where, during the pandemic, someone created a crochet kit and sold this online. They had designs for various items and created instructions on how to crochet them. This also became very popular as people tried to find things to do while stuck at home.

Using your skills and imagination to create things can be profitable, as the items you make are handmade and can't be found anywhere else.

- **Live streaming video games** – playing video games has become a lucrative business for teenagers. Twitch is a popular live streaming service where you can live stream the games you are playing for others to watch. You earn money through ads. The more viewers you have, the better your ad revenue will be. If you gain a good subscriber base, you can sign up as a Twitch.tv partner. This will give you a chance to earn $2.50 per month for every subscriber you have (Michaels, 2023).

In the Winter 2023 Toronto Met University Magazine, there is an article about a student named Sofia Beltran who took a course offered by the university called "Introduction to video game design" (Craig, 2023). One of her assignments was to begin live streaming on the Twitch platform three times a week for three hours, with the goal of building viewers along the way. Wait . . . What?? Playing video games as a school assignment? My astonishment grew . . . She had never been on Twitch before, but within three months, she had 2,500 subscribers! After that, she started to get more invested in this assignment. She decided to make short TikTok videos, which resulted in 60,000 followers on TikTok in five months! She then converted most of these followers to her Twitch account. WOW, really amazing! Just keep in mind that Sofia's results may not be your typical result on Twitch, but it is an option for a side hustle.

How to find side hustles

Upwork is a popular platform for those looking to make extra money online. People will post jobs on Upwork looking for help with writing blog posts, creating social media posts, logo designs, creating illustrations, or video editing. You bid for the projects you are interested in, but you have to be 18+ to be able to sign up for Upwork (Cheung, 2023).

If you win the job, you work on the project and get paid. Upwork, however, takes a cut of your fees. As of January 2023, if you earn less than $500, the fee will be 20% of your earnings. If you earn between $500 – $10,000 in earnings, the fee is 10%. If you earn more than $10,000, the fee is 5% (Upwork, 2023).

Fiverr is another popular platform for freelancers. It is similar to Upwork, except it's a marketplace where you sell your services instead of bidding for the posted jobs. You set the price of your services and do as much work as you want. You have to be 18+ to sign up, but if you are between 13–17, you can ask your parents to sign up on your behalf (Cheung, 2023). They will then be responsible for the work you do.

Fiverr takes a 20% cut of any money you earn (Fiverr, 2023).

Tracking your income

Since working as a freelancer or doing a side hustle is a business, you are responsible for reporting the income you earn in the year on your personal tax return as self-employment income. There are three ways of tracking your revenue:

1. Issue sales invoices to your customers. There are different online apps that you can use to create invoices. You can also create invoices using Excel or Word. Use Excel or Google Sheets to maintain a log of the sales invoices you've issued in the year. At the end of the year, add up all the sales invoices to come up with the gross revenue for the year.

2. Request a statement of earnings for a fully completed calendar year to determine the income you made in the year for tax reporting (Fiverr, 2023).

3. If you are a US person and earned income from sites like Fiverr or Upwork, you will need to complete a W-9 form. This is a one-page IRS form to provide your name, address, and SSN. The information on this form is used to issue you a 1099 form at the end of the year if you made more than $600. The 1099 form shows the gross income you earned in the year to report on your tax return. It does not reflect any fees you may have paid out or any refunds you may have issued to customers (Fiverr, 2023).

Whichever side hustle(s) you choose to pursue, you will need to decide on the appropriate method for tracking your revenue.

Deducting business expenses

An advantage of having a business is that you can deduct business expenses related to the business income that you earn to help reduce the income that you pay tax on. For example, if you used Fiverr or Upwork, you would have paid some fees to them that can be deducted as an expense of doing business. Common expenses like phone, internet, office supplies, materials, inventory, home office, travel, or other costs you incur to run your side hustle or business can also be deductible. Accountant's fees can be a deductible business expense as well.

I highly recommend speaking to your accountant before starting your side hustle to get an idea of what kind of expenses you can deduct for your particular business so you can begin keeping those receipts and tracking them on a regular basis. It's much easier to track things when you know what to look for, rather than wait until the end of the year to figure out what you can or cannot claim as an expense and then go looking for those receipts all at once. Planning ahead will save you time and stress.

You will need to keep the invoices or receipts for these costs and also track them on Excel or Google Sheets. If you are really serious about your side hustle, bookkeeping software/apps are available to help make tracking your revenue and expenses easier. These apps have a cost, but they are a deductible expense.

At the end of the year, provide your accountant with the Excel or Google Sheet with your business income and expenses so that they can properly report it on your tax return. If you're using an app, provide them with online access to your records.

Business payroll taxes

In Chapter 2, we discussed payroll taxes that get deducted from your paycheque as an employee. In the US, as a self-employed business owner, you will need to pay both the employee's share of the payroll taxes and the business' share of the payroll taxes, also known as self-employment tax. For 2022, social security is now calculated as 12.4% of net earnings. Net earnings are your gross income from self-employment minus your business expenses. Medicare is calculated as 2.9% of net earnings. For 2022, a total of 15.3% is to be remitted to the IRS. Half of the self-employment taxes are a deductible expense for the business (Orem, 2022).

In Canada, if you are self-employed, in 2022 you will pay the employee and business share of the CPP, which is 11.4% (5.7% x 2), on your net earnings (Government of Canada, 2022). The CPP gets calculated on your personal income tax return when you report your self employment income. You are not required to pay EI when you are self employed.

In both Canada and the US, income tax, which is separate from the payroll taxes discussed above, will also be calculated on your net earnings when you file your personal tax return. There may be a requirement to pay tax installments in advance, depending on where you live. Again, this would be a good topic to discuss with your local accountant.

Sales tax

Another tax to consider is sales tax. Again, depending on where you live and your business situation, you may need to charge sales tax on the goods or services you sell. Speak with your local accountant on whether this would apply to your business.

Other considerations

At some point, if your side hustle starts to make you some decent money and you're able to make it your full-time career, you should consider setting up a corporation for your business. There are more advantages to setting up a corporation for a business, like lower tax rates. However, there is more administrative work involved in having a corporation. Again, this is another conversation you would have with your accountant.

Mark Cuban – entrepreneur

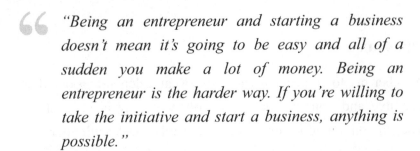

"Being an entrepreneur and starting a business doesn't mean it's going to be easy and all of a sudden you make a lot of money. Being an entrepreneur is the harder way. If you're willing to take the initiative and start a business, anything is possible."

— Mark Cuban

Mark Cuban is an American billionaire entrepreneur and TV personality on the show *Shark Tank*. He did not become a billionaire overnight. When he was 12, he ran his own side hustle selling garbage bags door-to-door. Later, he sold a variety of collectibles, from baseball cards to coins and stamps, to help pay for his college tuition. As a college student, he worked as a bartender and taught dance lessons to make extra money (Huddleston Jr., 2022). Everyone has to start somewhere.

Advantages of a business

There are some advantages to having a business:

- Your income is only limited by the amount of effort you put into the business. As a business owner, it's up to you to build your customer or subscriber base. The more customers you're able to get, the more revenue you can generate. With a job, you are limited by the wage or salary offered to you. You may get paid a bonus, but that depends on your employment agreement.

When I started working in an accounting firm, I saw many businesses' income and expenses. I was shocked that many companies were making millions in sales and were profitable! It was a real eye-opener.

- Business expenses can be deducted from your business income to reduce your income taxes.
- The hours can be more flexible as you make your own schedule, and you can also decide where you want to work.
- You control and make the decisions for the business.

Disadvantages of a business

The disadvantages of having a business:

- It takes time and effort to build your customer base. You will only get customers if you provide them with a product or service they need or want. You will have to research your customers and your competition. You'll have to invest in some marketing and manage social media.
- You're responsible for tracking your revenue and expenses and paying the appropriate amount of taxes. There's more administrative work involved.

- You may not make much money in the beginning, so you have to manage your cash carefully. You could be spending more than you are making. With a job, you get paid regularly, so you know when your money is coming in, but with a business, your sales can fluctuate.
- As your business grows, if you have employees, you will need to ensure you have good employees and make sure they get paid.
- If your customers have complaints, you will need to resolve them to keep your customers happy.
- There can be long hours and more stress as you have to deal with so many more things. With a job, once you go home, you don't need to think about your job again until your next shift. With a business, there really isn't a time you can stop thinking about your business.
- There is always the risk that your business cannot survive. If you're not able to get the customers to buy what you are offering, your chances of survival are not good. If your business doesn't survive, you could lose any money you invested in it. During the pandemic, many restaurants had to permanently close as they couldn't get customers to return to their restaurants.

Even though there is more risk and work involved in owning a business, most business owners, including myself, think the rewards outweigh the risks and disadvantages. It's now hard for me to imagine going back to work for someone else. I have to answer to my clients, but I have flexibility with my time and schedule.

If you plan to start a business, ensure that it's something you can do fairly easily without a lot of start-up costs. Find something you enjoy doing; otherwise, it won't work. Ensure you understand how to track your revenue and expenses for the business, as you will need to provide this information to your accountant for your tax filings.

It would be a good idea to have some money saved up first. If you plan to sell a product, you will need to pay for the cost of the materials or goods in advance before you can sell the product to your customer. In addition, you'll likely have to spend a bit on advertising to let people know about your business. Your savings will help to pay for these upfront costs.

How do we save? The details are in Chapter 4!

Chapter 4
Saving – Important, Yet Often Overlooked

"*The quickest way to double your money is to fold it over and put it back in your pocket.*"

— Will Rogers

"*Don't save what is left after spending, but spend what is left after saving.*"

— Warren Buffett

Now that you've made some money, what should you do with it? The first thing that comes to mind is to SPEND IT! We want to buy the latest fashions, electronics, games, movies, meals, and other things that we believe make us happy. We will talk about spending in Chapter 5. However, I would like to introduce the concept of saving, or "paying yourself first."

Saving is setting aside some of the money you have made so you can use it later. We'll discuss why this is so important and how to save. We'll look at how interest earned on savings is calculated. We'll also get into the different types of accounts in which you can save money, the tax advantages of saving, and how much to save. Unfortunately, many people don't save, which is one of the reasons they get into financial trouble.

Living paycheque to paycheque

According to a survey released by BDO Canada in 2022, 54% of Canadians live paycheque to paycheque (Dobson, 2022). In the US, as of December 2022, 64% of Americans live paycheque to paycheque (Dickler, 2023). Living paycheque to paycheque means you spend all your paycheque on needs and wants and do not save anything for the future. Your money comes in, and then it is all spent immediately. You must wait until your next paycheque arrives to have cash in your account again. This cycle keeps repeating, and people find it very hard to get out of living paycheque to paycheque.

Emergency savings

What will happen if you have a medical emergency and can't go to work? What if you lose your job because your employer can't afford to pay you anymore? When these things happen, you won't be able to get a paycheque. How will you pay for your groceries and rent?

Many are stressed and worried because their future is so uncertain, and they rely on their paycheque to survive. You need to prepare and plan ahead for medical emergencies and job losses so that you can deal with the problems as they occur. These situations are not in your control, but planning and preparing by saving *is* within your control. You can't just wait for the problem to hit and then react.

Imagine living in Florida, knowing hurricanes can destroy your home, but you have no action plan for what you will do when the hurricane does come. If you're living in Florida, you would already have supplies on hand to protect your house before the hurricane hits. In addition, you would have a plan detailing where to evacuate until the storm passes. Doing these things will ensure your safety and survival and the safety of your property.

We need to think and plan the same way when it comes to our money. We save or pay ourselves first before spending on things that are not critical. This money can be used in the future in case of an emergency. It provides a cushion you can fall back onto when a problem arises.

If you lose your job, you can apply for government programs for the unemployed, but the amounts you receive are not very significant, and they are only given for a short period of time. You really need some emergency savings in place to secure your financial safety and survival. If this isn't done, the results can be disastrous.

It's generally recommended to save 3 to 6 months' worth of your expenses in your emergency fund.

Saving for a specific purpose or goal

Another reason for saving would be for a specific goal or purpose. Perhaps you want to make a larger purchase in the future. You'll need to build your cash reserve to be able to pay for it later. College tuition or a new gaming console might be reasons to save.

How to save

Saving takes *time* and *discipline*. Consider opening a separate savings account, so you don't get tempted to spend all the funds in your chequing account. If you have income each month, the easiest way to save would be to ask your bank if they can make automatic monthly pre-authorized withdrawals from your chequing account to your savings account. This way, you don't need to think about saving as it is automatically done for you.

If you don't have income coming into your chequing account regularly, you will need to ask the bank teller or go into your online banking to transfer funds between the accounts.

If you get birthday money, allowance, or other cash gifts, put some of it in your savings account. Don't immediately spend it all.

Nuts about saving

I have an oak tree in front of my house. During autumn, the acorns fall to the ground. Squirrels gather them and hide them in my garden and wherever else they can find to store them so that they have food for the winter. One day my car wouldn't start, so I opened the hood to see what might be the problem. I found a bunch of acorns near the engine and several wires chewed up! I guess the thrifty squirrels wanted to keep their food warm. Squirrels are excellent planners and savers, but they are a big nuisance!

Interest income

You will earn interest if you put your money in a savings account. Interest is the price you pay to borrow money. In this situation, where you give your money to the bank to hold for you, the bank will pay you interest which is a reward or additional amount of money. The amount of interest paid depends on the interest rate, which constantly changes. At the time of writing this book, the interest rate on a savings account can be around 1 to 2% (MoneyGuide Network Inc., 2023).

Simple interest

There are different ways to calculate interest. One method is the *simple* interest calculation. Simple interest is interest on the amount you initially put in to save. For example, if $500 is put into a savings account for one year, which gives 1% interest, you would receive $5 of interest income ($500 x 1%). However, if you kept the $500 in the savings account for only two months, the amount of interest would be $0.83, which is a fraction of the $5 ($500 x 1% x 2 months/12 months).

The interest earned on savings accounts is usually not very much, but the primary purpose of the savings account is to set some money aside for future use.

Since interest is a type of income, you may have to pay tax on it in the year you receive it.

Compound interest – the snowball effect

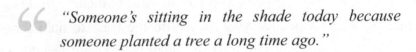

"Someone's sitting in the shade today because someone planted a tree a long time ago."

— Warren Buffett

Compound interest is another way to calculate interest. When interest compounds, it means you get interest on top of interest. Let's say you save $5,000 now in a retirement savings plan and keep it there for 40 years with an interest rate of 5% that compounds each year. In the first year, you would earn $250 of interest ($5,000 x 5%). You now have $5,250 in your account. In the second year, you earn 5% interest on the $5,250, which gives you $262.50 of interest. This represents interest on your original $5,000 deposit plus interest on the $250 of interest you earned in the first year. Each year, the interest keeps getting greater and greater due to the compounding. At the end of 40 years, you will have a balance of $35,199.95 in the retirement account! This means you made $30,199.95 in interest ($35,199.95 - $5,000) over these years without having to do anything except wait! This is referred to as passive income, as you did not have to perform any work to generate the interest income.

The formula for calculating the balance in your account after 40 years is $A = P(1+r/n)^{nt}$. P represents the principal amount you invested which is $5,000. R is the interest rate in a decimal format, which in this example is 0.05. N represents the number of times interest is compounded per year, which is once per year. T represents the time in years.

$$A = \$5,000 \, (1 + 0.05 / 1)^{(1)(40)}$$
$$A = \$5,000 \, (1.05)^{40}$$
$$A = \$5,000 \, (7.03999)$$
$$A = \$35,199.95$$

Note: There are various online compound interest calculators that you can use to check your calculations.

Let's change the scenario a bit. You invest $5,000 now and keep it in your retirement account for 40 years. You earn an annual interest rate of 5%, which compounds *monthly*. After 40 years, your balance will be $36,797.95.

$$A = \$5{,}000 \, (1 + 0.05 \, /12)^{(12)(40)}$$
$$A = \$5{,}000 \, (1.004167)^{480}$$
$$A = \$5{,}000 \, (7.35959)$$
$$A = \$36{,}797.95$$

By having interest compounded monthly (more often), that's $1,598 more interest than the previous example, where interest is compounded annually.

Now imagine that you invested $5,000 at the *beginning of each year* for 40 years in your retirement account, with an annual interest of 5% compounding *annually*. You would have $634,198.81 at the end of 40 years! This means you deposited a total of $200,000 of your money and earned $434,198.81 in interest income. The formula for calculating the future value (FV) of a series of payments (PMT) is:

$$FV = PMT \times \{[1 + r/n)^{nt} - 1] / (r/n)\} \times (1 + r/n)$$
$$FV = \$5{,}000 \times \{(1 + 0.05/1)^{(1)(40)} - 1] / (0.05/1)\} \times (1+0.05/1)$$
$$FV = \$5{,}000 \times \{(1.05)^{40} - 1] / 0.05\} \times 1.05$$
$$FV = \$5{,}000 \times 120.80 \times 1.05$$
$$FV = \$634{,}198.81$$

As you can see, this is huge! You can grow your money when you consistently save and invest regularly. Let your money work for you!

Let's say you don't start saving for retirement until later in life. Fast forward to the future, and you have 20 years before you want to retire. You decide you will deposit $10,000 at the beginning of each year for 20 years, for a total of $200,000. The annual interest rate is 5% compounded annually. Under this scenario, you would only have $347,192.52 in your account, of which $147,192.52 is interest.

$$FV = PMT \times \{[1 + r/n)^{nt} - 1] / (r/n)\} \times (1 + r/n)$$
$$FV = \$10,000 \times \{(1 + 0.05/1)^{(1)(20)} - 1] / (0.05/1)\} \times (1+0.05/1)$$
$$FV = \$10,000 \times \{(1.05)^{20} - 1] / 0.05\} \times 1.05$$
$$FV = \$10,000 \times 33.066 \times 1.05$$
$$FV = \$347,192.52$$

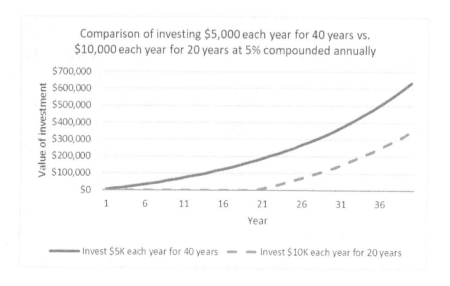

Comparison of investing $5,000 each year for 40 years vs. $10,000 each year for 20 years at 5% compounded annually

All the above theoretical examples illustrate the basic financial concept of the "time value of money." **The *more* you save, and** the *earlier* **you save, the more compound interest you can earn.** Investing the same principal amount of $200,000 later in life will result in $287,006.29 *less* interest. This is a very significant amount. Many individuals would have to work many years to earn this income, so why would you not want to save early? The more time you allow your money to grow, the more you will have at the end.

Here is a common analogy to help understand compound interest —think of it as a snowball rolling down a hill. Your initial savings is your first snowball. The compound interest is the snow that gathers as the ball rolls down the hill. The more it rolls, the bigger the snowball gets until it becomes a giant snow boulder.

Government pensions

In Chapter 2, we talked about contributing to the CPP in Canada or Social Security in the US, which is the federal pension plan that gets paid to you when you retire in your 60s. Although these pension plans pay you a monthly income, it will not be enough for you to live on. For example, in 2023, if you start receiving CPP at age 65, the government pays an average basic monthly retirement pension of $717.15 (Government of Canada, 2022).

In Canada, there is also the Old Age Security pension (OAS) that you may be eligible for if you meet the criteria, and it depends on your income at that time as well. For January to March 2023, OAS pays a maximum monthly payment of $687.56 if you are between the ages of 65 to 74 and have an annual income of less than $129,757 (Government of Canada, 2023).

If we combine the CPP and OAS, the possible monthly retirement pension the government would pay in 2023 if you meet the eligibility requirements is $1,404.

In the US, the average monthly social security benefit for January 2023 is expected to be $1,827 (Brandon, 2022).

Retirement savings

Government pensions aren't significant, so you will need to fund your own retirement to be able to cover your spending in your retirement years. In Canada, you can save for retirement through a Registered Retirement Savings Plan (RRSP). In the US, you can use an Individual Retirement Account (IRA).

There are also group retirement plans where your employer will contribute and possibly match the funds that you contribute to the group plan. In Canada, it's called a Group RRSP. In the US, it's the 401(k). Group plans are very advantageous, as your employer is helping you to save, and you can earn more income on the extra contributions. However, not all employers will offer these group plans.

RRSPs can be set up at a bank or other financial institution once you are 18 years old. For IRAs, there is no minimum age limit to set one up, but you need to have employment or self-employment income, and your parent will need to set one up on your behalf if you are under the age of 18 (Anspach, 2022).

Tax advantages for retirement savings

There are several tax advantages when you put money into these retirement accounts. You get a tax deduction on the amount you contribute to these accounts that reduces the income you have to pay tax on. Depending on your situation, you'll pay less or possibly no tax, and you could get a tax refund.

You can invest the money in a retirement account to give you interest or other types of income, such as dividends. The interest or other income you earn on the amounts you save does not get taxed while they stay in your retirement account.

Tax is paid when you take the money out, which is generally when you retire.

There are contribution limits based on your employment or self-employment income and government limits. The government has set some limitations on how much you can contribute to these savings accounts as they still need to be able to collect some tax from you to pay for the various services that everyone uses.

Roth IRA

You can put your money into other types of government savings plans. Contributions to *Roth* IRAs in the US are not tax deductible. But when you take the funds out of the Roth IRA, they do not get taxed as long as you are older than 59.5 years old and have held the Roth IRA account for at least five years (Woodfield, 2021).

Tax-free savings account

In Canada, if you are 18 or older, there is the tax-free savings account (TFSA) where your contributions are not tax-deductible. However, you can withdraw the funds from the TFSA at any age without paying tax and without penalty.

Both a Roth IRA and a TFSA can hold investments such as mutual funds, stocks, bonds, and cash. Any income that you earn while saving in these plans is not taxed. These plans also have contribution limits that vary. TFSAs are better savings accounts than regular savings accounts as you can invest in different types of investments, and the income you earn is tax-free.

Which is the best savings account?

If you had the option to save in a retirement savings account or a regular savings account, which would you choose?

If you save in a retirement savings account, you can take advantage of not having to pay tax on the interest while you save to get more compounded interest. You also get a tax deduction that helps reduce your income taxes in the year you contribute to the retirement savings account. If you get a tax refund, you can use the refund to invest further into your retirement savings.

If you save the $5,000 in a regular savings account, you would have to pay tax on the interest you earn each year, so you would have less money in your account and less for compounding interest, which generally means less money in your account.

However, you also have to consider your purpose for saving. The retirement savings account is the obvious choice if you are saving for retirement. On the other hand, if you are saving for an emergency fund or tuition, you should put your money in a regular savings account so you can get to it quickly, without any penalties or having to pay tax when you withdraw it.

How much should you be saving?

How much you save depends on your situation and stage in life. There's a popular savings rule out there called the 50/30/20 rule which is a way of splitting up your money into three categories. It states that 50% of your money should go to "needs," meaning basic things you absolutely need to pay for to live or survive, such as groceries, rent, utilities, and basic clothing. And 30% of your money should go to "wants," which are things that you want but don't necessarily need to live, such as restaurants, games, movies, and designer clothing. The wants make your life more enjoyable. The remaining 20% of your money would go to savings for the emergency fund, a big-ticket item, or retirement.

The 50/30/20 rule does not make sense if you are a teen living with your parents who support you. If your parents provide you with food, shelter, and clothing, you don't have any "needs" to spend on. That leaves "wants" and "savings" where you can allocate your money. This allocation depends on your money or savings goals.

When I worked as a cashier, I was fortunate to have my parents supporting me with my basic needs. I saved and then spent about

50% of my earnings on my university tuition, which was my "want." To my parents, it was more of a "need," as getting a higher education meant more opportunities for a higher paying job or career leading to future financial security. I could have lived without paying tuition. The level of importance on the "want" list was very high, though, as there was a future benefit for me.

About 15% of my earnings went to buying bus fare to get to school and my part-time job at CT. This again would be a want for me, but another high priority "want." I didn't need bus fare to live and survive, but it was very helpful to have this so I could get my education and get to work to pay for the education. For some people, the cost of transportation to get to work to earn income to pay for food and shelter would be a need.

About 10% went to buying the occasional lunch, drinks, and shopping at the Eaton Centre, a huge mall close to the university in downtown Toronto. This was another "want," as it wasn't necessary for me to get food at the food court. I could have made and brought my lunch, which I actually did most of the time. It also wasn't necessary for me to buy a leather coat that was on sale during Christmas, as I already had another winter coat that was perfectly fine.

The remaining 25% I saved in my RRSP and bank account.

It can be tricky to distinguish between a need and a want. This is where many people get confused. Many think they "need" the latest and greatest smartphone, but what is the reason for this need? Would they be able to survive and fulfill their basic communication needs using a smartphone from two or three years ago instead of the one that just came on the market? New smartphones are launched every year. Are you buying the latest smartphone as it seems like the popular thing to do?

What are your saving goals?

In a few years, you will become an adult and have to think about paying for your needs. Your money allocation may or may not be 50/30/20. What do you have in mind for saving?

Write down your saving goals and set a deadline for reaching these goals. Writing them down encourages you to plan for the future and gets you thinking about what you need to do to get there.

Key takeaways

Saving is an excellent habit to start forming now, as it will make life a lot easier for you in the future. When you put money aside, you can invest it to help grow your money. Saving early and on a regular basis will help to grow your money much faster than if you decided to save later in life. Depending on the account you save in, you can also save on taxes, which will also increase your cash. You will need to determine the appropriate amount to save based on your situation and your money goals. I recommend saving more than what you spend on your wants.

If you spend more than you make, you will get into a problem called debt, which is not a good road to go down.

Chapter 5
The Dark Side of Credit Cards, Spending, and Debt

 "Once you start down the dark path, forever will it dominate your destiny."

— Yoda

What is debt?

Debt results when you borrow money from someone else and need to pay them back. Why do people get into debt? One of the reasons why people get into debt is that they spend more than they have in income and savings. How is this possible? They will use a credit card, which is borrowed money. Credit cards are very easy to use but come with many rules that are not easy to understand. Some people don't understand these credit card rules, which gets them into a lot of financial trouble.

We will talk about the main things you need to know about credit cards so you do not find yourself in debt.

Another reason people get into debt is because of impulse shopping. They buy things without really thinking about whether they need them. They also don't keep track of their spending, so things can get out of hand very quickly. There are a number of reasons why people spend on impulse. We're going to discuss some of them so that you can be more aware of the triggers and use the tips provided to help control your spending so that you can keep more of your money in your bank account.

Credit cards

Credit cards make it very easy for us to spend money that doesn't belong to us. We can buy things now and pay for them later. It's just so convenient. In addition, the rewards and incentives on the credit cards, such as cash back and various loyalty points and discounts, lead us to think we are saving or getting back something for spending. The more we spend, the more we will be rewarded. To get your own credit card, you must be at least 18 years old and complete a credit card application (Equifax, 2023).

Credit report

Once the application is completed, the credit card company will review your credit report to determine if they will approve and give you a credit card. A credit report generally contains personal information such as your name and date of birth and a listing of other credit cards or other debt you may have. Credit reports can also show information about who has accessed your credit report, whether you filed for bankruptcy in the past, your debt repayments, and any debts you have not paid that have been turned over to collection agencies (Equifax, 2023).

You can request a copy of your free credit report from credit bureaus such as Equifax and TransUnion to check that the information in the report is accurate (Government of Canada, 2022).

Credit score

In addition to looking at the credit report, the credit card company will also look at your credit score to determine if they will give you the credit card. A credit score is a number from 300 to 850 that rates how well you handle debt (The Investopedia Team, 2022). The credit score is based on the information in your credit report. You can think of the credit report as a report card, and the credit score is the grade you receive on the report card relating to your debt history. Generally, a good credit score of 700 or higher means you have a good credit history and you pay back your debts. A lower credit score means you have a bad credit history and you don't pay back your debts.

Why is your credit score important? You'll get better loan interest rates with a good credit score. Lower credit scores will result in higher interest rates being charged on your loans and debt, as the lender is worried that you may not be able to pay them back. They charge more interest for this additional risk. Potential employers may also check your score to determine if you are reliable (The Investopedia Team, 2022).

If the credit card company sees that you have a lot of debt, or you haven't been paying your debts back, and you have a low credit score, they likely will not give you the credit card as there is a high probability you won't pay back the debt on the new credit card.

You can obtain your credit score for free from the credit bureaus or other online credit score companies to help you monitor your credit score (Equifax, 2023).

Credit limit

You will receive the credit card in the mail once you are approved. The credit card comes with a credit limit which is the amount being lent to you and the maximum that can be spent on the card. It's up to you if you want to spend some of it, all of it, or none of it. If you spend the limit, you will not be able to make any further purchases on the card until you pay back some or all of the balance on the card.

The credit limit is based on different factors like your credit score, income, debt, length of credit history, and rate of application for other forms of credit. For example, if you have a high credit score, high income, and low debt, you will likely get a higher credit limit as you are more likely to pay your bills on time (CIBC, 2023).

Billing period

Each month, at the end of the billing period, the credit card company will send you a statement, which is a report that lists all the purchases you made with the card during the billing period. The billing period is usually 30 or 31 days and can fall any time during the month. For example, you could have a billing period from January 6th to February 5th. This billing period has 31 days.

You will be given a "grace period," which is usually 21 days from the end of the billing period, to pay the credit card company back for the purchases you made without having any interest charged on the purchases. If the end of the billing period is February 5th, you will need to pay the credit card company by February 26th, which is also known as the due date, to avoid interest charges.

Interest charges

The credit card has an annual percentage rate (APR) of interest that will be charged if you don't pay for all your purchases by the due date. A typical APR is 20%, but this does not mean you get charged 20% interest once a year. If you always pay the balance on time before the due date, no interest will ever be charged. However, if you do not pay by the due date, the interest charge will appear on the next credit card statement. To understand how the interest is calculated, let's look at the following steps:

First, interest is calculated daily, so you will need to convert the APR to a daily rate. The credit card statement may already disclose the daily rate along with the APR. To calculate the daily rate, take the APR and divide it by 365 days in a year. In this example, 20% / 365 = 0.05479% daily interest rate (Lambarena, 2021).

Next, determine your average daily balance (Lambarena, 2021). It's the sum of your balances each day divided by the number of days in the billing period. There are online calculators you can use to help you figure this out. For this illustration, let's say the average daily balance is $10,000.

Then you multiply the average daily balance by your daily interest rate and then multiply by the number of days in the billing period (Lambarena, 2021). So, $10,000 x 0.05479% x 31 days = $169.85 of interest that would be charged at the end of the billing period. Depending on the credit card company, the interest can be compounded on a daily or monthly basis as well, so the interest would actually be higher than $169.85. Remember, this is one month of interest. Interest will continue to be calculated each month until the whole credit card balance is paid off.

Let's take a simple example to compare interest on debt vs. interest on savings. Let's assume the $10,000 credit card debt doesn't get paid for a whole year, and the interest at an annual rate of 20% compounds daily. The credit card debt at the end of the year would be $12,213.36, which means $2,213.36 of this is interest expense (Hazell, 2022).

If we only save $5,000 for a year with an annual interest rate of 5%, compounded monthly, the balance of our savings at the end of the year would be $5,255.81. Interest income would be $255.81 (Hazell, 2022).

Compound interest is good if we save money but bad if we have debt. As you will note, the 20% on credit card debt is a much higher rate than the 5% in our savings example. We will pay more interest on debt than we receive interest on the money we save. We also know that the higher the amount that interest is calculated on, and the more often it compounds, it will result in higher interest. The $2,213.36 interest on the debt is almost ten times more than the $255.81 interest on the savings due to the higher credit card balance and the compounding being done daily vs. monthly.

TIP

It is best not to incur debt, but if you do, it is advisable to pay down the debt first before doing any saving. Generally, the debt will cost you more than the income you will receive in savings.

Paying your credit card bill

You can pay the credit card balance using online banking, but don't wait until the actual due date to do this. Instead, try paying a few days before the due date to allow the bank time to process the payment, which could take up to a few days. If you pay on the due date and the bank takes two days to process the payment —perhaps because of a holiday or weekend when they are closed —you are considered to have paid late and will be charged interest on the balance until the payment gets processed. It is best to pay on time to improve your credit score and not get charged interest.

Alternatively, you can set up pre-authorized payments with the credit card company. The funds are automatically drawn from your bank account to pay your credit card balance on the due date, so you will never have a late payment.

Cash advances

You can go to the ATM and use your credit card to take out cash. This is called a cash advance. Transferring money from your credit card to your bank account can also be considered a cash advance even though you don't make a physical cash withdrawal. It's another type of lending that the credit card company provides (National Bank, 2023).

Please note that if you took cash advances out from your credit card, the cash advances would be charged at a higher interest rate, perhaps 2 – 3% higher than what would be charged on your purchases, as discussed above. You'll need to check your statement to determine the rate charged for cash advances. However, interest is charged from the day you make the cash advance, even if you pay your card balance in full by the due date (National Bank, 2023).

Cash advances also don't earn reward points or discounts (National Bank, 2023). It's an expensive way to borrow money, so I would not advise taking cash advances from credit cards.

Source: (Bonnet, 2020)

Retail store credit cards

Retail store credit cards have higher interest rates than typical credit cards. A typical credit card can have a rate of 20%, but a retail store card can have a rate as high as 30%! (Credit Cards Canada, 2023). Therefore, if you don't pay your balance off in full, you will pay more interest, and it will take you longer to pay the balance than a typical credit card.

Most people like retail credit cards as perhaps they are offered a good discount on their first purchase using the card, or they get a large number of points they can use for future purchases, or maybe they don't have to pay interest for a few months if they carry a balance.

You need to carefully weigh these benefits against the cost of a higher interest rate. If you can pay off your balance each month, getting discounts and points can be worth it. If you cannot pay your balance each month, steer clear of these cards, as the interest is just too high!

Minimum payment

On the credit card statement, it will show a minimum payment that you have to make. This is the minimum amount you must pay if you can't pay your balance in full. The minimum payment will be the higher of (i) a flat dollar amount, say $10, plus any interest and fees, or (ii) a percentage of your outstanding balance, perhaps 3%. Your credit card agreement will tell you how they calculate the minimum payment (Government of Canada, 2022). If you do not pay the minimum amount, you are at risk of having your interest rate increased. Your credit score may be negatively affected. You may also lose the benefit of any promotional rate offer you were given, or your credit card could be cancelled. You will also be charged late payment fees (Tsosie, 2022).

Paying just the minimum amount means it will take you longer to pay off your credit card balance, and you will pay more interest. Credit card statements will note on the statement how long it will take you to pay off your balance in full if you only make the minimum payment.

I came across a credit card statement that had a balance of $4,945.33. The APR was 20.97%, and the minimum payment was $108.79. The statement said, "*At your current rates of interest, if you make only your minimum payment by its due date each month, it will take approximately **50 years and 9 months** to repay the statement balance shown on this statement.*" That's a long time! You will not be able to retire if you only pay the minimum amount! Again, it's just best practice to pay your balance in full or pay as much as you can, as fast as possible, to avoid or reduce the interest charges, which are not beneficial to you.

Other credit card fees

Other credit card fees to watch out for are annual fees and foreign transaction fees. Some credit cards come with annual fees you must pay each year just for using the card. The cards that have more rewards are usually the ones that have annual fees. If you have a basic credit card that doesn't give you much incentive to use it, it will likely have no annual fee. The average annual fee can range from $99 to $150 (Choi, 2022).

My mom was offered a credit card by her bank, which she accepted. However, they did not tell her the card had an annual fee. When she received her statement, she was shocked to see the fee, so she immediately contacted the bank to cancel the card. She doesn't spend an enormous amount on credit cards, so the rewards or incentives she would have received for using the card would be less than the annual fee, which was not worth it for her.

Foreign transaction fees are fees charged by the credit card company if you make a purchase outside your home country. For example, if you buy something online from a foreign country using a credit card, you will be charged a foreign transaction fee that can typically be between 1% and 3% of the purchase amount (CIBC, 2023). So just be mindful of where you are purchasing items online, as we easily have access to a global marketplace, and you could end up having to pay foreign transaction fees.

Credit card statement

When you receive your statement, you need to review it as soon as possible to ensure there are no billing errors or fraudulent charges. One of my clients had some fraudulent Uber Eats charges placed on their card. I would review their statement each month and check the activity to the receipts and invoices. Two charges didn't have receipts. When I asked my client about this, they said they did not make those purchases. He then contacted the credit card company to let them know about this. He was later given credit on his account so that he did not have to pay for those charges.

It's a good idea to keep your receipts for at least two months to check the amounts to the credit card statement to ensure what was billed matches the receipts. If you notice some charges that should not be there or are inaccurate, you have up to 30 days to report them to the credit card company to resolve them.

Impulse shopping

In addition to using credit cards, another reason why people get into debt is by impulse shopping. Impulse shopping is when you buy something you didn't plan on buying. There are several reasons why people impulse shop. Marketing and advertising play a significant role in impulse shopping. Your emotions can also cause you to impulse shop. Social media or peer pressure can also be a factor.

Marketing and advertising

If you went to the mall to get a pair of sneakers, but you also bought a pair of jeans as they were on sale, that's an example of impulse shopping. *"Today only, 50% off!"* You already have ten pairs of jeans, but who can resist a 50% discount? That's a considerable saving! Well, you actually didn't save. You spent!

Stores will mark up their prices, then provide a discount to make you think you are getting a good deal. In addition, they put a time limit on the sale, creating a sense of urgency to buy immediately. Sales do end, but they come back at a later date. When you're about to buy something on sale, pause and ask yourself if you really need it at that moment or if you can wait to buy it. Try to objectively determine if this is a "want" or a "need".

TIPS

- *Pay for items with cash so you can see your money leaving your pocket. Avoid paying with debit or credit cards. They may be convenient and come with rewards, but they make us spend more. Only use credit cards if you are responsible enough to pay your credit card bills before the due date.*
- *Only spend what you can afford to pay back on time, as you do not want to incur interest charges.*

Have you ever bought some candy, chocolate, or a magazine while waiting in line at the grocery store? I have. I had no intention of buying those things when I went into the store, but somehow, I ended up buying them.

TIPS

- *I learned about this merchandising technique in the marketing class I took at university. Grocery stores strategically place these small items at the checkout because they know you will be waiting there. You may be hungry or bored while waiting, so the likelihood of you buying these items will be high. These items don't cost very much either, so we buy on impulse without thinking too much about it. "No big deal, it's just a few bucks!" Well, a few bucks here and there can add up over time. Since I learned about this technique, I stopped purchasing items at the checkout.*
- *Don't go grocery shopping on an empty stomach. If you shop when you are hungry, you will likely buy more than you need. Eat first before shopping!*

Emotions

Impulse buying can also happen based on emotion. When you are feeling down or need some cheering up, you think buying that designer top or that piece of jewelry will make you look and feel better. Many feel they need to buy something to make them feel joy or happiness. You may feel happy at the moment, but the happiness is short-lived. The next time you feel down, you shop again to lift your spirits.

When I was working in various CPA firms, their offices would be in areas with malls or shops. Often, during lunch, I would walk around the mall "window-shopping." This window-shopping was my relief from the stress at work. There was always something on sale. About 25% of the time, I made a purchase even though I did not need it. I would say to myself, "*I deserve a reward for working so hard.*" This resulted in a closet full of clothes, some of which I barely wore.

Over the years, I have donated some of these clothes to local charities so someone else could use them and keep them from landfills. In hindsight, it would have been better if I didn't purchase them in the first place.

Many now use online shopping to help temporarily cure their blues. With just a few clicks, you can have that item at your doorstep in a matter of days.

TIPS

- *To stop emotional impulse buying, put the items in your cart, but don't finalize the sale. Wait until tomorrow to come back to the cart to see if you still want to buy those items.*
- *In the meantime, try to talk to someone about your feelings and figure out what might be causing these emotions. Having a conversation may help you to feel better.*
- *You can write down your thoughts in a journal. I find journaling helps me when I'm trying to deal with many thoughts.*

- *We know online shopping is not a solution to your worries. It will only create financial problems, which will, in turn, create anxiety, stress, and more negative emotions. So emotional impulse shopping should be stopped.*

Social media

Social media is another reason why people impulse shop. With a tap of our phones, we are instantly connected to the world. We can see what our friends or favourite celebrities did on their latest Instagram and Facebook posts. Everyone seems to have the latest video game. They seem so happy and look like they are having so much fun! This makes us experience FOMO (fear of missing out). We want to fit in and don't want to feel left out, so we impulsively go and buy the new game as well.

Also, many businesses will have ads on social media to sell their goods and services. Businesses realize that many eyes are on social media, so it is no surprise that you will find many things to buy.

I gave my teenage son my old smartphone, which was several years old. He actually had no objections to using it. I was surprised he did not ask me for the latest and greatest phone. It was a relief that I didn't have to break my budget for new tech.

TIPS

- *Another thing you can do to stop impulse spending is to reduce the time you spend on social media. Instead, find a hobby or project you want to work on that will help to keep you busy. Maybe get that part-time job or start that side hustle.*
- *One trend in 2023, as reported by the show* Good Morning America, *is that some Gen Zs are now downgrading their smartphones to older model flip phones that can't access the internet. The people who have tried this say that they at first experienced FOMO, but the change has helped their mental health, and they can work on things they've been previously putting off because they were constantly on social media.*

Debt trap

Joe was a skilled tradesperson who made almost $100,000 a year. After taxes, he received about $75K. He spent 110% of the $75K, which means he spent more than he made. As a result, he was in constant debt. He racked up $20K of credit card debt, including interest that started to snowball, as he only paid the minimum payment required each month.

I advised him to get a line of credit from the bank (a type of loan) to pay off the credit card debt. The interest on the line of credit at that time was around 5%, which was much cheaper than what the credit card charged at 20%. This would help to cut down on the interest and make it easier to pay off the debt. Joe thought this was a great idea and immediately paid off the credit card debt with the line of credit.

I also advised him to stop using credit cards to make purchases. Guess what Joe did next? He started spending on the credit card again and racking up more debt!! Now he needs to pay the bank loan and the new credit card charges. This pattern went on for years. He didn't change his ways and can't escape the debt trap.

Environmental impact

This is something we don't really think about, but impulse shopping also has a negative effect on the environment. All the electronics, clothes, goods, etc. that we buy require the earth's resources to make them. These items are then put into landfills as waste in a few years or less when we no longer want them.

Here are a few facts regarding the negative environmental impact of the fashion industry (Earthday, 2023):

- The fashion industry produces 150 billion garments a year, and 87% (40 million tons) end up in a landfill where they smoulder and pollute the air or an incinerator.
- Only 1% of all discarded clothing is actually recycled.
- The average person buys 60% more clothing items than they did 15 years ago but keeps them for only half as long. The average garment may be worn as few as 10 times before disposal.

- Fashion is one of the most polluting of all industries. Clothing is manufactured with highly toxic dyes and heavy metals that are flushed into clean water streams, rivers, and aquifers, where they sicken people and animals, harm ecosystems, and cause biodiversity loss.

Here are a few facts regarding the negative environmental impact of technology (our electronic devices – smartphones, tablets, and laptops) (Okafor, 2022):

- Minerals need to be mined from the earth to make our electronic devices. Mining is responsible for deforestation, landscape degradation, water pollution, and the release of vast quantities of carbon dioxide, carbon monoxide, and other harmful gases and contaminants into the air.
- Miners are exposed to noise pollution and the toxic chemicals involved in mining, and many suffer from health problems.
- Manufacturers require a massive amount of energy to turn the materials into the electronic devices we use.
- Globally, we are throwing away $62.5 billion of electronic waste every year into landfills, or they are burned in dumps. These dumps emit methane and other carbon emissions. The discarded devices leach chemicals, including mercury, that blend with other wastewater contaminants, which can then get into waterways. The dumps are usually located out of sight, around some of the planet's poorest and most

vulnerable people, which again endangers human
health.

- A small proportion of electronic devices are recycled.

Not only is there a financial cost to us when we spend on things
we don't necessarily need, but there is also an environmental cost
that will hurt us in the future when our planet degrades further
and becomes uninhabitable. In addition, there is a human cost,
where people are exposed to dangerous chemicals and toxins and
suffer health issues.

Hopefully, we can consider all these things the next time we plan
to spend money on wants. The less we spend on wants, the more
we improve our financial future and the future of our planet.

Debt is a terrible trap to fall into. It's very hard to get out of debt
once it starts. We can avoid debt by doing the following:

- Pay for things with cash or debit instead of using a
  credit card, unless you are responsible enough to pay
  your credit card bill on time
- Limit the purchase of "wants" to only those we can
  afford to pay.
- Be mindful of impulse spending – watch your emotions,
  and look out for marketing tactics.
- Be confident and proud of the person that you are. Don't
  measure your worth by material items. Don't let peer
  pressure or other societal expectations dictate what you
  should do or buy.
- Manage and control your spending using a budget.

What's a budget? A budget is an excellent tool for helping you determine what you need to save and spend based on your money goals, income, and expenses.

Chapter 6
Budgeting – Where Did All My Money Go?

 "I'm stuck between 'I need to save money' and 'You only live once.'"

— Anonymous

What is a budget?

We've talked about making money, saving, and spending. So how can we organize or keep track of all this so that we have money saved, have enough to spend on our needs, and have some to spend on our wants? A budget is an excellent tool that can help us sort this out. We can create a monthly or annual budget. A budget is a planning tool that is made *before* you do your spending and saving. It's based on your money goals.

You will record the income you expect to come in, the expenses or purchases you plan to make, and the amount you plan to save. It helps prioritize your spending and ensures you have enough money to spend on the things you need. Once you have this plan for allocating your money, you will try to follow it as best as possible. The budget figures should be as realistic as possible.

After the month is over, you will go back to your budget and then write down the actual amounts you earned, spent, and saved. Any large differences between what you budgeted and what actually happened should be reviewed carefully and adjusted for in the next budget you do. The more specific you can be about the items you are spending on, the better, so you can see exactly where the money is going.

Let's look at how we can prepare a budget, revise it, and track it to our actual spending to better manage our money. We'll also look into inflation and its impact on our budget.

Sarah's first budget

Let's say Sarah just finished high school and has a full-time job paying $30,000 a year, which is about the average annual salary for a recent high school graduate in the US and Canada (Statista, 2022) (Talent, 2023).

Let's also estimate that payroll and income taxes will be about $6,000 for the year, which means her take-home pay is $24,000/year or $2,000/month. She doesn't have any debt, and she lives with her parents. Her parents have asked her to pay them $750 for rent, $38 for internet, and $75 for utilities each month. She will need to buy her own groceries and pay her other costs. She plans to go on a vacation and travel at the end of the year.

She makes her first attempt at creating a budget which looks something like this:

Monthly budget – First attempt	Budget	% of income
Income after taxes	$2,000	
Expenses – needs		
Rent	750	
Groceries	300	
Utilities (gas, water, electricity)	75	
Cell phone	75	
Internet	38	
Transit fare	150	
Basic clothing and shoes	100	
Personal hygiene products	50	
Total needs	1,538	77%
Saving		
Regular saving – emergency fund	100	
Regular saving – vacation	100	
Retirement saving	100	
Total saving	300	15%
Expenses – wants		
Restaurants, clubs	200	
Haircut	50	
Additional or designer clothing, bags, accessories, shoes	200	
Games	100	
Movies	20	
Gym membership	50	
Other	50	
Total wants	670	34%
Total payments	2,508	
Overspending	($508)	

Based on this budget, Sarah's income after taxes is $2,000/month, but her spending is estimated to be $2,508/month. Therefore, there is an overspending of $508, so some items need to be reduced or eliminated.

Where do you think the spending can be reduced? Needs are the basic essentials you have to pay for to live. There may be a possibility that she could ask her parents to lower the rent since they are her family.

In terms of savings, we know it's important to save for emergencies and retirement, so she shouldn't get rid of those amounts. On the other hand, vacations are discretionary spending, meaning it's not absolutely necessary, so perhaps this may need to be eliminated for this year. Maybe she can plan for that vacation next year.

The wants are where we have the most flexibility for adjusting our budget. These are the items we would like to have but are not critical. Each person will need to review their priorities in terms of their wants and adjust their budget accordingly. Sarah can eliminate some things entirely or significantly reduce some costs. Her lifestyle will change slightly, but it's wise to live within her means instead of overspending and going into debt. These changes won't significantly impact her life.

Some of you may think that Sarah's life is boring and not fun as she can't spend much on her wants. Well, Sarah can go out to restaurants and clubs to have some fun, but less often than she would like. She has the internet and her cell phone, which she can use to chat with her friends, and can watch all types of media. Sarah will need to keep an open mind regarding the changes.

When the COVID-19 pandemic was declared in March 2020, nonessential businesses had to shut down. People had to isolate themselves as much as possible, only going out for necessities such as food and medical needs. Many people were getting laid off from their jobs, which meant a paycheque was not coming. The government stepped in to provide some financial assistance to those that qualified.

Like many, my family was affected by the shutdowns. I had advised my sons' father that we needed to cut costs like cable TV to stay financially afloat during this pandemic. He was upset when I suggested this and was not happy at all. He couldn't believe that we could not afford to pay for cable TV. What was he going to watch while we were all stuck at home?

I cancelled the cable TV. A week later, I didn't hear any complaints. We had the internet to stream the news and other shows. We saved $60/month by cutting an expense we did not miss and have never reinstated.

Change is not easy, but if you keep an open mind, it could actually be a good thing.

Sarah's revised budget

Monthly budget – Second attempt	Budget	% of income
Income after taxes	$2,000	
Expenses – needs		
Rent	750	
Groceries	350	
Utilities (gas, water, electricity)	75	
Cell phone	75	
Internet	38	
Transit fare	150	
Basic clothing and shoes	100	
Personal hygiene products	50	
Total needs	1,588	79%
Saving		
Regular saving – emergency fund	100	
Regular saving – vacation	–	
Retirement saving	100	
Total saving	200	10%
Expenses – wants		
Restaurants, clubs	100	
Haircut	25	
Additional or designer clothing, bags, accessories, shoes	–	
Games	50	
Movies	–	
Gym membership	–	
Other	37	
Total wants	212	11%
Total payments	2,000	
Overspending	$ –	

As Sarah cannot control most of the costs related to her needs, you'll notice that most of the wants in the revised budget have been eliminated or reduced, including the vacation plans. In addition, groceries have been increased to replace some of the restaurant meals that were removed. In the wants, there is an amount for "other." This is just a small reserve for unexpected costs.

There isn't a lot in the savings, but it is better than nothing.

Her budget is now balanced, meaning her income, or money in is equal to her expenses, or money out. This is just one variation of what her budget could look like. Each person will need to determine where they will adjust their budget based on their personal circumstances and goals.

Following the budget

Now that Sarah has her revised budget, she needs to follow it. This means that if she wrote in her budget that she would spend $100 on restaurant meals and drinks this month, she should only spend up to $100 on meals and drinks. She can spend less than $100, but not more. If she spends more, the chances of her going into debt are higher because the amount of income she's receiving does not change, so she needs to spend according to her plan.

She'll also have to consider how many restaurant meals the $100 can cover. Fast-food restaurant meals are priced lower than those at an upscale or full-service restaurant where you have a waiter or waitress serving you. This means she can eat out more often at fast-food restaurants than at a full-service restaurant. For example, she might spend $15 for one meal at a fast-food restaurant, so she could potentially have about six meals in a month at a fast-food restaurant. At a full-service restaurant, she may spend $50 for one meal. If she had eaten at a full-service restaurant twice that month, she would have spent her restaurant budget and should only eat out again the next month.

Waiters and waitresses typically receive tips if they provide good service. You will need to factor in tips as part of the cost of a restaurant meal. It's up to you how much you want to tip a server. The general consensus is to tip your server between 15 – 20% of the pre-tax amount on the bill (Gillespie, 2022). Some tip less than that range if they feel the service wasn't great. Some will tip more than 20% if they feel they had an excellent experience at the restaurant. Just double-check that your bill doesn't already have a tip or gratuity automatically charged by the restaurant. You may not want to tip extra if the tip is already part of the bill.

Comparing actual costs to the budget

At the end of every month, Sarah should track what she actually spent and compare it to her budget. This will help her to identify any potential money problems that could occur. She will need to take out her receipts for the items she spent that month.

It's a good idea to keep all monthly receipts in an envelope or folder to easily find them in one spot. Sort the receipts by the type of expense, e.g., grocery receipts in one pile and restaurant bills in another. Then add the receipts in each pile and put the totals each month into the "actual" column of the budget. Some things like the rent and utilities she pays her parents will not have receipts. She will just record the amounts she paid them. Once all the amounts she spent have been recorded, she can see where she may have veered off the path.

Here's what Sarah's budget to actual comparison looks like:

Monthly budget – actual vs. budget	Budget	Actual	Variance
Income after taxes	$2,000	$2,000	$ –
Expenses – needs			
Rent	750	750	–
Groceries	350	300	(50)
Utilities (gas, water, electricity)	75	75	–
Cell phone	75	75	–
Internet	38	38	–
Transit fare	150	150	–
Basic clothing and shoes	100	75	(25)
Personal hygiene products	50	30	(20)
Total needs	1,588	1,493	(95)
Saving			
Regular saving – emergency fund	100	100	–
Regular saving – vacation	–	–	–
Retirement saving	100	100	–
Total saving	200	200	-
Expenses – wants			
Restaurants, clubs	100	200	100
Haircut	25	–	(25)
Additional or designer clothing, bags, accessories, shoes	–	–	–
Games	50	–	(50)
Movies	–	–	–
Gym membership	–	–	–
Other	37	20	(17)
Total wants	212	220	8
Total payments	2,000	1,913	(87)
Extra money	$ –	$ 87	$87

The variance column is the difference between her actual and budgeted spending. There is a negative $50 in groceries, which means she spent $50 less than what she planned to spend on groceries. Part of this is because she ate out more than she had anticipated. She spent $200 eating out, but her budget was $100. She needs to be careful of her spending on meals in the future. She also cut her grocery bill by using some coupons and price matching. And luckily, some of the groceries she needed were on sale that month. She decided to forego the games and haircut this month, which saved her $75. She can always get these in another month.

In the end, she saved a total of $87 from overall less spending! She spent $100 more on meals but made up for this by spending less on other things. This extra money should go toward her emergency fund savings.

Inflation

Something else you may have noticed about Sarah's revised budget is that her needs are a significant portion of the budget – 79%, which is more than the suggested 50%. This is, unfortunately, the reality we all face now. The cost of living has drastically increased over the past few years. Due to inflation, things generally cost more now than they did in the past. Inflation is a persistent rise in the average level of prices for goods and services over time (Bank of Canada, 2020).

The chart below shows how inflation has changed the price of a cup of coffee over time. As you will notice, the price continues to increase as the years go on.

Year	1970	1980	1990	2000	2010	2022
Price	$0.25	$0.45	$0.75	$1.00	$1.25	$1.85

Source: (Fernando, 2023).

To measure inflation, we look at the consumer price index (CPI) and how quickly it is rising. The CPI tracks how much the average household spends and how that spending changes over time. The government has a virtual shopping basket that includes the typical things people buy or pay for, such as food, rent, transportation, utilities, clothing, and medical care. Each month the total cost of this basket is added up, and the changes in price each month are tracked. The percentage change in the CPI is a measure of inflation (Bank of Canada, 2021).

For example, one year, the basket of goods and services the CPI uses costs $100. The following year, the same basket costs $102. This means the average annual inflation rate is 2% as the cost of the basket of goods increased by $2 ($2/$100 = 2%). The central bank likes to keep the inflation rate between 1 – 3% (Bank of Canada, 2020).

The central bank is the head bank of the country. It controls the production and distribution of money, meaning they print our money. It also sets the interest rates. The central bank will raise interest rates to slow down people's spending, encourage people to save, and reduce inflation. They will lower interest rates if they want people to spend more. The central bank also makes the rules for the member banks. The member banks are the banks we visit to do our banking, such as opening a bank account, getting a loan, and depositing or withdrawing money (Segal, 2022).

Inflation becomes a problem when the income we earn does not increase as much as the price of the goods and services we buy. If inflation is 2%, but we receive a 4% pay raise, we are not worried because we have more spending power. However, if inflation is 2% and we do not get a pay raise, we will need to use more of our own money to pay for things. Our spending power is declining (Dillow, 2023).

Canada's inflation rate for November 2022 is 6.8% (Rate Inflation, 2023). The annual inflation rate for the US is 7.1% for the 12 months that ended November 2022 (Coin News Media Group LLC, 2023). The average national base salary increase in 2022 was 4.2% in both Canada and the US (The Canadian Press Staff, 2022) (O'Brien, 2022). Inflation and the loss of spending power are why many people are currently worried about their finances.

In Sarah's situation, since her income is limited, she really has to watch her spending as inflation reduces her spending power.

Can you afford to live on your own?

If we look at the cost of rent, the median cost for a one-bedroom apartment in the US was US$1,876 as of Jun 2022. This is a 23.9% increase from June 2020 (Thompson, 2022).

The average rent for a one-bedroom apartment in Canada in November 2022 was just over C$2,000, which is 12.4% higher than last November (CBC News, 2022).

Rent and transportation costs will vary depending on where you live. Rent is higher in the major cities, but you probably won't have to travel too far to get to your place of work or other amenities. On the other hand, if you live further away from the city but work there, your transportation costs will be higher.

Rents have increased so significantly for several reasons. One of the reasons for the increase is rising interest rates. Another reason is that there is not enough supply of rental units or housing to keep up with the demand.

Interest rates, which change periodically, have been increased by the central banks to try to reduce inflation. They want to slow the demand or purchasing of goods and services. Interest gets charged if you borrow money.

In our economy, many businesses will borrow money to build, manufacture, or produce goods to sell to us. Now that the interest rates have increased, it costs more for these businesses to borrow money and produce the goods. Home builders, condo developers, and construction companies have decided that since the interest rates have increased and the borrowing cost is much higher, they don't want to build now (CBC News, 2022). This means apartments and condos are not being built for people to live in.

In addition, people are not buying houses due to the increased interest rates. When you buy a house, you get a mortgage from the bank, which is a loan to buy the house. The cost of borrowing or getting a mortgage has increased, so people have decided not to buy a house at this time. These people now need to find a place to rent and live in. As a result, the demand for purchasing houses has decreased, which is one of the objectives of increasing interest rates, but the need for rental units has increased (CBC News, 2022).

Also, new immigrants coming into the country each year need a place to live. University and college students are now back to in-person school, with those attending school away from home needing to rent a place to live.

With the limited places to rent due to a low supply of real estate and housing and the increase in demand by people looking for a place to rent, this drives up the price of rent (CBC News, 2022). This makes it very unaffordable to live on your own.

A little bit of effort goes a long way

Although my parents did not plan on having seven children, they did plan out their finances using a budget so that we could live a simple yet enjoyable life. We didn't have a lot of material items, but we were still happy.

Budgeting does take some time in the beginning, but as you get more experienced with it, it will be much easier. It will definitely keep you on track with your finances and point out any areas you need to watch carefully. Without a budget, we can easily spend our way into debt, which we should try to avoid if we want to keep our financial freedom. In addition, creating a budget for saving and reducing spending will help to cope with inflation.

TIP

You can find free budget templates online or in Excel to help you get started on your budgeting. Alternatively, as a gift to my readers, you may go to my website and download a free copy of the Excel budget templates from this book!

https://www.janekwancpa.com/personal-finance-for-teens

Another way to adjust the budget

Another way to adjust Sarah's budget would be to increase her income. She could get a second job or start a side hustle to do this. A college education can provide better job or career opportunities, which leads to more income. However, more income doesn't mean she can start spending more on wants. If she went to college and took out a student loan, she would need to incorporate the payments for the loan into her budget.

Is it worth it to go to college or university?

Chapter 7
University and College – Is It Worth It?

" *"The best investment you can make is an investment in yourself . . . the more you learn, the more you'll earn."*

— Warren Buffett

There is a debate about whether going to college or university is worth it, as tuition and student debt are increasing each year. We just talked about how debt is a bad thing. However, some debt, like student loans, can be considered "good debt" if we are incurring it to make more money afterwards. If we are able to make more money than we borrow, we can pay the debt off and then reap the rewards of a higher education.

My university education enabled me to get better opportunities for work, which in turn helped me to earn higher salaries. Not only did it benefit my work life, but I was able to use what I learned to benefit my personal life and save on taxes. My university education was like a boost . . . a power-up.

However, education is not limited to college or university. You could educate yourself by reading books (like this one). You can look at educational sites on the internet, blogs, online courses, or YouTube videos about topics you are interested in. There are also podcasts you can listen to. My education did not stop once I graduated. I've learned many things from working at various companies, working with different people, reading books and listening to the news. The world is constantly changing. Once we leave school, we need to keep educating ourselves.

Let's look into various factors we should consider to help us figure out if getting a postsecondary education is worth the time, effort, and cost.

Brainstorm career ideas

If you are in Grade 9 or 10, you'll want to start thinking about what type of career you would like to pursue to determine if you even need to go to university or college. If you don't have any idea, I suggest speaking with your family and guidance counsellors at school to find out what careers may suit you. Think about your interests, abilities, and personality. Are you the type who likes to do things with your hands to create something, or are you the type to focus on academics and theory? Are you better at language rather than math? Are you an extrovert or an introvert? There are various free career aptitude tests you can take to help guide you in determining what careers might be suitable for you.

Once you have an idea of the type of career that might be right for you, determine if the career is in demand. You want to study in an area where there are a lot of job opportunities. There is no point in studying something if there are not many jobs in that field. The main purpose of getting an education is to use what you have learned to help you earn income. Do some research and find out which fields are in demand. Currently, there is a need for people to fill jobs in information technology (IT), healthcare, finance, and skilled trades (Affordable Schools, 2023).

Once you've narrowed your list of possible careers, you can research or ask guidance counsellors whether you need to go to college or university to pursue these careers. If you require post-secondary education, ask what courses you must take in Grades 11 and 12 to help you get into the appropriate program. Please keep in mind that colleges and universities don't accept everyone who applies for their programs. To increase your chances of getting accepted, you will have to do well in your high school courses.

University

Universities are larger institutions offering both undergraduate and graduate programs, granting bachelor's, master's, and doctoral degrees. They focus on analytical abilities as well as academic and professional programs. For example, if you wanted to become an accountant, engineer, lawyer, or doctor, you would choose to attend university. To get a bachelor's degree, you usually spend four years in a university in an undergraduate program.

Even though I knew I wanted to be an accountant, the business program required me to take courses in marketing, economics, IT, accounting, and business law, as part of the first year. I also had to take an elective, so I chose psychology. I majored in accounting in my 3rd and 4th years.

If you plan to get a master's or doctoral degree, you must spend a few more years in university.

College

Colleges are smaller institutions with fewer course offerings than universities. Class sizes are smaller, focusing on developing skills for the career or job you want to pursue, so you wouldn't be taking any courses outside of what you want to learn. They grant diplomas in Canada. In the US, they're called associate degrees (Best Colleges Staff Writers, 2022). Certificates are also issued. Depending on your program, you can graduate in one to two years (Yocket Editorial Team, 2022). If you are interested in skilled trades like becoming an electrician, mechanic, robotics technician, dental hygienist, or technician in the healthcare field, you can choose to go to college. Some of these skilled trades don't absolutely require a college education, but your chances of securing better employment increase with more education.

Tuition fees

For the fall of 2022, Canadian students attending university in Canada in a bachelor program will pay, on average, C$6,834 of tuition for the academic year, up 2.6% from a year earlier (Statistics Canada, 2022). Tuition will vary depending on the specific program you take and the province you live in. The average Ontario college diploma program tuition for one academic year is C$2,400 (Ontario Colleges, 2023).

Average undergraduate tuition fees for Canadian full-time students, by province or territory, 2022/2023

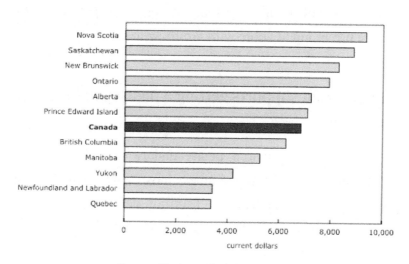

Source: (Statistics Canada, 2022).

In the US, at public four-year institutions providing an undergraduate degree, the average in-state tuition and required fees total US$9,377 per year (Hanson, 2022). On average, a two-year, in-state public college tuition is US$3,501 per year (Hanson, 2022).

According to Statistics Canada, international students paid, on average, three times more in undergrad tuition than Canadian students during the 2019/2020 year (Statistics Canada, 2022). Therefore, if you are an international student looking to study abroad, you will need to factor the higher tuition fees into your budget.

Other costs to consider

Other postsecondary costs to consider are books, supplies, school fees, and cost of living (rent, food, utilities, transportation, etc.) if you are not living at home with family who can support you.

Evidence that supports getting a postsecondary education

There is evidence that a postsecondary education results in higher salaries. Studies in Canada have shown that bachelor's degree graduates earn about half-million dollars more than those with a high school diploma over a 15-year follow-up period (roughly between the ages of 30 and 45) (Statistics Canada, 2022). In the same studies, men with graduate degrees in Canada earn at least C$800,000 more, and women with a graduate degree earn at least C$680,000 more than those with a high school diploma (Frenette, 2019).

Studies from the US Social Security Administration have shown that men with bachelor's degrees earn approximately US$900,000 more in median lifetime earnings than high school graduates. Women with bachelor's degrees earn US$630,000 more. Men with graduate degrees earn US$1.5 million more in median lifetime earnings than high school graduates. Women with graduate degrees earn US$1.1 million more. In this study, lifetime earnings are total accumulated earnings over 50 years from age 20 to 69 (Social Security, 2015).

One thing to keep in mind is that these studies were done over a long period of time and prior to 2020. Salaries and wages have since increased, so the earnings gap would have increased between what a person with a degree makes compared to someone with a high school diploma. But generally, the idea is that you will make more money if you have a postsecondary education.

Student loans

Incurring a huge student loan debt is worrisome for many students as they wonder how they will be able to pay this back.

If you have a Canada Student Loan, you'll have a six-month non-payment period after graduation. During that period, you won't have to make payments and won't be charged interest on your loan. The repayment rules of provincial student loans will vary by province (Government of Canada, 2021).

In November 2022, the Canadian federal government announced that they will no longer charge interest on student loans starting

April 1, 2023, which will provide some relief to students. However, interest will still apply to provincial loans (The Canadian Press, 2022).

With US government loans, you don't have to begin making payments until six months after graduating. Interest will not be charged until after graduation for subsidized loans but starts getting charged immediately for unsubsidized loans (Farrington, How Student Loans Work: Applying, Borrowing, and Paying Back, 2023). Subsidized loans are available to undergraduate students who demonstrate financial need. Unsubsidized loans are available to undergraduate and graduate students, and there is no requirement to demonstrate financial need (Farrington, Subsidized vs. Unsubsidized Student Loans, 2022).

You can also apply for a student loan through your financial institution. Interest will have to be paid on the money you borrow while you're still in school. After you graduate, the financial institution may give you a period of time where you just pay the interest. After this, you repay the debt based on a repayment schedule (Government of Canada, 2021).

Let's look at Jacob's situation to see if it's financially possible to pay off his student loan.

Jacob's budget – attending a local university

Let's say Jacob is fortunate enough to live at home with his parents, who support his living costs while he is in school. Once he graduates, he estimates he will have $40,000 in debt. He plans to get a government student loan. The interest rate currently charged is 7% per annum, compounded monthly. Jacob hopes to land a job fairly quickly after graduation with a starting annual salary of $60,000, as his field of study has a high demand for workers. His take-home pay after taxes is estimated to be $46,000. He plans to continue living with his parents but will pay for his share of living expenses. Jacob prepares a budget to help determine if going to university will be financially feasible for him.

Monthly budget – Jacob	Budget	% of income
Income after taxes	$3,833	
Expenses – needs		
Rent	500	
Groceries	350	
Utilities (gas, water, electricity)	75	
Cell phone	75	
Internet	50	
Transit fare	150	
Basic clothing and shoes	100	
Personal hygiene products	50	
Total needs	1,350	35%
Saving		
Regular saving – emergency fund	100	
Regular saving – vacation	–	
Retirement saving	–	
Total saving	100	3%
Loan repayment	1,800	47%
Expenses – wants		
Restaurants, bars, clubs	300	
Haircut	25	
Additional or designer clothing, bags, accessories, shoes	–	
Games	50	
Movies	25	
Gym membership	50	
Other	133	
Total wants	583	15%
Total payments	3,833	100%

Jacob has allocated 47% of his income toward paying down the debt. By doing this, he is reducing the total interest he has to pay on the loan and will be debt free sooner. Using an online loan calculator, he found out that with a monthly payment of $1,800, he is able to repay the whole loan in just under two years! The total interest that he pays will be about $2,966.

Of course, he doesn't spend very much on his wants, and there are almost no savings during these two years. Nevertheless, he is willing to make sacrifices during this period of time. Once the debt is paid off, he can revise his budget.

Jacob's budget – moves away from home to attend university

Let's change the scenario and say that Jacob is considering moving to another city to attend the university he wants. He has to pay for his own living costs, and he plans to work while in university. His parents saved $40,000 in an education savings plan for him. He estimates that his tuition, other school costs, and living costs will be $140,000 over 4 years. With the education savings and his part-time income, he estimates his total borrowing will be $80,000. He plans to get a student line of credit from the bank to cover the $80,000, but he'll need his parents to help co-sign the loan. Co-signing means his parents will be responsible for paying the loan if he is not able to pay. The interest on the line of credit will be 7% compounded monthly.

Using the same budget from the previous example, if he makes monthly payments of $1,800 towards the debt, it will take him about 4 years and 4 months to pay off the $80,000, and he will have paid about $13,000 in total interest. Is he willing to sacrifice for about 4.5 years to pay off debt?

If he instead decides to make monthly payments of $900 towards the debt, it will take him about 10.5 years to pay it off, and total interest will be about $33,000. That's an extra $20,000 in interest.

We haven't considered the pay increases Jacob will receive as he gains more experience each year. However, with a pay increase, he will pay more income taxes. In addition, we don't factor in inflation in our example, so the cost of living will likely increase as time goes on. Lastly, as he took out a loan with the bank, the interest starts getting charged as soon as he borrows the funds. He will need to pay this interest while he is still in school.

Is it worth it for him to live on his own during his time in university to incur this extra debt? If he can receive the same education at a local university, it's probably not worth it to study out of town. Each student will need to assess their own situation in answering this question.

Other ways to pay for college or university

- Apply for scholarships and grants – apply for as many as possible to increase your chances of getting one. Make sure you follow all the directions on the application so that you can qualify. Most applicants don't follow the directions, so they get disqualified (Farrington, How To Save For College: Order Of Operations For Parents, 2022).

- Ask your parents or guardians if they have saved any funds for your postsecondary education or if they can contribute some funds for your tuition.

Some states give tax deductions or tax credits for 529 plan contributions (Farrington, How To Pay For College: The Best Order Of Operations, 2023). The 529 plans are college savings plans in the US where parents can contribute money into the account. It will grow tax-free to someday pay for their child's education (Farrington, How Much Should You Have In A 529 Plan By Age, 2022).

In Canada, the registered education savings plan (RESP) is used to help save for a child's postsecondary education. Parents contribute to this savings plan. To provide an incentive for saving, Employment and Social Development Canada (ESDC) provides a Canada Education Savings Grant (CESG) of 20% of the annual contributions made to eligible RESPs to a maximum of $500 each year for each student in the savings plan (Government of Canada, 2022). Income on the contributions grow tax-free. There is no tax deduction for the contributions. When it's time to take the money out to pay for the tuition, the income that was earned is reported on the student's tax return (Government of Canada, 2022). The contributions are returned tax free. When the tuition is paid, if the student does not have any taxable income in that year, they can transfer a tuition tax credit to their parents, which will help reduce the parent's tax bill.

- Use your savings.
- Get a part-time job or side hustle. Some jobs on or around campus allow you to work around your class schedule. During my final year in university, I found a part-time bookkeeping job near the school. The job was posted at the university's career center.

Is it worth it to get postsecondary education?

Each person's situation is different. You'll have to think about what you want to do after high school. Look at your interests, abilities, and talents. Speak with family, friends, guidance counsellors, and those already doing what you might want to pursue. Get their perspectives to help guide you in the right direction.

Prepare a budget to see if you can afford to pay for postsecondary education. Look into all the options for helping to pay the tuition. If you can earn and save more than you spend on your education, it will be worth it. If you are going to have a massive debt after graduation and don't think your career will be able to help you pay it off in a reasonable amount of time, then maybe rethink your plans.

Perhaps you just want to start working after high school to take some time to think about whether postsecondary education may be beneficial for you. Or you may want to start a business and invest your time in building your business.

There isn't a definitive answer, as each person's situation is different. Consider all the factors we've discussed and make a decision that is right for you.

In high school, my parents were the ones who suggested I become an accountant. They were convinced that this was the right career for me. I had no idea what I wanted to do, so I followed their suggestion.

My parents had an accountant to help them with their income taxes and investments, as they knew nothing about investing. Investing was another way my parents could earn extra income to support our family.

Chapter 8
Investing – Let Your Money Work for You!

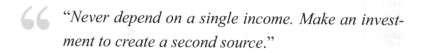 *"Never depend on a single income. Make an investment to create a second source."*

— Warren Buffett

What is investing?

Most people think of the stock market when they think about investing, but it's more than that. Investing is when you use your money to buy other things that can increase in value and/or provide a future source of income. Investing is when you make your money work for you to create more money.

Of course, to invest in the stock market or any type of investment, you need to have the money. Investing is only done when you have extra cash to spare. In your budget, you've paid for your needs, put some money in your emergency fund, and allocated funds for your wants. If you've allocated some money to be saved for retirement, this money can be invested.

Investing is a vast topic. There is a lot to know about investing, but we will cover the fundamentals. We'll discuss various types of investments, return on investment, and the kind of income you can earn on these investments. Costs associated with investing and other factors you need to consider in determining the best type of investment for you are also discussed. In addition, we'll look at how to make these investments and which investments to avoid.

Return on investment

Return on investment (ROI) is a calculation that tells you how much profit you are making on an investment, expressed as a percentage.

$$\text{ROI} = \frac{\text{current value of investment} - \text{cost of investment}}{\text{cost of investment}}$$

You are able to fight inflation if you can invest your money to earn an ROI that is more than the inflation rate.

Example: Trey bought shares in Company A for $1,500. He then sold all the shares a year later for $1,700. His ROI is ($1,700 - $1,500)/$1,500 = 13.3%.

If the inflation rate is 7%, he is able to earn more than the inflation rate, meaning his money has more spending power.

If Trey sold his shares for $1,400 instead of $1,700, he would have a negative ROI or a loss.

What can you invest in?

There are a number of things you can invest in, but some of the more common investments would be stocks, exchange-traded funds, index funds, mutual funds, bonds, and term deposits.

Term deposits

In Canada, term deposits are also known as guaranteed investment certificates (GICs). In the US, they are called certificates of deposit (CDs) (Wikipedia, 2022). Term deposits offer a guaranteed rate of return over a fixed period of time. The investment is usually issued by banks. As the rate of return is guaranteed, term deposits have little to no risk, meaning that the amount you invest will get returned to you with interest.

Example: You can buy a $2,000 term deposit for a five-year period with an interest rate of 5%. This means the interest you will receive on your money is 5% each year. There can be compounding of interest. You need to keep the money in the term deposit for five years to get all the interest and your $2,000 principal back. A penalty will normally be charged if you have to take the money out early.

Bonds

Bonds are a loan from an investor to a government or a corporation with a fixed term for the borrower to repay the investor with interest. The interest is called a coupon and can be paid throughout the life of the bond. At maturity, which is the due date of the bond, the principal is returned to the investor (Lioudis, 2022).

For example, if you invested $5,000 in a 10-year bond with a coupon rate of 6%, the issuer would send you a coupon (interest) payment of $300 every year (or $150 semi-annually) for 10 years. At the end of the 10 years, you will get your $5,000 back.

There are also zero-coupon bonds which receive no payments until the bond matures. Investors buy the bond for an amount less than face value. When the bond reaches maturity, they are paid the full face value of the bond. Zero coupon bonds are also known as discount bonds. Treasury bills (t-bill) and savings bonds are two examples of zero-coupon bonds (Lioudis, 2022).

For example, a t-bill has a face value of $1,000, but you are able to buy it for $950. The t-bill matures in one year. At the end of the year, you will get paid $1,000. Therefore, you received an extra $50 more than what you paid for the t-bill, which is your income. In this case, you earned 5.3% ($50/$950) on your investment.

Bonds don't necessarily provide the biggest returns, but they are a stable and reliable investment, which makes them low risk.

Bonds can be purchased from a bond broker or directly from an issuing government. Bonds cannot be purchased on the stock market (Rolfe, 2022).

Stocks

You can invest in stocks or shares of a company. Owning a share or stock means you own a part of that company. You become a shareholder. There are different types of shares, but the main ones are common shares and preferred shares. A company can give different rights to the shares, but generally, you would have the right to vote at the shareholders' meetings and be a part of the company's decision-making if you are a common shareholder.

Dividends

You can earn dividends on the shares you own. If a company has profits and wants to share them with its shareholders, it can declare and pay a dividend. Dividends can be paid on a quarterly, semi-annual, or annual basis.

Not all companies will pay dividends. Some companies will use the profits to help make the business more profitable. Perhaps they'll do more marketing to help increase sales or hire more staff to perform services to help generate more sales. They may buy more equipment or technology to help get things done faster or produce products more quickly to sell more.

Companies that pay dividends usually have a long history of being in business and have enough cash to consistently pay dividends to their shareholders. Banks are an example of where they are profitable and have been in business for a long time. Since so many businesses borrow money and individuals have mortgages on their homes where they need to pay interest, the banks earn quite a bit of interest income. They have profit and cash, so they decide to pay their shareholders dividends. However, banks do have debt as well. By just being an owner of the bank, you can get paid dividends regularly without having to do anything.

Dividends are paid based on how many shares you have. For example, if you have 10 shares and a dividend of $0.50 per share is declared, you get a dividend of $5. If you own 200 shares, your dividend would be $100.

Dividend income has to be reported on your income tax return, and you may need to pay some tax on it. In Canada, you will receive a T5 slip from the company, which shows how much dividends you were paid so that you can report it on your tax return. In the US, you will receive a 1099-DIV form for dividends above $10 (Maverick, Is Dividend Income Taxable?, 2023).

Capital gains or losses

The price of shares fluctuates each day based on the market. You may have bought a share for $100, but maybe next year, the share will be worth $105. You've theoretically made $5 of profit. You will only get that profit if you sell the share.

If the share price drops to $90, theoretically, you have a loss of $10. However, you will only lose $10 if you sell the share for

$90. If you just hold it and wait until the share price goes up to, say, $100, then you won't have a loss anymore.

Usually, people buy more than one share of a company. For example, if you bought 10 shares in the bank at $100/share, your cost would be $1,000. If you sold those shares next year for $105, you would receive $1,050. You made a $50 profit, which is called a capital gain. If you sold the shares at a loss, you have a capital loss.

Capital gains and losses need to be reported on your income tax return. The financial institution where you do your trading should be able to provide you with a summary of your capital gains and losses each year.

Stock exchanges

You would buy and sell shares on the stock market or stock exchange. There are multiple stock exchanges. The largest stock exchange is the New York Stock Exchange, with a market capitalization of US$27.6 trillion at the end of 2021 (Rolfe, 2022). Market capitalization is the total value of the outstanding shares of all the companies on the exchange.

TMX Group Ltd. operates the TSX, TSX Venture, and Montreal exchanges. TMX Group stock exchanges collectively rank 10th in the world by market cap at C$3.3 trillion (Rolfe, 2022).

Other examples of stock exchanges are the Nasdaq, London Stock Exchange, Shanghai Stock Exchange, and Canadian Securities Exchange. Companies can be listed on multiple exchanges. However, not all companies are listed on a stock exchange. Only those that have applied to the exchange to have their shares on the public market and who meet certain criteria set by the exchange can be approved for trading.

Financial reports

Once a company is approved to be listed on the exchange, it will be required to provide audited financial statements to the shareholders every year. In addition, the companies will also need to provide quarterly, unaudited financial statements to keep the shareholders updated regularly on what is happening with the company.

Financial statements are reports of the business that summarize its financial activities for a period of time. These reports help the shareholders and other people interested in the company's finances to understand whether or not the business has been doing well and how they have been using their money.

Audited financial statements have an audit report attached to them. The audit report is prepared by an accounting firm licensed to perform audits. It states that the accounting firm has verified the financial information in the financial statements based on a set of generally accepted accounting rules. This assures the investors or anyone else looking at the financial statements that the information is fairly accurate.

One of the financial statements is the profit and loss statement, also known as an income statement. It shows the revenue and expenses of the company and whether there was a profit or loss.

A profit is when the revenue or sales are greater than the expenses. A loss is the opposite, where expenses are greater than sales. The profit and loss statement can report revenue and expenses monthly, quarterly, or annually. As an investor, you would like to see companies with a lot of profit and a long history of profits.

Another financial statement is the balance sheet or statement of financial position that shows three main categories. First, it shows the *assets*, which are the items the company owns that can help them generate more sales or provide them cash. It also shows the *liabilities*, which are the debts they have to pay. In addition, the balance sheet shows the *equity*, which is the amount of money that investors have invested in the company, along with how much profit or loss the company has accumulated since they've started the business. The balance sheet is reported at a point in time.

If a company has more assets than liabilities, this is good. Cash in the bank is considered an asset as they can use this to buy equipment or invest in technology that will help them to increase their sales. The equipment or technology can also be considered assets. Another example of an asset is something called *accounts receivable*. This represents the cash that still needs to be collected from their customers. The company may sell their products and give its customers 30 days to pay.

If a company has more debt than it does assets, this is *not* good. As discussed, debt is not a good thing if you don't pay it off on time, as you will need to pay interest, and you eventually need to pay the debt back. However, it is common for businesses to borrow money as they need the funds to get the business going. They will borrow in hopes that the business will have a lot of sales and profit, which they can then use to pay back the debt.

The interest expense in a business is generally a deductible expense, meaning that it can be used to reduce the income of the company, so it pays less tax. This is a good thing if the money they have borrowed is helping them to increase their sales and business. I would avoid investing in companies with a lot of debt that don't have the income to support paying the debt off.

The third statement is the cash flow statement or statement of changes in financial position. The cash flow statement reports the cash activity for the year. This shows where the company spent or received its money. This is similar to the budget format we've discussed, where you show the money that came in, then subtract the money that was paid out for purchases and the money saved or invested. The end result will be a positive cash balance or a negative cash balance. A positive cash balance is good as this means you have cash remaining after all the spending and investing. A negative cash balance, also called an overdraft, means that the company spent more cash than it had, so it borrowed money temporarily from the bank to cover the overage it spent.

It's good to know how a company is managing their cash. If they keep spending a lot on expenses but don't collect money from their customers, they will have to borrow money to keep the business going, which is not preferable. Perhaps they have a lot of cash in the bank because they borrowed a lot of money. Again, we know this is not ideal. If they invested the cash into buying technology or equipment to help them make more products to sell, this would be a good thing.

There will also be reports from the company's management that discuss and explain the financial results and the business plans. This report is called management, discussion, and analysis (MD&A).

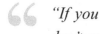 *"An investment in knowledge pays the best interest."*

— Benjamin Franklin

When investing, it's best to educate yourself. Research and analyze your potential investments before making any decisions. Don't just buy the stocks that are trending on social media.

Meme stocks

"If you aren't willing to own a stock for 10 years, don't even think about owning it for 10 minutes."

— Warren Buffett

GameStop Corp. is an American video game and electronics retailer. Their stock price rose more than 10,000% from US$3.25 in April 2020 to US$347.50 in late January 2021, then quickly dropped afterward (Masterson, 2022). The share price did not increase because the business was performing well. Instead, it increased because people read and talked about the stock on social media. The stock went viral and became known as a meme stock. The more people bought the shares, the higher the share price became. Eventually, some decided to sell their shares to reap the profits of the high share price. Once people started selling, the share price started to drop (Masterson, 2022). GameStop's share price was US$19.61 on January 20, 2023 (Yahoo Finance, 2023).

Purchasing meme shares is really risky as you don't know when the price will increase or fall. There is no stability or predictability. Some people did make some money, but those who perhaps bought the shares at a price of US$300 have a huge loss. The share price is not likely to get back over US$300 for them to make their money back. This is a form of gambling. They were hoping to make quick money but did not understand what was really going on in the stock market. Sadly, these people probably don't have much money in the first place, so they now have bigger financial problems.

Stock market index

A market index tracks the performance of a specific group of stocks meant to represent a sector or the bigger market. It helps investors understand whether or not the market is doing well (Rolfe, 2022).

Each stock market index has a different method of figuring out which companies to include in their index.

The S&P 500 is a market cap-weighted index of the 500 largest public companies in the United States (Rolfe, 2022). To be in the index, companies need to have a minimum market cap of US$14.6 billion, trade on the stock market for at least a year and be listed on a select group of exchanges, among other requirements (Rolfe, 2022).

Its Canadian equivalent is the S&P/TSX Composite Index which represents roughly 70% of the total market capitalization on the Toronto Stock Exchange, with about 250 companies included in it (Wikipedia, 2022).

The Dow Jones Industrial Average is an index of 30 prominent companies listed on stock exchanges in the US (Wikipedia, 2023).

The Nikkei is the index for the Tokyo Stock Exchange. It measures the performance of 225 large, publicly owned companies in Japan from a wide array of industry sectors (Wikipedia, 2022).

Mutual funds

A mutual fund is a group of different investments, like stocks and/or bonds, in a single "basket" or fund. Investors will put their money into the fund, which is pooled together with money from other investors who also want to invest in the fund. This large pool of money is then used to buy the stocks and/or bonds that are in the fund.

Let's say the fund has shares in three banks, three healthcare companies, three tech companies, and three oil and gas companies. It also has various government bonds and corporate bonds.

Let's also assume that 50% of the fund is made up of shares and the other 50% of bonds. If you were to buy all these types of investments yourself, it would cost you a lot. Let's assume you buy 10 shares of each company, and each share costs $100. The total cost would be $24,000.

With a mutual fund, you are sharing the cost with others in the fund, so you benefit from having some ownership in each of these investments at a fraction of the cost. You can choose to invest however much you would like in the mutual fund. Some funds may have a minimum amount you need to invest, like $500 or $1,000. In this illustration, you could invest $1,000. If the mutual fund is trading for $5 per unit, you will receive $1,000/$5 = 200 units in the mutual fund.

Option 1:	
Investment	Cost
Three banks	$3,000
Three healthcare companies	$3,000
Three tech companies	$3,000
Three oil and gas companies	$3,000
Government bonds	$6,000
Corporate bonds	$6,000
Total	$24,000
Option 2:	
Mutual fund with same investments above	$1,000

The mutual fund is *actively* managed by professional money managers. This means these experts will try to get positive returns, even if the market is doing poorly. They will frequently trade the investments in the fund to try to make money.

Management expense ratio (MER)

Since the fund is actively managed, there are fees for managing the fund. The fund also has some other operating costs like legal, accounting, and administrative fees. Taxes also have to be paid. The fees and operating costs of a fund are represented in the management expense ratio (MER). If a fund has a MER of 2%, this is the estimated cost of owning the fund. MERs for mutual funds typically fall between 0.5% and 2% (CFI Team, 2023).

Distributions

Any income, such as dividends and interest income, that the fund receives on these investments will be distributed to the unit holders after paying out the fund's costs. Depending on the fund, these distributions can be made monthly, quarterly, semi-annually, or annually (Cussen, 2022).

How to buy mutual funds

Mutual funds are not traded freely on the market as stocks, but you can easily get them from your financial advisor or an online brokerage (Boyte-White, 2022). You can only purchase mutual funds at the end of the trading day, so the fund prices do not fluctuate throughout the day. Frequent trading of mutual funds is discouraged as it causes the fund's administrative and operational costs to increase, increasing its MER (Boyte-White, 2022). There are no trading fees when you buy or sell the mutual fund, as there are with stocks or ETFs.

ROI in mutual funds

If you own mutual funds and the fund makes a return of 6% in the year from the investments it holds, and the MER is 2%, your net return is 4%. If the return on the fund is 4% and the MER is 2%, your net return is 2%. MER is charged whether or not a fund performs well. The return earned is reported net of the MER. Mutual funds can also have negative returns. Just like stocks, there is some risk involved when you invest in mutual funds.

Other fees

Depending on the fund, you may pay sales commissions when you buy mutual funds. Watch out for any funds that are "front-end load" or "back-end load." If you are considering purchasing mutual funds, you would want to buy funds with no load.

TIP

The lower the MER, the better, as your investment return will be higher. Over time, the costs eat away at your income, as you are not able to benefit from the compounding growth you could have had on the money you paid in fees.

Index funds

Index funds are a type of mutual fund that is *passively* managed. They generally aim to match the performance of a particular stock index, like the S&P 500. The investment managers buy and hold a representative sample of the securities in the target index and then leave them alone unless the index itself changes. As a result, there isn't much work involved in managing this type of fund which translates to a lower MER (Maverick, What Is a Good Expense Ratio for Mutual Funds?, 2021).

The typical MER for index funds is about 0.2% (Maverick, What Is a Good Expense Ratio for Mutual Funds?, 2021).

If the index fund makes a return of 6% in the year from the investments it holds, and the MER is 0.2%, your net return is 5.8%.

Index funds, like mutual funds, can only be traded at a set price point at the end of the trading day. You can buy index funds through your brokerage account or financial institution.

TIP

Do actively managed mutual funds perform better than passively managed index funds?

You would think the answer is yes since professionals are spending their time trying to figure out the best investments. However, this isn't true. It has been found that in most cases, over a long period of time, passively managed index funds provide higher returns and lower costs than their actively managed counterparts (Marquit & Reilly-Larke, 2022). If you are trying to decide between mutual funds or index funds, go with index funds.

Exchange-traded funds (ETF)

Exchange-traded funds are similar to index funds. They are a collection of securities that aim to replicate an index or sector's performance as closely as possible (Rolfe, 2022). ETFs can also focus on specific sectors. Examples of sector ETFs would be gold ETFs, where they focus on gold or the shares of companies that mine gold (TD, 2023), and cryptocurrency ETFs, which track the price of one or more digital tokens (Reiff, How Do Cryptocurrency Exchange-Traded Funds (ETFs) Work?, 2022). ETFs focusing on just one sector is riskier than if you held a wide array of stocks in the ETF.

ETFs are also passively managed, so the fees are comparable to index funds. Most ETFs won't have an MER greater than 0.25% (Weyman, 2023). Some MERs can go as low as 0.05%! (Weyman, 2023).

If the ETF makes a return of 6% in the year from the investments it holds, and the MER is 0.05%, your net return is 5.95%.

Distributions

Any income, such as dividends and interest income, that the ETF receives will be distributed out to the unit holders after paying out the costs of the ETF. These distributions can be made monthly, quarterly, semi-annually, or annually (Mackenzie Investments, 2021).

How to buy ETFs

ETFs are traded daily on a stock exchange where the price fluctuates throughout the day. You would open a discount online brokerage account and do the trading yourself.

Cryptocurrency

Cryptocurrency is a digital or virtual currency. Bitcoin is the most popular and valuable cryptocurrency. Bitcoin originated in 2009 and has since become quite popular. (Frankenfield, What is Bitcoin? How to mine, buy, and use it, 2022).

The value of Bitcoin fluctuates very significantly. Bitcoin had a price of US$7,167.52 on December 31, 2019, and a year later, it appreciated more than 300% to US$28,984.98 (Frankenfield, What is Bitcoin? How to mine, buy, and use it, 2022). It continued to surge in the first half of 2021, trading at a record high of US$68,990 in November 2021 (Frankenfield, What is Bitcoin? How to mine, buy, and use it, 2022). Then it started falling in price in 2022 and has continued to do so. On January 22, 2023, one Bitcoin was worth US$22,720.42 (Yahoo Finance, 2023).

Other cryptocurrencies are Solana, Binance Coin, Ethereum, and Cardona (Frankenfield, Cryptocurrency Explained With Pros and Cons for Investment, 2023).

Cryptocurrency is a very risky investment. Most people buy it just because they see the high valuations and hope to sell and get a huge capital gain. Cryptocurrency does not provide you with any interest or dividends.

You can buy cryptocurrency on online markets known as cryptocurrency exchanges. These exchanges are entirely digital and are at risk from hackers, malware, and operational glitches (Frankenfield, What is Bitcoin? How to mine, buy, and use it, 2022).

FTX

In November 2022, a cryptocurrency exchange called FTX had to file for bankruptcy. A significant investor had decided to sell all the cryptocurrency it had with FTX. FTX was then not able to pay other investors the cash for the cryptocurrency when they wanted to sell, so FTX declared bankruptcy. It is suspected that there was a hack of the FTX system where possibly US$477 million was stolen (Reiff, The Collapse of FTX: What Went Wrong With the Crypto Exchange?, 2023). As of the writing of this book, the case is under investigation.

There are stories where people have made millions from trading cryptocurrencies, but you can also lose millions as well. Many people don't understand how cryptocurrency works and the risks involved. Putting your money in cryptocurrency is gambling rather than investing.

Risk tolerance

Knowing your risk tolerance helps determine what kind of investments would suit you. Risk tolerance refers to how much loss an investor is prepared to handle when it comes to their investments. You can classify this into three categories – conservative, moderate, and aggressive.

As a conservative investor, you don't like risk. You're uncomfortable if your investments lose value for a certain period of time. Low risk investments will have lower gains or returns compared to riskier investments. Term deposits, where the principal of the investment is guaranteed, are low risk investments. Bonds are typically considered low risk investments as you can earn a predictable return through the coupon payments.

Aggressive investors take huge risks and understand the stock market will have ups and downs. They will get great returns when the market is up but will have huge losses when it is down. However, they won't panic sell when the market goes down as they understand that overall if they hold their investments for the long term, their return will be good. A significant amount of their investments can be in stocks. Stocks are riskier than term deposits or bonds but can also come with higher returns. The S&P 500 has averaged a 10.46 % annualized return since 1926 (Rolfe, 2022).

Moderate investors are less risk tolerant than aggressive investors. They take on some risk but balance their investments between risky and safe. They earn less than aggressive investors when the market does well but do not suffer huge losses when it falls. Moderate investors would buy a mix of stocks, ETFs, bonds, and term deposits.

The question to ask yourself when considering buying shares is: *"Would you still be able to sleep at night knowing that the stock market has declined?"* If so, then you can consider investing in stocks. Otherwise, do not bother, as you will only worry about it.

The next question would be: '*How much money are you willing to lose?"* If you are not afraid to lose all your money to be able to possibly make double your money, then you are likely an aggressive investor. It's usually wealthy investors that are aggressive as they have other sources of income to fall back on if they lose their money in the stock market. If you cannot afford to lose all your money, determine how much you think you would be comfortable losing . . . 20%? 30%? Figuring this out will help to determine how much of your money should go to stocks and how much should go to safer investments.

Younger investors have a longer time horizon to recoup any losses in the stock market than older investors, so they have a higher risk tolerance. If you start investing in the stock market when you are young for a long-term goal, say retirement, you will experience the ups and downs of the stock market. However, since you have a lot of time before you retire, any losses you may experience will have a higher chance of being recovered later. So, it may be worthwhile to take some risks investing in the stock market when you are young.

Investment goals

Knowing your goals is also essential in determining what to invest in. If you need the funds in the short term, in less than a few years, do not invest in the stock market. Instead, put your money in a high interest or high-yield savings account, a short term GIC, CD, or a short term bond. This way, you can access your entire principal and interest when needed.

If you want to invest the money for retirement, buying a house, or some other long-term goal that is more than five years down the road, then you'll want to consider investing in stocks, index funds, or ETFs. Over a longer period of time, these types of investments can earn greater returns.

"Don't put all your eggs in one basket"

When you have investments, you should try to buy different types of investments and not focus on one type of investment or one sector. This is called *diversification*, and it helps to balance the risk and rewards in your portfolio of investments. We know that stock prices can go up or down at any given time. This fluctuation in prices is known as volatility. The bigger the swing in prices, the more volatile, and risky an investment becomes.

Let's say you only have shares in two banks for a total investment of $10,000. In Bank A, you invested $2,000; in Bank B, you invested $8,000. One day, there is an announcement that Bank B has gone bankrupt! (Banks have gone bankrupt in the past as they also borrow money to run their business). Since most of your money was in the shares of Bank B, you will have lost 80% of your investment portfolio.

Let's change the scenario and say you invested $1,000 in Bank A, $1,000 in Bank B, $1,000 in a tech company, $3,000 in bonds, and $4,000 in a term deposit, for a total investment of $10,000. If Bank B goes bankrupt, you will only have lost 10% of your investment portfolio. By spreading your money out into different types of investments and industries, you are helping reduce the risk that comes with investing. You will then still have the ability to earn income from the other investments that haven't been affected by the bank's bankruptcy.

TIP

ETFs and index funds can provide diversification as they are a basket of different investments. They are a great low-cost way to start investing, to be able to achieve some decent returns, and get exposure to the stock market. With stocks, you would have to buy many of them to achieve diversification. This can get expensive, especially when you are a new investor.

Ways to invest and the associated costs

There are fees associated with buying and selling investments on a market. The fees will vary depending on how you trade.

Professional investment advisors

Fees will be higher if you have a professional advisor do the trading for you, as someone with experience will charge more.

These advisors can help you make investment decisions, and monitor and make changes to your portfolio. They will also give investment advice and provide tax planning and consultation. A commission or trading fee will be charged each time you trade stock, whether you buy or sell. Trading fees for a full-service broker can be around 1% to 2% of the money being managed (Ganti, 2022).

For example, if you wanted to buy 50 shares of Company Z at $100 per share, your trading fee would be 50 x $100 = $5,000 x 1% = $50. The total cost you would need to pay for the trade is $5,000 + $50 = $5,050. This is a good option for those with a large amount to invest and require tax and financial advice on managing their money.

Self-directed online discount brokerage accounts

You can open a self-directed online discount brokerage account and trade shares, ETFs, mutual funds, and index funds. The fees will be lower as you are doing it yourself. Each trade you make will have a fee to be paid. The fee can vary, but a typical fee would be $9.99 per trade.

Be careful of how much you trade. If you have $5,000 to invest and you trade 10 times, you will pay fees of $100. That's a 2% cost ($100/$5,000) in addition to the MER (if you are trading ETFs and index funds). It's best to research good investments to buy and then keep them for the long term so that you don't have to keep trading and incurring trading fees.

Some online brokerages do not charge trading fees, but they charge a management fee instead. This fee is based on a percentage of the value of the assets in your account.

If you are confident about your investing knowledge and ability, you could manage your investment portfolio on your own. A survey from the Royal Bank of Canada in February 2022 found that 48% of Canadian do-it-yourself investors between the ages of 18 and 34 started investing after the onset of the pandemic (Rolfe, 2022).

It's not difficult to place the actual trade, but you need to be knowledgeable about what you will buy and when you should sell. Refrain from buying or selling based on emotions or what the market is doing, as you can easily lose money this way.

If you are under 18, you will not be able to open a brokerage account on your own. However, custodial accounts can be opened where your parent or guardian opens the account in your name and makes the transactions on your behalf until you turn 18 (Farrington, How To Start Investing In High School, 2023) (Mydoh, 2023).

Robo-Advisors

There are robo-advisors which are an automated hands-off option that typically costs less than working with a broker or financial advisor. A robo-advisor will typically charge 0.25% to 0.89% of the money being managed (Henricks, 2022). Once a robo-advisor program has your goals, risk tolerance level, and other details, it automatically invests for you. They don't buy and sell individual stocks for you. Instead, they use an algorithm to put together a portfolio of diversified ETFs (Rolfe, 2022).

TIP

For those interested in learning more about trading stocks and ETFs but don't want to risk their own money, there are stock trading simulators that can be used where you practice trading with virtual practice money.

We've covered the basics of investing. If you have extra money saved in your budget for a long-term goal, it would be a great idea to invest it so that you can make more money. A small amount invested now will make a big difference later, as you can use the power of compounding to increase your wealth. Investigate what might be the best investments to suit your risk tolerance, your investment goals, and your budget. Avoid the very risky investments like meme stocks, cryptocurrency, or any new type of investment that is poorly understood. You're gambling your money away if you buy these "investments".

Final Thoughts

> *"Knowledge is power: you hear it all the time but knowledge is not power. It's only potential power. It only becomes power when we apply it and use it. Somebody who reads a book and doesn't apply it, they're at no advantage over someone who's illiterate. None of it works unless you work. We have to do our part. If knowing is half the battle, action is the second half of the battle."*

— Jim Kwik

For us to ever achieve something, including wealth, we need to set a goal, make a plan on how we will reach that goal, and then take action to make the plan a reality.

Many people do not take the time to plan things in advance, which is a recipe for disaster. Instead, they spend all their money as soon as they receive it. They don't consider saving and investing until it is already too late. As a result, they are not able to take advantage of the time value of money and the incredible compounding effects. This is why many people live paycheque to paycheque and live in a world of debt and stress.

You can avoid financial worries. I've given you a guide on how you can get a job to start making money. There are jobs out there. You just have to know where to look for them. Jobs are not always glamorous or exciting, but they are an easy way of making consistent money as long as you show up and do well. Also, use the tips provided for getting the resume and cover letter done and how to prepare for the interview. Finally, don't be afraid to ask for help.

You also have information on how to start a side hustle, along with the financial, tax, and business matters to consider. If you have an idea for a product or service you want to provide and believe there could be a market for it, give it a try! Talk with a trusted adult about your business plan to see if they can help you out or offer any advice.

When you do make your money, prepare a budget to figure out how much you can spend and how much you can save. Spending is very hard to control as so many factors make it easy for us to spend. It takes some discipline and sacrifice to control spending in your early years, but things will get easier as you build up your cash reserve. The more you can save and invest at an early age, the more you can get your money working for you. You will then be able to retire without being stressed about your finances.

Deciding to go to college or university also requires a plan. Postsecondary education will give you a chance to increase your income, but you'll need to determine what kind of career you want to have to figure out if you need to go to college or university. If you do, next look at the cost and then ways you can pay for the tuition. Create a budget and see if it all financially makes sense and would be worth it.

As you can see, you are actually in control of your actions and financial future. It doesn't have to be all doom and gloom. Be a game changer! You don't have to follow the crowd, spend yourself into debt, and work until ripe old age. Plan your strategy, play it out, and adjust it where necessary, and you will be a winner!

I hope all this information has been beneficial.

Speak with your parents or guardians about the topics we've discussed. Ask them to help you open the various bank accounts (if you are under 18). Lastly, apply the knowledge, secrets, and tips I have provided to continue on your personal finance journey.

Wishing you all a lifetime of financial success!

Jane

Works Cited

ADP. (2023, n.d. n.d.). *Payroll tax*. Retrieved from ADP: https://www.adp.com/ resources/tools/tax-guides-and-forms/state-and-local-tax-guides/state-tax-guide.aspx

Affordable Schools. (2023, February 4). *The 20 Most In-demand Jobs Over the Next Decade*. Retrieved from Affordableschools: https://affordableschools.net/ faq/in-demand-jobs-over-next-decade/

Anspach, D. (2022, December 8). *Minimum and maximum age limits for IRA contributions*. Retrieved from thebalancemoney: https://www.thebalance money.com/minimum-and-maximum-age-limits-for-ira-contributions-2388696#toc-minimum-age-limit-for-ira-contributions

Bank of Canada. (2020, August 13). *Understanding inflation*. Retrieved from BankofCanada: https://www.bankofcanada.ca/2020/08/understanding-inflation/

Bank of Canada. (2021, May 19). *Understanding the consumer price index*. Retrieved from BankofCanada: https://www.bankofcanada.ca/2021/05/under standing-consumer-price-index/

Bank of Canada. (2023, February 10). *Central bank digital currency (CBDC)*. Retrieved from BankofCanada: https://www.bankofcanada.ca/research/digital-currencies-and-fintech/projects/central-bank-digital-currency/

Best Colleges Staff Writers. (2022, November 4). *College vs. University: What's the Difference?* . Retrieved from Bestcolleges: https://www.bestcolleges.com/ blog/difference-between-college-and-university/

Bonnet, F. (2020, June 17). *Suburban Fairy Tales*. Retrieved from Francisbonnet: https://francisbonnet.com/archive/sft/suburbanfairytales/06-17-2020/

Boyte-White, C. (2022, January 20). *A Guide to Mutual Fund Trading Rules*. Retrieved from Investopedia: https://www.investopedia.com/articles/investing/ 121715/guide-mutual-funds-trading-rules.asp

Brandon, E. (2022, November 15). *How much you will get from social security*. Retrieved from Money.usnews: https://money.usnews.com/money/retirement/ social-security/articles/how-much-you-will-get-from-social-security

CBC News. (2022, December 14). *Average rents in Canada soar above $2K for* *first time ever, new data suggests.* Retrieved from CBC: https://www.cbc.ca/news/canada/toronto/rental-costs-canada-1.6685602

CFI Team. (2023, February 1). *Management Expense Ratio (MER).* Retrieved from corporatefinanceinstitute: https://corporatefinanceinstitute.com/resources/wealth-management/management-expense-ratio-mer/

Cheung, G. (2023, n.d. n.d.). *10 remote jobs for high school students.* Retrieved from Wizeprep: https://www.wizeprep.com/blog/10-remote-jobs-for-high-school-students

Choi, B. (2022, July 15). *When is a credit card annual fee worth it?* Retrieved from Nerdwallet: https://www.nerdwallet.com/ca/credit-cards/credit-card-annual-fee-worth-it

CIBC. (2023, n.d. n.d.). *Foreign currency transactions with your credit card.* Retrieved from CIBC: https://www.cibc.com/en/personal-banking/credit-cards/articles/foreign-currency-credit-card.html

CIBC. (2023, n.d. n.d.). *What is a credit limit?* Retrieved from CIBC: https://www.cibc.com/en/personal-banking/credit-cards/articles/credit-limit-overview.html

Coin News Media Group LLC. (2023, February 4). *Current US inflation rates: 2000-2023.* Retrieved from USinflationcalculator: https://www.usinflationcalculator.com/inflation/current-inflation-rates/

Craig, L. (2023). Game Changers - transforming how we teach, learn, work and play in the virtual world. *Toronto Met University magazine,* 14-21.

Credit Cards Canada. (2023, n.d. n.d.). *The pros and cons of retail credit cards.* Retrieved from Creditcardscanada: https://www.creditcardscanada.ca/education-centre/credit-card-basics/pros-cons-retail-credit-cards/

Cussen, M. P. (2022, January 16). *Investopedia.* Retrieved from How Mutual Funds Pay Dividends: https://www.investopedia.com/articles/investing/082415/how-mutual-funds-pay-dividends-overview.asp

Dickler, J. (2023, January 31). *64% of Americans are living paycheck to paycheck - here's how to keep your budget in check.* Retrieved from CNBC: https://www.cnbc.com/2023/01/31/share-of-americans-living-paycheck-to-paycheck-jumped-in-2022.html

Dillow, C. (2023, n.d. n.d.). *What is...inflation?* Retrieved from ING: https://www.ing.com/Newsroom/News/Features/Features-old/What-is...-inflation.htm

Dobson, S. (2022, September 30). *High inflation sees more Canadians living paycheque to paycheque.* Retrieved from Hrreporter: https://www.hrreporter.